To Zarin
with much love
from Jess and Mair

BIRDS OF THE WORLD

BIRDS OF THE WORLD

OVER 400 OF JOHN GOULD'S CLASSIC BIRD ILLUSTRATIONS

MAUREEN LAMBOURNE

STUDIO EDITIONS

LONDON

PUBLISHER'S NOTE

Birds of the World brings together a selection of more than four hundred illustrations chosen by Maureen Lambourne from John Gould's books on the birds of the Himalayas, Australia, Asia, Great Britain, and New Guinea and his monographs on toucans, trogons, partridges of America, and humming-birds. This volume is organized in ten chapters, each covering one of the original works, and the plates appear in the order in which they were first published. Each plate is accompanied by text written by Maureen Lambourne which combines recent information with quotations from Gould's text.

Gould identified all of the illustrations with both scientific and common names, but many of these have now been altered. To avoid confusion, and because the text includes quotes from the original volumes, Gould's names have been retained but changes in scientific nomenclature and common name have been added where applicable.

Example:

WHITE-TAILED (SEA) EAGLE – common name
HALIAEETUS ALBICILLA – scientific name used by Gould
Haliaeetus albicilla (Linnaeus) – present scientific name and author

The brackets in the first line separate the common name which was used by Gould i.e. Sea Eagle from that accepted today i.e. White-tailed Eagle. The authority for the scientific nomenclature has also been given, but where this name appears in brackets this indicates that the genus has changed since the species was initially named. Therefore, although *Haliaeetus* is the genus used by Gould in *The Birds of Europe* and is still in use today, it is different from the original nomenclature, *Falco Albicilla*, given by Linnaeus in 1758.

To aid the identification of each illustration the plates have been numbered in the order in which they appear in this volume. The caption underneath each illustration gives this number, the common name and the initials of the artist: – Elizabeth Gould, William Hart, Edward Lear, Henry Constantine Richter and Joseph Wolf.

Birds of the World
first published in 1992 by Studio Editions Ltd.
Princess House, 50 Eastcastle Street
London W1N 7AP

Printed and bound in Hong Kong

ISBN 1 85170 761 1

Contents

PITTA CONCINNA, *Gould.*

Elegant Pitta *Pitta concinna.* The illustrations on pages 10–13 show the processes that a picture
passes through from the original sketch to become the hand-coloured lithograph shown here.

INTRODUCTION

JOHN GOULD (1804–1881) 'The Bird Man'

John Gould's life was devoted to birds and books. Endowed with great energy and organizing ability, he did not work single-handedly but master-minded a skilful production team. This book is a tribute not only to Gould but to his artists, including his wife Elizabeth, Edward Lear (later of 'nonsense' fame), Joseph Wolf (a wildlife painter) and two highly accomplished illustrators, Henry Constantine Richter and William Hart. The sheer quantity of Gould's bird prints may give the impression of sameness but a closer study reveals the artists' differing styles and personalities, and the changing taste in natural history illustration as the century progressed.

John Gould was born in 1804, at Lyme Regis in Dorset, the eldest child, with four sisters, of John Gould, a gardener, and Elizabeth Clatworthy. When he was still an infant his parents moved to Stoke Hill near Guildford, and his boyhood was spent bird-nesting and exploring the surrounding Surrey countryside. Although nothing is known of his education, and it may well have been rudimentary, he later evolved a highly literate, if ponderous prose style.

In 1818, Gould's father was appointed a foreman gardener at the Royal Gardens, Windsor. Young Gould trained there in the same vocation, and as the Royal Gardens were then under a central authority, he probably worked in Kew Gardens as well as at Windsor. J.W. Thomson, in *Reminiscences of an Old Kewite*, 1893, related that Gould was one of the many 'light-hearted, merry fellows' who were gardeners at Kew and later rose to eminence. Gould later disclaimed any great knowledge of botany, simply remarking: 'I've gathered many a bunch of dandelions for Queen Charlotte's [George III's wife] German salads.'

As a youth Gould became proficient at egg-blowing and taxidermy. At Eton, across the river from Windsor, he traded eggs and birds to the College scholars, for natural history collecting was then a popular hobby. He also became expert at preserving mammals, and after eighteen months as a gardener at Ripley Castle, Yorkshire, set up his own taxidermist practice in London. He received several royal orders, and his most notable commission was to assist in the stuffing of George IV's pet, the first giraffe to live in England, which had unhappily died less than two years after its arrival from Egypt.

When Gould was twenty-three, he was appointed 'Curator and Preserver' of the museum at the newly formed Zoological Society of London. There he met the foremost natural history scientists, and his first publication *A Century of Birds from The Himalayas* illustrated by his wife's lithographs, paved the way for his future career as a publisher and ornithologist.

Gould's artistic skills have often been debated: some assume he did all the illustrations himself, while carping critics claim he was incapable of drawing anything, and took all the credit from others. The truth lies between these two premises, for Gould, although he did not have any art training, drew hundreds of powerful sketches which were the inspiration for the finished illustrations. From the outset of his career he made diagrammatic sketches from which his wife Elizabeth created careful watercolours. After her death, he trained the young H.C. Richter to work from vigorous composition-

A watercolour of John Gould by Marion Walker, 1875.

al drawings which he drew on paper the same size paper as the published pages. Richter closely adhered to Gould's designs, as can be seen by careful comparison between Gould's rough sketches and the finished pictures. In 1842 Prince, Gould's secretary, wrote that for the *Monograph of the Partridges of America*, Gould 'executed many very beautiful drawings in an entirely new style being a mingling of pencil and crayon the effect of which is astonishingly superior to anything he has yet done'. For the later series Gould often drew corrections of the birds characteristics. Some sketches are a fascinating palimpsest showing Richter's careful work, Gould's quick scribbles and numerous written annotations.

Gould never lost interest in the depiction of birds. Shortly before his death he was visited by Sir John Millais, P.R.A., who was inspired to paint a picture of the elderly naturalist surrounded by his bird skins. *The Ruling Passion* or *The Ornithologist*, was based on this occasion but using different models. In the foreground sits a young girl with a quetzal on her lap, on the coverlet are birds of paradise and a scarlet ibis. The scene was much romanticized, but for John Ruskin, the art critic, it was 'perfectly beautiful . . . the old man with his birds around him'.

But let us leave Gould with an anecdote related by Sir Richard Owen, the eminent naturalist, which shows Gould enjoying bird life and song at Owen's home, Sheen Lodge, Richmond Park. Owen described a visit by Gould who 'possessed in a remarkable degree the faculty of imitating the various notes of all our vocal species. He bade us sit still and be silent, then began. After emitting a particular "motivo" for a few minutes, he would quietly point to a little bird which had flown from an adjoining bush upon the lawn, and was there hopping to and fro, gradually nearing the locality of the specific song. We could then recognise the species to which Gould gave the name. This attraction and its result was repeated, and we enjoyed the same instructive amusement on subsequent summer vacations . . . '.

ELIZABETH GOULD (1804–1841)

Gould's early success was attributable to his own business acumen, scientific knowledge, and his wife Elizabeth's artistic talent. Elizabeth Coxen, called by her husband Eliza, was born at Ramsgate, Kent, of a naval and military family. She had numerous siblings, but many died in infancy. Two brothers Stephen and Charles later emigrated to Australia and Elizabeth became a governess. A moving letter to her mother from James Street, London, reveals that she felt sad and isolated, although her charge, a nine-year-old girl, to whom she taught French, Latin and music, was 'a perfect child in mind and manners'.

It is not certain how Elizabeth met her future husband, but it may have been through a Mr Coxen 'the Birdstuffer', perhaps a relation, and a colleague of Gould. Gould was then a curator and taxidermist at the Museum of the Zoological Society of London. They married at St. James Piccadilly; both were aged twenty-four, although Elizabeth was two months older than John.

The story of how Elizabeth came to illustrate her husband's first book was related over forty years later by Gould to his biographer R. Bowdler Sharpe. After a discussion of the project and the need for illustrations by the new method of lithography, Elizabeth inquired, 'But who will do the plates on stone?' 'Who?' replied her husband, 'Why you, of course.' So began a partnership which lasted through many joint ventures, including the monographs of Himalayan birds, toucans and trogons, the *Birds of Europe* and *Australia*.

For Elizabeth, who loved her children, it was a great wrench to be parted from the three youngest during the two-year expedition to Australia with her husband. Her son and two daughters were left behind in England under the care of her mother and niece, while the eldest Henry, aged seven, travelled with his parents. During the voyage Elizabeth made valuable studies of seabirds caught by Gould when lowered down to sea in the ship's boat during calm weather. In Tasmania the Governor and his wife, Sir John and Lady Franklin, both keenly interested in natural history, received the Goulds with great hospitality. There Elizabeth gave birth to another son Franklin, 'a little Tasmanian' whom she proudly described to her mother in a letter as 'a prodigious fellow'. During her pregnancy she painted local plants, captive birds, and specimens shot and collected by Gould on his field expeditions.

In August 1839 the Goulds left Tasmania for New South Wales to visit Elizabeth's brothers. They sailed to Newcastle via Sydney, then travelled up the Hunter River in a steamer to Maitland, and by bullock cart to the Coxens' property at Yarrundi. Elizabeth continued to draw while Gould set out into the bush on his most ambitious journey discovering new species.

Soon after their return the Goulds commenced the publication of *The Birds of Australia*, for which Elizabeth produced eighty-four

An oil painting of Elizabeth Gould, painted after her death. Artist unknown.

illustrations and many studies and drawings which later provided invaluable reference material. In May 1841 Gould obtained a cottage at Egham by the Thames, where he hoped the family would benefit by a holiday in the country. But the pressure of work, added to the responsibility for her young children, combined to undermine Elizabeth's health, for tragically she died in August, aged thirty-seven, from puerperal fever five days after the birth of Sarah, her eighth child and the sixth to live past infancy.

Elizabeth's gentle and sympathetic personality compensated for Gould's assertive ways and bustling manner. Although modest about her own talents and retiring by nature, her letters reveal her pride in her husband's success and support of his achievements. Her life provides a classic demonstration of the immense problems involved in combining the roles of wife and artist in Victorian England before the notion of the career woman existed. Was she overstretched due to her compliancy to Gould's demands? Her name has been much overshadowed, for after her death Gould continued to work for a further forty years and when he died in 1881 her contribution had almost been forgotten.

EDWARD LEAR (1812–1888)

Edward Lear is best remembered for his comic verse and illustrated limericks, especially such fantasies as 'The Owl and the Pussy Cat' and 'The Quangle-Wangle's Hat'. He did not expect to receive lasting fame from such dotty nonsense, which was first created to amuse the children and adults at Knowsley Hall, where he illustrated the rare birds and mammals in the Earl of Derby's menagerie.

Although Lear excelled at amusing young children, his own

childhood was clouded with unhappiness. Born at Upper Holloway, a suburb of north London, he was the twentieth of twenty-one children, many of whom died in infancy, and he was looked after by elder sisters. His father, a stockbroker, suffered from severe fluctuations in fortune. Lear was often ill from asthma, bronchitis, epilepsy and bouts of depression. As he was short-sighted he had to wear glasses, later caricaturing himself as an owl with large spectacles.

During his unsettled childhood Lear received little formal education, but he enjoyed painting and copying the animal pictures in the family volumes of Buffon's encyclopaedic *Histoire Naturelle*. At about fifteen he settled with his sister Ann (twenty-two years his senior) in London, earning his living by colouring prints (at 9d to 4s each), painting fans and screens, and making 'morbid disease drawings, for hospitals and certain doctors of physic'.

In June 1830 Lear, aged eighteen, applied for permission to draw the parrots belonging to the newly founded Zoological Society, which were housed in a temporary aviary at Bruton Street, and it was probably there that he first met John Gould, the young curator. Lear hoped to compile a book of all the parrots then known, and he made preparatory studies of living birds for his finished watercolours at the zoo and private collections. Many of these have a breathtaking reality quite distinct from rigid formal eighteenth-century pictures drawn from stuffed specimens.

Lear decided to use the new method of lithography, or 'drawing on stone' to reproduce the pictures for his *Illustrations of the Family of Psittacidae, or Parrots*. He drew the outlines of the parrots on stone, had these printed at Hullmandel's workshop, and arranged for them to be hand-coloured by experts using his vivid paintings as a guide. The parrot prints were a brilliant artistic achievement for a man of eighteen to twenty, but unfortunately were not a commercial success, and Lear abandoned the production. Gould bought the remaining stock with the idea of completing orders and finishing the last parts, but these plans were never fulfilled.

Gould greatly admired Lear's work and employed him as an illustrator for *The Birds of Europe* and *A Monograph of the Toucans*. Lear worked with Elizabeth Gould, whom he described as 'exceedingly pleasant and amiable', and assisted her 'in all her drawings of the foregrounds'. He helped her discard the stiffly drawn clichés of eighteenth-century tree stumps and mounds for more loosely delineated naturalistic branches and foliage. Although he contributed striking illustrations for *The Birds of Europe*, his work was not always acknowledged, and some plates signed 'E. Lear del' on the picture itself were credited to 'J. & E. Gould'. Gould, keen to promote his own name did not wish Lear's to be too prominent and regarded commissioned work as his own property. Like other publishers of the time he was often careless about checking that the credits on the plates were to the correct artists.

Lear's illustrations were highly regarded among naturalists, and he also worked for Lord Derby, Sir William Jardine, P.J. Selby and T.C. Eyton. But as a draughtsman he received little acknowledgement or status and poor pay. He longed to escape from the restrictions of hired employment for a freelance life as artist and painter – a precarious profession but one that could command wealth and respect in Victorian England. In October 1836, in a letter to Gould from Knowsley, he complained of the cold and the strain of detailed work, writing that his eyes had become 'so sadly worse that no bird under an ostrich shall I soon be able to see to do'. He decided to give up zoological illustration for landscape painting in warmer climates and set off for Italy in July 1837.

Lear sent the Goulds amusing, chatty letters from Rome, and asked about their journey to Australia. 'Why will you continue to walk topsy-turvy so long?' he inquired. 'For every one knows that the people in the Antipodes, being on the other side of the world, must necessarily have their heads where their heels should be. When you come back you will all be puzzled to walk properly.' He invited Gould to visit Rome: 'I can give you a spare bed if you like to put up with the roughness and fleas and procupines flesh and snails for dinner . . . Good wine though. Come.'

Although Lear no longer illustrated natural history books, bird memories peopled his nonsense world, and funny owls, parrots and pelicans (but strangely not toucans) appeared in his comic stories and verses. During his travels he often stayed at hotels and amused children by drawing crazy birds or comic alphabets with spotted ducks, hissing geese or white-headed eagles.

In old age Lear had unhappy memories of Gould, for he wrote after Gould's death in 1881, 'He was one I never liked really, for in spite of a certain jollity, and bonhommie, he was a harsh and violent man. At the Zoological Society . . . ever the persevering hard-working toiler in his own [ornithological] line.' Lear often had bitter and crabbed opinions in his last years and was resentful of successful businessmen; but he probably still held fond memories of Elizabeth Gould, for after her death forty years earlier, he had asked her husband for 'a little sketch . . . as a memorial of a person I esteemed and respected so greatly'.

A drawing of Edward Lear aged 28 by Wilhelm Marstrand.

EDWIN CHARLES PRINCE (1809/10–1874)

Edwin Prince was Gould's private secretary, accountant, reception-ist, salesman and publicity agent. He wrote letters for Gould, transcribed his texts, balanced accounts and collected subscriptions; he was a 'valuable right hand', as Lear so aptly described him.

Prince, unlike Gould, had an urban background, for he was born in Westminster, and throughout his life had London addresses. His contact with ornithology was entirely academic and acquired through a forty-year long association with Gould. In 1838, when Gould set out on his two-year expedition to Australia, Prince was left in charge of his business affairs, including the taxidermy practice which was a valuable source of income. Prince was extremely conscientious and in twenty-nine letters written to Gould, now in the Mitchell Library, Sydney, he recorded receipts and expenditure in an almost daily account of his trials and tribulations.

While Gould was away, Prince obtained subscriptions, main-tained supplies, and ordered further copies of the recent plates of *The Birds of Europe, Toucans* and *Trogons*. Prince felt responsible for promoting Gould's name and sales during his absence. He arranged the Zoological Society's list of Fellows into streets and districts, and called on each person, sometimes leaving prints for inspection. He wrote over 300 letters and made more than 100 visits but found the results very disappointing. In March 1840 Prince used the new prepaid penny post system to send prospectuses to 140 gentlemen living in the country. This early instance of sending unsolicited mail met with some resistance, however, for by the next month two had been returned and no answer had come back from 135 letters!

Prince lived at Gould's house, 20 Broad Street, Soho, during his absence and prepared a room as storage for the cargoes of birds and mammal discoveries from Australia. In October 1839 he was dismayed to find that skins sent by the *Cheviot* were so damp that it was necessary to distribute them over the house and keep large fires going to dry them – a platypus had lost its fur and a large owl's wings were in fragments. Another cargo from the *Marianne* was also so damp that he had to remove the mildew from each specimen.

All the household contracted severe colds and coughs during the winters, and Prince, suffering from chest pains, complained bitterly of the house's damp conditions. He wrote in March 1839 to Gould, 'I do hope you will not attempt to reside here on your return for I am thoroughly convinced that the house itself is a positively unhealthy one, in fact, so old and full of draughts is it, that it is next to impossible to escape illness.' In spite of this unhealthy environment the Gould family remained there for another twenty years. Broad Street featured in Dr John Snow's 1854 study of a cholera epidemic, when over 500 people died in the neighbourhood.

On his return, Gould thanked Prince in the preface of *The Birds of Australia*. Prince continued to decipher Gould's untidy scrawl, compile notes, correct spelling and polish the literary style of the texts, making 'fair copies' for the printers. He also checked scientific names of species writing them on the proofs of the illustrations.

Prince's health was very poor during the preparation of *The Birds of Great Britain* and caused Gould much anxiety. Sharpe recalled that when Prince was ill, Gould, although unwell himself, used to drive out every day to take everything he could that might do good to the sufferer. Prince died in 1874 of asthma and bronchitis, and was buried at Kensal Green Cemetery.

Sharpe found Prince 'a most amiable and conscientious man', who related 'many anecdotes of his patron's early struggles', whereas Wolf, Gould's illustrator, described the diligent secretary as a 'long-suffering slave'. Prince seems to have been too intelligent to be merely servile, but was a worthy member of the team, devoutly dedicated to the success of Gould's career and his publications.

CHARLES JOSEPH HULLMANDEL (1789–1850)

Charles Hullmandel was an important and innovative figure in the printing world of the early nineteenth century. He promoted the new process of lithography or 'drawing on stone', a method which Gould used for all his publications. Indeed, for a whole generation of artists the lithographic printing presses of Hullmandel ensured the production of their finest works, which included *Subjects drawn from Life* (1821) by Théodore Géricault, *Celebrated Horses* (1824) by James Ward, *Views of London* (1842) by Thomas Shotter Boys, and David Roberts's famous series *The Holy Land* (1842–1849).

Hullmandel was born in London of Alsatian and French emigré parents. As a young man he studied art in Paris, and during a sketching tour which ended in Munich he met Aloys Senefelder, the inventor of lithography. Lithography is a method of surface printing, initially used as a cheap way of reproducing music scores. It does not require the skills necessary for engraving into metal or cutting in wood. It is based on the principle that grease is antipathetic to water, and consists of drawing with special greasy chalks on a prepared slab of limestone (although today zinc or aluminium plates are used). The stone is then treated with a wash of dilute acid, coated with gum arabic and finally thoroughly wetted with water. When printing ink is applied with a roller, it adheres only to the parts of the stone covered with the drawing, and is repelled by the remainder of the wet surface.

In 1817/18 Hullmandel established a lithographic workshop at Great Marlborough Street, London, just around the corner from Gould's premises in Broad Street. It was thus very convenient for

Rough watercolour sketch, probably by Gould.

Gould to hire the heavy stones, have them brought to his house where his artists could draw on them, and then send them back to be printed on Hullmandel's presses. He was also close at hand to see the latest proofs and discuss any corrections. As Hullmandel employed draughtsmen for lettering the headings, specialists were available to write the titles on the stones in the final stages before printing. These, of course, had to be written in reverse as the prints were mirror images. Hullmandel's workshop had a high reputation, and Gould was assured that from each 'drawing on stone' an edition of many hundred fine prints would be available.

A manual entitled *The Art of Drawing on Stone*, published in 1824 and written by Hullmandel, described the different effects which could be achieved by light or dark shading with the chalks used for lithography. The title page showed an elegant young lady seated at a desk holding a lithographic pencil – an indication that 'drawing on stone' was a suitable accomplishment for any aspiring lady artist. This book may well have been used by Elizabeth Gould as a guide for her first attempts in lithography. Hullmandel promoted lithography not merely as a mechanical reproductive process, but also as an exciting artistic medium, and he made many experiments in tint and colour printing. Gould, however, was uninterested in these aspects and all his prints were hand-coloured.

Hullmandel died aged sixty-one in 1850, on the eve of the Great Exhibition where his firm exhibited examples of lithotint printing, and Gould's colourists showed experiments with gold colouring for the hummingbird plates. The establishment was carried on by his partner, J.F. Walton. Gould's later plates were printed by Walton, Walter and Cohn, T. Walter, and Mintern Bros.

Ink and watercolour drawing by Hart.

GABRIEL BAYFIELD (1781–1870)

'Bayfield, the colourer' has until recently been a mysterious figure. His name appears in the prefaces of Swainson's *Zoological Illustrations* and Gould's *Birds of Europe*, where he is profusely thanked for his skill and care in colouring. He has now been identified as Gabriel Bayfield, artist, then living in Walworth, South London. His daughters, Mary Ann Bayfield and Maria Elizabeth Gordon, were later also colourists in watercolour.

Bayfield's expertise in *The Birds of Europe* was highly regarded by other eminent naturalists, who asked Gould to arrange for Bayfield to colour their own publications. But Bayfield's prices were high and Darwin asked Gould to negotiate for terms 'at something less than 5d. a piece', for colouring the plates in *The Zoology of H.M.S. Beagle*. Sir William Jardine commented that the production and colouring of the twelve etchings in his elephant folio *British Salmonidae* had been so costly that it was unlikely to make a profit.

From 1831 to 1861 the bulk of Gould's work was coloured under Bayfield's direction, and the number of plates has been estimated at the enormous figure of 350,000. Gould next issued the popular *Birds of Great Britain* (1860–1873), but by then Bayfield was in his eighties and had probably retired. Gould remarked that he engaged 'all the colourers in London' to colour by hand every sky and bird's feather in about 280,000 plates using as a guide to the correct tints, coloured proofs or 'pattern plates' to copy. Some patterns for the toucan plates have survived and are now owned by Henry Sotherans Ltd, London. The *Andigena nigrirostris*, for the second edition of *Toucans*, has special instructions to Mr Bayfield. He is asked to 'alter the sky' using the following colours: 'Here pinky so as to relieve the blue and white, blending the pink into the orange yellow below'. Colour washes for the skies were very important, and it required great skill and experience to paint them satisfactorily. Although colouring was the final stage in production, it could either make or mar the efforts of author, artist and printer.

HENRY CONSTANTINE RICHTER (1821–1902)

Although H.C. Richter was Gould's artist for over thirty years and contributed more than 1,600 illustrations, he remains a shadowy, unobtrusive figure. He came from an artistic family. His grandfather came to England in the late eighteenth century and was an artist, engraver and scagliolist (maker of imitation marble). Richter's father was also a notable artist and engraver, becoming President of the Associated Artists in Watercolour 1811–1812. Henrietta Sophia Richter, an older sister, exhibited miniature portraits at the Royal Academy from 1842 to 1849. In spite of these artistic surroundings, Henry Constantine does not appear to have exhibited his work consisting entirely of natural history illustrations.

In 1841, after his wife's sudden death, Gould searched diligently for an illustrator and was fortunate to find in Richter, then aged about twenty, the perfect interpreter of his requirements. At first Richter was asked to make watercolour studies, and at London Zoo he painted from life kangaroos and wallabies for Gould's *The Mammals of Australia* (1845–1863). Gould originally intended to employ a specialist draughtsman for the drawings on stone, but was delighted to find that Richter himself could do this work and persuaded him to take up lithography. For *The Birds of Australia* Richter worked from Gould's roughly sketched compositions and Elizabeth's Australian studies, and was able to draw directly on the stones without having to make preliminary careful watercolour pictures. Richter and Gould worked side by side and were dependent on each other. Gould wrote to Jardine in August 1842 that he had scarcely left town as 'my friend Richter always requires me to be at his elbow and as it were compels me to stay at home'.

Until the mid-1870s, Richter portrayed Gould's hummingbirds, toucans, trogons and birds of Asia. Some of his most delightful illustrations are of the smaller brownish birds, such as the partridges of America and the warbling birds of the English hedgerows. Richter was mentioned in Gould's will and bequeathed £100 for 'the purchase of a ring or any other article'. He died in 1902, a bachelor aged eighty-one, twenty-one years after his master.

JOHN GILBERT (1812–1845)

Gould could not have accumulated such an extensive list of Australian birds without the assistance of his field-worker John Gilbert. Almost all the new information which Gould used in his descriptions of west and north Australian birds was based on the observations, notes and specimens supplied by this able naturalist-explorer.

At the age of sixteen, Gilbert became a taxidermist at the Zoological Society, London, where Gould was already employed. When Gould needed an experienced assistant to collect and preserve new specimens in Australia, he employed Gilbert, who accompanied him on the *Parsee*. The two naturalists explored in Tasmania and then set off in different directions, Gould travelling to east and south Australia, and Gilbert to the west and north. During ten months in the scrubs and forests of west Australia

Transfer tracing incorporating comments from Gould.

Gilbert amassed some hundreds of specimens of birds and mammals. From Perth he sent to London a box of his finds, 175 birds, 17 quadrupeds, 95 skeletons, 9 reptiles and a fish.

Gilbert and Gould hoped to meet again in Sydney, but much to Gilbert's disappointment this reunion did not take place for Gould rushed home to continue with his publications. Gilbert set off for Port Essington, Australia's most northerly port, a remote settlement in Northern Territory. During eight months in this area before his return to England, he made many exciting discoveries, including the Gouldian Finch and the incubating mounds of the Scrubfowl.

Gould was delighted with his collector's achievements and plans were drawn up for Gilbert to make a second journey to Australia. An agreement was signed whereby Gilbert was to undertake further explorations for the same salary as before, £100 a year plus travelling expenses. Back in west Australia Gilbert journeyed hundreds of miles by foot and horse in the brushland and also visited the Houtman's Abrolhos Islands where he was amazed by the vast numbers of congregating seabirds. Planning then to revisit the north, Gilbert on his own initiative made the fatal decision to join an ill-assorted group of convicts, aborigines and naturalists on a poorly prepared expedition from Moreton Bay to Port Essington led by Dr Leichhardt. Tragically, in a remote area of northern Queensland, Gilbert was killed by local natives who, it is thought, were angered by the treatment of their women by aborigines in the party.

Fortunately, Gilbert's research during this final journey was not in vain. His journal and skins were kept safely by Leichhardt and sent to Gould in London. Many of these carefully labelled specimens have been used to describe new species and are still preserved in Liverpool Museum, the Natural History Museum, London, the Academy of Natural Sciences, Philadelphia, the Royal Albert Museum, Exeter and other institutions.

WILLIAM MATTHEW HART (1830–1908)

William Hart was the illustrator of Gould's final volumes. He drew and lithographed plates after about 1872, and eventually replaced H.C. Richter. According to Sharpe, Gould's biographer, Hart first worked for Gould as a colourist in 1851, 'making the patterns for the Humming-birds and colouring the metallic parts of the birds'.

William Matthew Hart was born in Limerick, Ireland, the son of a watercolour painter. His life and personality have been little recorded but unlike Richter, who was a bachelor, he had a large family of at least seven children to raise. He was frequently impoverished and lived at various addresses in Walworth and Camberwell, in south London. Gould left Hart £200 in his will to support his large family, and £50 was added in a later codicil.

Whereas Richter's role was that of the perfect interpretive illustrator, Hart had ambitions to become a freelance artist. His illustrations for Gould and Sharpe have pictorially elaborate landscape backgrounds, and in his oil paintings he used the rich colours and detail so loved by late Victorians. He may have optimistically hoped that by selling paintings he could earn more money than the meagre wages of a natural history draughtsman.

As William Hart spent most of his life in London in straitened circumstances, it is probable that he never saw in the wild the birds he portrayed so magnificently. It is sad to realize that his pictures are mostly based on dried specimens and topographical landscapes in travel books. A few decades ago Hart's bird of paradise pictures so captivated an aspiring young naturalist, David Attenborough, that he was determined to see for himself the birds in the New Guinea mountains. Sir David's nature films and commentaries have brought to life the astounding displays and glorious colours of these extraordinary birds in their natural settings.

JOSEPH MATTHEW WOLF (1820–1899)

Joseph Wolf would probably have disliked being counted as a member of Gould's team, for he preferred to be regarded as an independent freelance wildlife artist and a rugged individualist. Brought up in a small village of the Rhineland Moselle valley, Germany, from an early age Joseph Wolf enjoyed drawing birds and mammals. The wilder aspects of nature particularly appealed to him, and he captured birds of prey to use as subjects for his first paintings. At sixteen he was apprenticed as a lithographic draughtsman to a firm of advertisers, where he drew trade headings and bottle labels. This exacting work, although tedious, increased the accuracy of his studies from nature, in which he carefully recorded the minute markings of plumage and the formations of feather tracts.

In 1844 Wolf supplied life-size illustrations for a lavish book on falconry by Schlegel and Wulverhorst. His powerful presentations impressed English naturalists, and Gould later acquired the water-colour of a magnificent hooded Greenland Gyrfalcon perched on a falconer's fist. Wolf left Germany to study painting in Antwerp, but political unrest brought life to a standstill, and in 1848 he left for England. At the British Museum, London, he illustrated the last parts of G.R. Gray's *Genera of Birds*, but he found the work uninspiring and was unimpressed by the museum scientists. He complained that these naturalists only knew dried specimens and would not recognize 'a bird when they see it flying'.

Gould greatly admired Wolf's work and commissioned an oil painting, *Woodcocks seeking shelter*, which was exhibited at the 1849 Royal Academy. He was keen to include Wolf's work in his publications, and during the following thirty years Wolf's water-colours of birds of prey, game, pheasants and water birds were reproduced in *The Birds of Asia* and *The Birds of Great Britain*. Wolf was often dissatisfied with the lithographs and thought the colours vulgar and harsh compared to the subtle shades of watercolours.

In the summer of 1856 Gould and Wolf travelled to the high mountains in the Dovrefjell district of Norway to see the Willow Ptarmigan and breeding Fieldfares. Wolf claimed that he was the better field naturalist for he could find birds by identifying their calls and lead the way to their nests. Later he described Gould as 'a shrewd old fellow, but the most uncouth man I ever knew', and related to his biographer A.H. Palmer many anecdotes about Gould's keen eye for a bargain. His anecdotes told of Gould's indefatigable passion for acquiring new skins, which he would borrow for comparison, and then take to Wolf's studio. There he would help himself to a cigar and walk restlessly round the room while a drawing or watercolour was made. 'Gould was the most restless fellow who would never sit down except when he was fishing at Maidenhead when he would sit for hours.'

Wolf regarded the majority of Gould's illustrations as prosaic and expressionless. He preferred to paint wild birds in dramatic situations with such titles as *The Proud Bird of the Mountains* or *A Dying Partridge*. When Wolf first exhibited his paintings in England Sir Edwin Landseer prophesied: 'When a good many artists of the present generation are forgotten, Wolf will be remembered.'

RICHARD BOWDLER SHARPE (1847–1909)

Richard Bowlder Sharpe was only fifteen when he first met Gould as he fished, aged fifty-eight, at Cookham on the Thames. Both had a passionate interest in birds and struck up a friendship which lasted until Gould's death nineteen years later.

Sharpe, born in London, was expected by his father, a publisher, to join the army or enter university. Instead he left school to work at the bookshop W.H. Smith and later for the antiquarian bookseller Bernard Quaritch. At twenty he became the first librarian at the Zoological Society, London, and a year later published the first parts of *A Monograph of the Alcedinidae, or family of Kingfishers*, for which Gould lent many specimens.

In 1872 Sharpe was appointed Keeper of the bird section of the British Museum, where vast numbers of skins and eggs were arriving from outposts of the expanding British Empire. These discoveries were excitedly discussed at Zoological Society meetings and with Gould at his home. After Edwin Prince died, Sharpe helped Gould prepare his manuscripts, becoming an almost daily visitor. Towards the end of his life Gould was frequently unwell but found comfort in Sharpe's companionship. The younger man's knowledge and interest helped to compensate for the loss of his sons Henry and Franklin, both medical doctors, who had assisted with his books but had died aged twenty-five and thirty-three, one in Bombay and the other at sea after a visit to India. Gould's other son Charles, a geological surveyor in Tasmania and author of *Mythical Monsters* travelled abroad and seldom revisited England.

Sharpe was a prodigious worker, publishing monumental catalogues and handbooks of birds in the British Museum, lavishly illustrated volumes of the birds of paradise, and chatty books based on a popular series of lectures. After Gould's death he completed three unfinished sets of Gould's volumes, wrote his short biography and indexed all the illustrations. During his conversations with Sharpe in his final years, Gould would point to his portrait and mention the words that he would like for his epitaph. These would form the simple inscription: 'Here lies John Gould, the "Bird Man".'

Lithograph print, before the text was added.

A Century of Birds from the Himalayas

One volume (1830–1833), 80 plates depicting 100 birds.

As curator and taxidermist to the museum of the newly founded Zoological Society Gould had access to the latest exciting discoveries of birds throughout the world and shared in the enthusiasm among naturalists for classifying and describing new species. A valuable collection of bird skins from the mountainous districts of northern India was stuffed and mounted by Gould and discussed at the Scientific Committee of the Zoological Society. They aroused such interest that Gould decided to present them in the form of a book of illustrations.

Gould was not a skilled artist, but his wife Elizabeth, who was gifted in drawing and watercolour painting, made careful studies of the mounted birds under his scientific guidance. She also drew their outlines with wax pencils on the prepared limestone slabs ready to be sent for printing at Charles Hullmandel's lithographic workshops. The first prints, made in late 1830, depicted small owls, finches and tits, similar to European birds. These small tightly drawn birds were very tentative compared to the more confident and richly coloured Himalayan pheasants illustrated a year and a half later. All the plates were issued with the plants and backgrounds uncoloured, but rare copies have survived with both birds and settings coloured.

Elizabeth Gould's early, careful, but stilted bird studies, now in Spencer Library, University of Kansas, and at Knowsley Hall, depict the specimens displayed on small wooden props or perches. In the finished plates the birds are positioned on stumpy branches, small mounds or tree-trunks in the traditional convention evolved by bird illustrators of the eighteenth century. The size of plates, imperial-folio (559 × 406 mm), was the same format that Edward Lear had introduced for his pioneer work *Illustrations of the Family of Psittacidae, or Parrots* (1830–1832). This became a successful standard for Gould's later productions and was large enough for life-size illustrations of the majority of bird species.

Nicholas Vigors MP, Secretary to the Zoological Society of London, wrote the text, which was added more than eighteen months after the illustrations were completed. Vigors named a beautiful little sunbird after Elizabeth Gould, *Cinnyris Gouldiae*, in recognition of her valuable contribution to ornithology.

Gould dedicated the book to King William IV and Queen Adelaide. As with all his books Gould was his own publisher. He initiated a list of two hundred subscribers, and efficiently organized the production so that it was financially successful.

During the preparation of the book an interesting event took place in the history of bird illustration. At the first meeting of the British Association for the Advancement of Science, held in York in September 1831, Gould exhibited the Himalayan specimens and copies of his work; also present was Robert Havell, who displayed drawings of birds for 'Mr Audubon's great work on American Ornithology'.

NUCIFRAGA HEMISPILA.

Drawn from Nature & on Stone by E. Gould.　　　　　　　Printed by C. Hullmandel.

1　*Himalayan Nutcracker* (EG)

GREATER PIED OR CRESTED KINGFISHER
ALCEDO GUTTATUS

Ceryle lugubris guttulata Stejneger

PLATE 3

In her first bird illustrations Elizabeth Gould adopted the eighteenth-century formula of depicting the bird in profile on a perch. This silhouetted kingfisher with its few colours has an almost naive simplicity, which contrasts greatly with the multicoloured elaborate compositions of Gould's final works. The picture is almost monochrome, for the bird's plumage is black and white and the foliage and tree-stump are in pencil grey. The beige and pink washes on the beak, feet and belly are the only indications of colour. This illustration is in keeping with the period trend for simple colouring, as can be seen in its similarity to early nineteenth-century fashion plates which feature ladies in delicate white muslin dresses, dark trimmings and lightly tinted complexions.

Vigors, who wrote the description, mentions that only two skins of this large spotted kingfisher from northern India were known in England, and that it was nearly equal in size to the black and white kingfisher of Africa. In India it was said to feed on fish and aquatic insects, and was called 'Muchee-bag', which meant 'Fish-tiger'. It made a nest composed of mud lined with grass 'adhering to the side of a stone similar to the nest of a swallow', where it laid four eggs 'coloured like itself'.

ALCEDO GUTTATUS.

3 Greater Pied or Crested Kingfisher (EG)

GARRULUS LANCEOLATUS.

2 Lanceolated Jay (EG)

HIMALAYAN NUTCRACKER
NUCIFRAGA HEMISPILA

Nucifraga caryocatactes hemispila Vigors

PLATE 1

Gould was intrigued to find that some of the birds collected from the Himalayas appeared to be closely related to European species, varying only by slight differences in colouring and markings. It was thought that the nutcracker living in Europe was a unique species of its genus, but the Himalayan Nutcracker seemed very similar. The only difference was that the Indian bird had spots 'confined to the upper part of its plumage', whereas the European bird had spots all over its breast and belly. Vigors wrote: 'the *Nucifraga hemispila* may be considered as one of those remarkable objects of nature, which, with a decided identity of form and character, but with slight though permanent distinctions, are placed in remote countries as representatives of the same group.'

The nutcrackers live in thick woods, and their diet consists mainly of nuts and pine seeds which they extract from shells with great skill. In autumn they hide and store food in holes in the ground for excavation during the cold winter. H.C. Richter's picture of the nutcracker in *The Birds of Great Britain*, made in 1865, shows the bird vigorously pecking at cones in a pine forest.

17

Lanceolated Jay
Garrulus lanceolatus

Garrulus lanceolatus Vigors

PLATE 2

Vigors remarked that this jay from the Himalayas had a close affinity in form and colour with some species inhabiting the U.S.A. and Mexico. This was another example of the fact that 'similar forms of ornithology are found in countries widely separated from each other whose temperatures are similar'.

Elizabeth Gould's meticulous watercolour study for the jay, now in the Spencer Library, Kansas University, shows the bird posed on a tiny bar perch. Gould would have carefully positioned the stuffed and mounted jay on a prop ready for his wife to draw. She painted the colours of the jay in exquisite detail and her picture would have been used by the colourists as a guide for tinting the plates. Vigors described the jay as having a black-crested head, throat covered with white elongated lanceolate feathers, and the wing- and tail-feathers barred in blue and black, each feather tipped with white.

Elizabeth Gould probably knew the coloured engravings of jays in Levaillant's *Histoire naturelle des oiseaux de paradis* (1801–1806), based on paintings by Jacques Barraband. The birds in these luxurious French prints were stiffly perched on tree-props in the traditional manner without landscape backgrounds. In contrast, John James Audubon's roguish blue jays in the magnificent aquatints of *The Birds of America* (1827–1838) were depicted in the act of stealing eggs. Elizabeth Gould may have seen some of Audubon's preparatory paintings but it is unlikely that she would have seen the print of jays, as the monumental aquatints were then in course of publication.

Red-billed Blue Magpie
Pica erythrorhyncha

Urocissa erythrorhyncha (Boddaert)

PLATE 4

This brilliant blue magpie was described as exceeding all other magpies in the beauty of its plumage and grace of its proportions. 'Seen among the foliage of the trees, it is recorded as forming an elegant and conspicuous object, flitting from bough to bough, with long flowing tail and full of vivacity in every movement.'

Elizabeth Gould had difficulty in coping with the scale of this bird, which she depicted two-thirds of its natural size, and its long central tail-feathers almost fall off the page. In one of her drawings, signed Eliza Gould 1829, now in Knowsley Hall Library, the magpie's tail is so long that a separate drawing was made of its tip. Some thirty years later in *The Birds of Asia*, Richter's more successful and dramatic composition depicts the blue magpie flying diagonally downwards, and in the distance smaller birds fly across the centre of the picture.

Vigors remarked that a captive magpie kept by Mr Shore, who had provided valuable notes on Himalayan birds, was fierce and tyrannical, refusing all food except for live birds which it pounced on and devoured with alacrity.

PICA ERYTHRORHYNCHA.
⅔ Nat Size.

Drawn from Nature on Stone by E Gould.

Printed by C Hullmandel.

4 *Red-billed Blue Magpie* (EG)

GREAT HORNBILL
BUCEROS CAVATUS

Buceros bicornis Linnaeus

PLATE 5

Elizabeth Gould's picture is the only example of a hornbill in all Gould's books. This grand bird, originally presented at half natural size, was entirely black and white, except for its 'dirty straw-coloured neck' and the huge bill which was yellow,

becoming scarlet at the tip. Vigors noted its unusual feet, which had broad fleshy soles and three united strong front toes.

Its powerful grip enables it to perch and leap agilely from branch to branch among the trees where it lives. Today it is found in the lowland forests of the Himalayas from India to south China, Burma, Thailand and Indonesia to Malaysia and Sumatra. In many areas the species has declined, mainly due to deforestation.

The hornbill's diet is omnivorous and

consists primarily of fruit, berries, various insects and small mammals. With their large bills they are able to reach out to awkward places and pluck insects or fruit, which they often toss in the air before catching and swallowing.

BLACK AND YELLOW GROSBEAK
COCCOTHRAUSTES ICTERIOIDES

Mycerobas icterioides (Vigors)

PLATE 6

'This richly coloured species of Grosbeak, which may be considered a typical example of the genus, is one of the most valuable recent additions to science. It is a bird of extreme rarity in our Museums; the female, indeed, of the pair which we were fortunate enough to procure, is the only specimen of that sex, we believe, which has hitherto been brought to this country.'

The grosbeaks, like the hawfinches of Europe, have large powerful conical bills and can break open the toughest nuts. They are shy and retiring birds, and live in the interior of thick woods and forests in the western Himalayas and north-eastern Afghanistan.

The male has a black head and wings, while its rump and underparts are rich yellow. In contrast, the female is a light tawny colour.

These grosbeaks were one of Elizabeth Gould's first published illustrations. The pair were placed on a bending branch one above the other so that their prominent large beaks and contrasting plumage could

BUCEROS CAVATUS.

COCCOTHRAUSTES ICTERIOIDES.

5 *Great Hornbill* (EG)

6 *Black and Yellow Grosbeak* (EG)

7 *Mrs Gould's Sunbird* (EG)

a valuable addition to science.

Nearly forty years later Richter was commissioned by Gould to illustrate this species in *The Birds of Asia*. The contrast between Elizabeth Gould's rather flat depiction and Richter's later livelier version shows both the change from an earlier artificiality to a greater realism, and the increasing proficiency of Gould's artists. This change can be seen also in the treatment of the plants in the two plates: Elizabeth Gould depicts some indistinguishable foliage for a background, whereas Richter uses the exotic flower *Nepenthes ampullaria* as an integrated and integral part of the composition.

It is interesting to note that Mrs Gould's Sunbird *Aethopyga gouldiae* has retained the correct name of Mrs Gould. The Austra-

lian bird named in dedication to her by her husband is known as the Gouldian Finch, despite the nomenclature of *Amadina gouldiae*, which denotes by the ending -*ae* that it is named after a woman. Ironically, it is often thought that the Gouldian Finch commemorates not Elizabeth Gould but Gould himself.

IMPEYAN PHEASANT OR HIMALAYAN MONAL

LOPHOPHORUS IMPEYANUS

Lophophorus impejanus (Latham)

PLATE 9

Vigors marvelled that such a beautiful bird should live in remote rocky areas of the

be clearly depicted. Some eight years later Elizabeth Gould illustrated the curiously different beaks of the Galapagos Islands Finches for Darwin's *Zoology of the Voyage of the Beagle*. In 1838 Gould classified the specimens Darwin brought back from his world trip, and noticed that finches from different Galapagos islands had varied beaks, some as large as a hawfinch's, others as small as a warbler's, according to whether their diet consisted of nuts, cacti, or insects. Gould's descriptions and Elizabeth's illustrations led to further investigations and eventually contributed to Darwin's momentous theories of evolution by natural selection, which were formulated many years later.

MRS GOULD'S SUNBIRD

CINNYRUS GOULDIAE

Aethopyga gouldiae (Vigors)

PLATE 7

This little sunbird was dedicated to Mrs Gould by Nicholas Vigors, the first secretary of the Zoological Society, who wrote the classifications and text for *A Century of Birds in the Himalayas*.

Vigors wrote that the sunbirds of India were very like the hummingbirds of America, for they were small, beautiful, and fed on tiny insects among flowers with open blossoms. The *Aethopyga gouldiae*, from the high Himalayan mountains was an exceedingly rare species and its discovery was

8 *Satyr Tragopan* (EG)

LOPHOPHORUS IMPEYANUS.

Male. ⅔ Nat. Size.

9   *Impeyan Pheasant or Himalayan Monal (EG)*

upper Himalayas. 'Is it not singular that the elevated regions of the Himalayas, verging upon the limits of perpetual snow, should present us with a tribe of birds [the family of the Phasianidae] which are distinguished almost beyond all others by the brilliancy of their plumage?' The Impeyan Pheasant was particularly remarkable for the 'intense metallic lustre of its colours'.

This pheasant or monal (a Nepalese name for this bird) was dedicated to Sir Elijah Impey, who was Chief Justice in Bengal from 1774 to 1789, and Lady Impey, who brought some living birds from India. This attempt to introduce them to England was unsuccessful, but it was hoped that further attempts would be made to establish them in aviaries where they would form 'a splendid ornament to our woods and lawns'. By mid-century many were successfully breeding in European zoos, and Joseph Wolf painted in oils a pair at the Zoological Gardens, London; this was used as an illustration in *The Birds of Asia*.

Vigors pointed out the great contrast between the plumage of the adult male and female. The adult male was resplendent with tints of burnished green and purple changing with every light. The general colour of the female was of a deep brown, variegated with markings of white and rusty brown.

These pheasants live in the upper valleys, forests, scrub and alpine meadows of the Himalayas, where they dig up tubers, roots and insects with their powerful beaks. They rarely descend below about 6,500 feet (2,000 metres) even in winter.

SATYR TRAGOPAN

TRAGOPAN SATYRUS

Tragopan satyra (Linnaeus)

PLATE 8

This tragopan was named after the mythical Greek satyr, a deity depicted as half-man and half-beast, with a goat's horns, hind-legs, ears and tail. The name *satyrus* refers to the satyr-like fleshy erectile horns on the head of the male.

These tragopans are secretive birds living in the higher forests of the Himalayas, moving lower in winter. They feed on insects, leaves, buds, tubers and roots and scratch about among the bamboo and

TRAGOPAN HASTINGSII.
⅓ Nat. Size.

Drawn from Nature and on Stone by E. Gould.   *Printed by C. Hullmandel.*

10   *Western Tragopan* (EG)

rhododendron undergrowth in the ravines and gullies. The male has an extraordinary but rarely seen courtship display; it inflates the two slender blue horns on its crown, and puffs out the fleshy bib under its throat which looks like a piece of blue silk with sage green margins edged with patches of brilliant red.

Elizabeth Gould's illustration was of a young male, originally produced at two-thirds life size. She depicts with great expertise its elaborately spotted and mottled colouring. The back is brown with irregular spots of white, and its under-surface varies from blood-red to scarlet-maroon with numerous white spots encircled in black.

This pheasant was also illustrated by Richter over thirty years later in *The Birds of Asia*.

OTIS NIGRICEPS.
⅓ Nat Size

11 Great Indian Bustard (EG)

Western Tragopan

Tragopan hastingsii

Tragopan melanocephalus (Gray)

PLATE 10

This species was named in honour of the Marquis of Hastings (1754–1826), Governor General of India from 1813 to 1823. Vigors described it as similar to the *Trago-pan satyrus*, but slightly larger in size, and with distinctive fiery orange feathers on the lower part of its throat. However, the bird drawn by Elizabeth Gould is now thought to be a male Western Tragopan, *Tragopan melanocephalus*, though the face and lappet coloration is not correct. The rich mottled colouring of the young male pheasant is depicted in great detail, the brown or maroon feathers are each tipped with black with a large spot of white in the middle.

All the plates in *A Century of Birds from the Himalayas* are described as 'Drawn from Nature and on Stone by E.Gould'. In the early nineteenth century drawing 'from Nature' was a token of authenticity, since it meant working from a bird model, either a specimen or a captive bird, rather than copying from another illustration or making a picture from a written description. It was not until later in the century that artists made bird illustrations from field studies of wild birds in their natural surroundings.

Great Indian Bustard

Otis nigriceps

Ardeotis nigriceps (Vigors)

PLATE 11

Vigors wrote that although this bustard came from the highlands of the Himalayas, it was not confined to that area. Large numbers lived in flocks throughout the wide and open plains of north-west India, where they were hunted and considered a great culinary delicacy.

The Great Indian Bustard is now confined to grassland areas of western India, and is now known as an endangered species. The range of its habitat has been reduced by agricultural development and livestock grazing. It is still hunted for food; its ability to run rapidly formerly provided sport for horsemen but today's method of shooting from vehicles allows it little chance of escape. Wardened reserves have been established for its protection, and recent conservation efforts seem to be stabilizing the remaining population.

The male bustard has an elaborate display, during which the neck feathers are fluffed out, an inflatable pouch of skin is expanded, and the tail is spread and elevated. The height of the bustard is about 4 feet (120 centimetres). Elizabeth Gould coped with the problem of depicting its large stature by reducing it in her original illustration to one-third of its natural size.

THE BIRDS OF EUROPE

Five volumes (1832–1837), 448 plates.

Encouraged by the success of *A Century of Birds from the Himalayas*, Gould embarked on a larger project, *The Birds of Europe*. He wrote a prospectus, dated October 1831, announcing that the forthcoming work, limited to 300 copies, would be issued in parts of twenty-five plates at three-monthly intervals, for £3 per part to be paid by subscribers on delivery. A letterpress, describing the birds' habits and changes of plumage, would be made to accompany the pictures. This was different from the Himalayan volume, where the text was published separately, and Gould followed this revised plan of production for all his subsequent publications.

Gould wished to include familiar British birds and also lesser known species from Continental Europe. To study specimens and collect the latest information he travelled with Edward Lear to visit zoos, private collections and museums in Amsterdam, Rotterdam, Berne and Berlin. In 1835 Gould and his wife Elizabeth went on a tour of Leyden, Frankfurt, Munich, Vienna and Salzburg.

Lear contributed sixty-eight plates, mainly of the larger birds such as eagles, storks, cranes, herons, flamingoes, owls and pelicans, the two latter categories producing some of his most striking bird portraits.

The smaller, pretty, but also most of the duller birds were depicted by Elizabeth Gould from sketches and designs by her husband. Sometimes her birds seem stiff and awkwardly positioned, but the chaffinch, golden oriole, and stonechat are portrayed among flowers and foliage. Her skill of linking birds with plants was later perfected in *The Birds of Australia*.

In his preface Gould acknowledged the work of both artists, but his highest praise was for the 'unceasing attention' of Mr Bayfield, under whose expert direction the plates had been 'carefully and accurately coloured'. As the names of colourists were not usually mentioned by publishers, Gould's profuse thanks show his high regard for their skill and their importance in the success of his enterprises.

Strangely, Gould included some North American birds, such as the Bald Eagle and Barred Owl, among the European species. This was probably due to the interest aroused in England by J.J. Audubon's magnificent *Birds of America* (1827–1838) which was then in the course of production in London.

The Birds of Europe was dedicated to all the 'Noblemen and Gentlemen forming the Council of the Zoological Society of London', and its eminent president, the 13th Earl of Derby.

VOLUME I

CINEREOUS OR BLACK (CINEREUS) VULTURE

VULTUR CINEREUS

Aegypius monachus (Linnaeus)

PLATE 13

'The European habitats of the Cinereus Vulture are the vast plains of Hungary, the mountainous district of the Tyrol, the Swiss Alps, the Pyrenees and the middle of Spain and Italy'. Today the Cinereous or Black Vulture is a rare breeder in Spain and Greece, also eastwards through the Middle East and Asia.

Gould wrote that this dark brown vulture had downy feathering on its head and neck, a kind of beard under the throat, and bluish bare skin on its neck, bill, legs and claws. It had powerful curved claws which were strong enough to carry off live animals, but it fed mainly on putrid carcasses.

Lear's later comic drawings and verse often portrayed animals. An alphabet letter V for Vulture has a lively sketch and the tongue-twister: 'The Visibly Vicious Vulture who wrote Verses to a Veal-cutlet in a Volume bound in Vellum.'

Although the original plate, one-third life-size, is signed prominently 'E. Lear del' on the vulture's perch in Lear's own handwriting, the inscription underneath reads 'Drawn from Nature & on Stone by J & E Gould.' Gould was not always careful about ascribing the correct credits to his artists, and used the Gould name almost as a trademark on several plates which were in fact Lear's work.

WHITE-TAILED (SEA) EAGLE

HALIAEETUS ALBICILLA

Haliaeetus albicilla (Linnaeus)

PLATE 14

'Although not so alert and sprightly as the Golden Eagle, it is nevertheless vigorous and resolute, its powers of flight enabling it to soar with great majesty and ease through the upper regions of the air, whence it often precipitates itself upon its prey, or any intruder near its nest, with great force and velocity.'

Gould write that the Sea Eagle was the 'most common of all the European Eagles, and perhaps the most widely dispersed'. The White-tailed Eagle was then frequently seen 'along the rocky shores of England, Ireland, Scotland and the adjacent islands'. Since then there has been a marked decline in its range, due mainly to persecution, and in many countries including Britain it has become extinct. However, recent attempts to introduce eagles from Norway to breed in West Scotland have been successful; and in 1985 a young White-tailed Eagle flew from a Scottish eyrie after an interval of some seventy years, and in 1991 seven young were raised by four pairs at carefully guarded nests.

Lear's illustration shows an adult eagle in the foreground with its mature plumage of pale brown head, neck and chest, yellow bill and striking white tail. The young bird lacks the white tail and has a blackish-brown bill and dark brown plumage.

A watercolour sketch by Lear of these powerful eagles is in the Blacker-Wood Library, McGill University, Montreal. The birds, with their layers of brown feathers strongly outlined, are surrounded by many colour notes written by Lear in pencil, such as: 'Chin very light, head & neck pale umber. Thighs dark brown, legs yellow.'

13   *Cinereous or Black Vulture* (EL)

14   *White-tailed Eagle* (EL)

BALD (WHITE-HEADED) EAGLE

HALIAEETUS LEUCOCEPHALUS

Haliaeetus leucocephalus (Linnaeus)

PLATE 12

Although the White-headed Eagle, or Bald Eagle, is found only in North America, Gould introduced it into *The Birds of Europe* because its young had brown feathering similar to the immature Golden and Sea Eagles and could easily be confused with those species. The adult Bald Eagle, well-known as the national bird of the United States, was unmistakable with its chocolate-brown plumage, white head, neck and tail, but these distinctive colours were not acquired until its third or fourth year.

Gould wrote that the Bald Eagle hunted for itself but also ate fish caught by the osprey. 'Though preying indiscriminately on every kind of animal, especially mammalia, and not even refusing carrion when pressed by hunger, the White-headed Eagle gives the decided preference for fish. Not that he obtains his prey by his own exertions as a fisher . . . he watches the labour of the Osprey, and forces that industrious fisher to give up his booty.'

The eagle's eyrie at the top of lofty trees was formed of a mass of 'sticks, sods and grass' increased, repaired and used annually

15 *Marsh Harrier* (EL)

until it became 'of such magnitude as to be observable at a great distance'. The young were fed with fish, which often lay 'scattered in a putrid state round the tree, infecting the air for a considerable distance'.

The adult male and immature bird were illustrated one-third life-size. Recently the Bald Eagle has declined in numbers but it is still widespread in Alaska and western Canada, and in parts of central Canada, central and southern U.S.A.

MARSH HARRIER

CIRCUS RUFUS

Circus aeruginosus (Linnaeus)

PLATE 15

Gould wrote that the Marsh Harrier was widespread in low marshy areas of Europe; its large size made it such a conspicuous bird in the air that it could not fail to attract attention. 'Like the rest of the Harriers its flight is buoyant and sweeping, but generally at a low elevation, it traverses over moors and marshes in search of its

prey, which consists of frogs, lizards, mice and even fish.'

Gould thought that most Marsh Harriers seen in England were probably not native bred birds, but had flown over from

BARN OWL.

16 *Barn Owl* (EL)

Europe. During this century, through drainage, persecution and the use of pesticides, harriers have become uncommon in many areas of western and central Europe. Lately, in England, some recovery has taken place, and harriers are now nesting in East Anglian bird reserves.

The adult bird in the foreground, depicted in the original at three-quarters life-size, has a yellowish-white head, delicate grey on its wings and tail, and a rufous brown belly. Although some immature birds are almost all brown, others, as in the illustration, have buff heads, cheeks and shoulders.

BARN OWL

STRIX FLAMMEA

Tyto alba (Scopoli)

PLATE 16

Gould described the Barn Owl as a resident species widespread throughout Europe, which spent the day in barns, ruins, church towers and hollow trees, leaving at dusk in search of food. 'Dazzled by the light of day, for which their powers of vision are not adapted, they remain motionless and inanimate in their retreats.' Their eyes were protected from the light by a 'thin membraneous veil', which looked like a third eyelid.

At night the owl emerged from its daytime lethargy. Then, 'intent on their search, they skim over meadows with every sense alert . . . so rapidly, indeed, do they pounce upon their victims, that even the little mouse is seized before aware of its approaching fate.'

Barn Owls have recently greatly declined in numbers, as roosting and nesting places in hedgerow trees and old barns are disappearing in the countryside; attempts are being made to encourage farmers and others to provide Barn Owl nesting boxes in lofts and outhouse conversions.

This plate is signed 'E.Lear del' under the ledge in the left corner, but is one of several prints by Lear bearing an inscription credited to the Goulds. On the bottom left is printed: 'Drawn from Life & on Stone by J & E Gould.'

EAGLE OWL

BUBO MAXIMUS

Bubo bubo (Linnaeus)

PLATE 18

'Perched upon some branch, and obscured by the shadows of evening, it marks its ill-fated quarry, — the fawn reposing among the fern, — the hare nibbling the grass, — the grouse crouching among the heath; — silently and rapidly down it pounces, strikes its talons into its victim, and commences the work of destruction. Less noble game, such as moles, rats and lizards, may also be ranked among articles of food.'

This majestic owl, the largest and most powerful in Europe, lived in the great forests of Norway, Sweden and Russia; it was also seen in Germany and Switzerland, but was a scarce vagrant in France and England. Today it is rare over much of its large range of mainland Europe. In its forest environment it is difficult to spot as it is mainly nocturnal and its brown colouring forms a protective camouflage.

Gould explained that the feathered tufts, usually called ears, had no connection 'whatever with its true organs of hearing'. The Eagle Owl had remarkable vision and could see in dull daylight and moonlight as well as in the dusk and darkness.

Lear's illustration from a stuffed specimen was three-quarters life-size. Its large, staring, yellow eyes give it a quizzical, penetrating and disturbing appearance. Perhaps something of Lear's strange personality is reflected in this extraordinary bird portrait.

17   Snowy Owl (EL)

18   Eagle Owl (EL)

Snowy Owl

Strix nyctea

Nyctea scandiaca (Linnaeus)

PLATE 17

Gould wrote that the Snowy Owl lived in the Arctic regions, but during extreme weather moved southwards, to Russia, Sweden, Norway and occasionally the Faeroe, Orkney and Shetland Islands. They were occasionally found in England, and the ornithologist Prideaux John Selby owned a fine pair which were killed near Rothbury, Northumberland, in January 1823 during a severe snowstorm. In the long hours of the arctic summer the owls hunted by day and preyed on alpine hares, rabbits, rats, lemmings, grouse and even foxes. Today they still live in the Arctic, but with marked fluctuations in numbers and movements which are related to the fluctuations in the numbers of their main prey. Rather surprisingly, breeding occurred in Fethar, Shetlands, between 1967 and 1975, but not since.

The Snowy Owl's dense plumage, which covers its face and legs, provides a useful insulation against cold weather. The colouring varies according to age, from the brown bars of the young birds to the pure white of the older males. Lear's original illustration shows an adult in front of a two-year-old bird, both about a third life-size.

Lear was an expert at depicting the smooth texture of downy plumage with the grey shading of lithographic pencil. The fluffy feathers of the white owl look so soft one is almost tempted to stroke them!

Barred or Mottled Owl

Strix nebulosa

Strix varia Barton

PLATE 19

The Barred Owl lives in central and eastern North America and Mexico. Gould included it in *The Birds of Europe* because he believed the species occasionally migrated to Norway, Sweden and Russia.

Gould quoted from J.J. Audubon's *The Birds of America*, which described the owls' discordant screams at dusk of 'whah, whah, whah-aa' in the woods of Louisiana. Audubon reported that the owls appeared not to see well during daytime: 'I have observed that the approach of the grey squirrel intimidated them, if one of these animals accidently jumped on a branch close to them, although the Owl destroys a number of them during the twilight.'

Gould thought that the owl's noiseless flight was due to its soft, yielding feathers,

19 *Barred or Mottled Owl* (EL)

20 *European Bee-eater* (EG)

which enabled it to steal up on its victim without warning. Its prey consisted of young hares and rabbits, mice, small birds, frogs and lizards.

In different regions the owl's plumage varied from dark to very light colours. Lear's owl, which in the original is almost life-size, was barred on its upper body with brownish-grey, greyish-ash and yellowish-white markings.

VOLUME II

EUROPEAN BEE-EATER (BEE-EATER)

MEROPS APIASTER

Merops apiaster Linnaeus

PLATE 20

Gould wrote that the bee-eaters were similar to the kingfishers and swallows. Like the kingfishers they had long bills, short legs, brilliant plumage, and nesting sites in sandy banks. They resembled the swallows in their gregarious habits, flying agility and dexterity in catching insects on the wing.

Bee-eaters were migratory birds, flying to the warmer parts of Europe, especially Italy, Spain, Greece and Turkey in large numbers. Sometimes they strayed to England but did not often breed there because of the uncongenial climate. They caught flies, gnats, and particularly wasps and bees in the air whilst flying backwards and forwards.

The bee-eaters scooped out deep holes by river banks for nesting. In Australia, some few years later, Gould saw the bee-eaters', or rainbow-birds' long tunnels which led to underground rooms where the females reared chicks.

Elizabeth Gould illustrated the 'adult male in its finest state of plumage' against a distant landscape of rocky shore and water. In *The Birds of Great Britain* H.C. Richter elaborated this scene into a congregation of birds in the trees by a sandy river bank.

ROLLER.
Coracias garrula. *(Linn.)*

21 European Roller (EG)

EUROPEAN ROLLER (ROLLER)

CORACIAS GARRULUS

Coracias garrulus Linnaeus

PLATE 21

Gould wrote that the Roller was one of the most beautiful birds of Europe. He recorded that it was often seen in England and in the oak forests of Germany, Denmark and Sweden. Today in Europe it is a scarce species present only in the south and east, and found in wild landscape where there are hollow trees for nesting. The rollers migrate to East Africa in the winter.

The Roller's name derived from its somersaulting and aerobatic flight; in Europe the species was called *garrulus* because of its restless noisy chatter.

Elizabeth Gould illustrated the majority of perching species, while Lear drew the larger birds of prey and water birds. Her careful; precise touch was suited to the delineation of small birds; Lear preferred to work on a larger scale for he had delicate sight and detailed work caused him eyestrain.

22 *Common Kingfisher* (EG)

COMMON KINGFISHER (KINGFISHER)

ALCEDO ISPIDA

Alcedo atthis (Linnaeus)

PLATE 22

Gould wrote that the kingfisher looked as if it had strayed from the tropics, when it flashed past 'like a meteor' displaying its brilliant metallic colours. It was usually a solitary bird, perching motionless for hours on a branch overlooking a stream, patiently waiting for a favourable moment to dart like an arrow upon a fish within reach. Its wedge-shaped body, sleek plumage, and long pointed bill seemed especially adapted for plunging into the water. When it returned to its perch with its catch in its bill, it shifted the fish, grasped it by the tail, smartly knocked its head on a stone or branch and finally swallowed it head first.

The shimmering azure and green kingfisher is still found throughout Europe along slow-running streams and rivers.

GREAT GREY OR NORTHERN SHRIKE

LANIUS EXCUBITOR

Lanius excubitor Linnaeus

PLATE 23

The Great Grey Shrike was a 'bold and courageous bird, attacking others much larger than itself, and destroying mice, frogs and small birds for its food, of which, however, we believe the hard-winged

insects constitute a considerable portion'. It killed prey with its strong bill, and used its claws to grasp its victims, which were then impaled on thorns before they were torn to pieces and eaten.

Linnaeus named the shrike *excubitor*, or sentinel, because it watches for prey from a high post in a hedge or tree and also drives off any intruders into its territory.

This shrike was 'one of the migratory birds of Great Britain, appearing by no means regularly . . . being in some seasons very scarce and in others very abundant, and that only in the months of autumn and winter'. It is still an uncommon winter visitor to England but breeds extensively in Continental Europe.

23 *Great Grey or Northern Shrike* (EG)

GOLDEN ORIOLE

ORIOLUS GALBULA

Oriolus oriolus (Linnaeus)

PLATE 25

Gould wrote that the male Golden Oriole of Europe was striking for its beautiful rich yellow and black contrasting plumage, but it was not to be confused with the similarly coloured American Oriole which belonged to an unrelated genus *Icterus*.

The Golden Oriole was an occasional summer visitor to England but abundant in central and southern Europe. Today it is found in the upper parts of trees in deciduous woodlands of Continental Europe, south to north-west Africa and

throughout western Asia. It is a shy bird and, although brightly coloured, is difficult to see among the foliage. Sometimes it can be traced by its loud melodious song.

Elizabeth Gould illustrated a pair, the bright yellow and black male with a prominent black eye streak, and the female with duller colours. Her yellow breast was 'clouded with an olive tinge' merging below into greyish-white.

STONECHAT

SAXICOLA RUBICOLA

Saxicola torquata (Linnaeus)

PLATE 24

Gould wrote that the Stonechat 'may be observed in all seasons on commons, moorlands and shrubby heaths' in the British Isles and throughout Europe. Its habits were 'restless and noisy, flitting from bush to bush, or rock to rock, and not unfrequently perching on the tops of the flower of the thistle or highest twig of the whinbush'. This sprightly bird's name was derived from its unusual call, which sounded like 'the clicking of two stones struck together at repeated intervals'. Its main diet was insects which it caught on the wing, but it also ate worms and larvae.

The male and female 'in perfect plumage' are depicted on two separate sprays, and the upper bird is on a thistle. This picture is an early example of Elizabeth

24 *Stonechat* (EG)

25   Golden Oriole (EG)

26 *Chaffinch* (EG)

Gould's practice of illustrating the bird with an appropriate flower from its habitat, which is also mentioned in the text.

The male has a deep black head and throat, pure white collar and reddish-brown chest; the female has duller colours with a brown head.

VOLUME III

CHAFFINCH

FRINGILLA COELEBS

Fringilla coelebs Linnaeus

PLATE 26

'Our plate represents the birds in their spring plumage, although we must acknowledge our inability to do justice to the rich and harmonious tints which pervade the feathers of the living bird, and which afford so much attraction and ornament to our lawns and shrubberies.'

The Chaffinch is one of Europe's commonest birds, found in deciduous and coniferous woods, gardens and parks. Gould noted that during autumn these birds deserted the gardens and orchards for fields and hedgerows, but returned in early spring to sing, pair and nest. Their neat nests lined with fine hair and feathers were built in tree forks and carefully camouflaged on the outside with lichen stripped from apple trees.

The sexes have different colouring, the male has a rich grey crown and nape, chestnut-brown back, white bars on the wings and pinkish-brown chest. The female also has white wing bars but is mostly pale grey and yellowish brown. In winter the male has a duller plumage.

RAVEN

CORVUS CORAX

Corvus corax Linnaeus

PLATE 28

'The largest and strongest of its genus, and bold as well as cunning, it is always an object of suspicion to shepherds and husbandmen, from its daring attacks upon the young and weak among their flocks and herds.' The Raven was also regarded as a bird of ill-omen by the superstitious, 'its hoarse croaking being supposed to announce some impending calamity'.

Ravens were found throughout Europe, on rocky shores and mountains, and in woods and large fields, especially pasture land. They fed indiscriminately on small mammals, eggs, reptiles, dead fish, grain and carrion.

The male and female, said to mate for life, were often seen together. Their nest, made of sticks, wool and hair, was built in high trees or rock crevices and used for many years in succession.

If captured young, the Raven could be tamed and taught to pronounce various words correctly. It was also notorious for hiding shiny pieces of metal.

Lear's glossy blue-black bird was originally depicted three-quarters life-size.

27 *Wallcreeper* (EL)

WALLCREEPER

TICHODROMA PHOENICOPTERA

Tichodroma muraria (Linnaeus)

PLATE 27

The Wallcreeper was found in middle and southern Europe in high mountains, such as the Alps, Apennines and Pyrenees. 'Among these towering rocks, where the ruins of castles and fortresses are not unfrequent, this pretty bird is seen flitting from crevice to crevice, enlivening the solitude of the scene by its presence.'

With their short rounded wings, tenacious feet, and long slender bills they fluttered, hopped and probed among rocky crevices in an incessant search for insects. As their tails were too short and feeble to be used as a support for climbing, their flitting actions were very different from the up and down movements of treecreepers and woodpeckers.

Wallcreepers are now found in mountainous areas of southern Europe, southwest and south-central Asia. Often heard but not seen they are relatively common in parts of their range. They have grey heads, necks and backs, bright crimson on their wings, and black tails tipped with white. The male and female are illustrated in summer plumage when the male has a black throat and slightly darker grey head than at other seasons.

On the lower right corner is the signature 'E.Lear del. 1833'. Lear did not illustrate many insect-catching birds, which were often small and sombre, but this species had bright, almost tropical colouring.

VOLUME IV

RAVEN.
Corvus corax (Linn)

28   *Raven (EL)*

WOODPIGEON

COLUMBA PALUMBUS

Columba palumbus Linnaeus

PLATE 29

The Woodpigeon was well known throughout Europe, and lived in woods and forests feeding on 'all kinds of grain, the leaves of some plants, corn, beech-nuts and acorns'.

Early in spring the pigeons paired and made a flat nest of small sticks loosely put together in trees about 12 to 16 feet (3.6 to 4.8 metres) from the ground. The young birds were fed from 'the softened contents of the parents' crop', and two or three pairs of young birds were generally produced in a season.

The Woodpigeon has bluish ash-grey head and wings, with a neck and breast of mauvish pink colour and a large patch of white on either side of its neck surrounded by green and bronze glosses. The illustration depicts a mature bird and a young pigeon, which lacks the white on its neck and glossy colours of the adult.

Lear also made drawings for thirty engravings published in a small volume of pigeons, including the attractive fan-tailed and blue-crowned varieties, for Sir William Jardine's series *The Naturalist's Library*, 1833–1843. Lear had a high reputation as an animal artist, and was in demand both from Gould and from several other natural history publishers.

COMMON OR EURASIAN CRANE

GRUS CINEREA

Grus grus (Linnaeus)

PLATE 31

Gould wrote that cranes were once common in England according to accounts by falconers, who in the past had hunted them for sport with gyrfalcons and peregrines. Since then the crane had disappeared, except as an occasional winter visitor, due mainly to the draining of marshes and the cultivation of land in enclosures.

In Europe, the cranes lived in northern latitudes and migrated south in autumn. 'Flocks of these birds are seen at stated times in France and Germany, moving southwards or northwards as the season may be, in marshalled order, high in the air, their sonorous voices distinctly sounding . . . Occasionally they descend, attracted by new-sown fields, or the prospect of finding food in the marshes . . . but generally they continue their flight unchecked towards their destined restingplace.'

The cranes, apart from their red crowns, have greyish black plumage with elongated feathers hanging from their backs almost halfway to the ground. Lear's adult bird, depicted nearly half life-size in the original volume, stands in a romantic landscape of

BLACK STORK.
Ciconia nigra (Bellon)

30 *Black Stork* (EL)

29 *Woodpigeon* (EL)

a mountain lake, windswept trees and grasses. Some fifteen years later during his travels as a landscape painter in Albania, Lear noted in his journal on 17 May 1849: 'There were great grey cranes, too, the first I ever saw enjoying the liberty of nature. These birds seem made for the vast plains of Thessaly.'

PURPLE HERON

ARDEA PURPUREA

Ardea purpurea Linnaeus

PLATE 32

The Purple Heron resembled the Common Grey Heron with its long slender neck,

PURPLE HERON.
Ardea purpurea. (Linn.)

31   *Common or Eurasian Crane* (EL)

32   *Purple Heron* (EL)

flowing head plumes and sharp pointed bill. Its habitat was more like that of the bittern, for instead of wide expanses of water it preferred seclusion among the 'dense coverts of reed-beds, morasses and swamp lands'. Unlike other herons which built nests in lofty trees, the Purple Heron nested low on the ground among thick vegetation.

Gould wrote that the Purple Heron ranged over most of Europe; it was abundant in Holland and France but rare in England. He suspected that those found in England were escaped captive birds which were brought alive 'accompanied by hundreds of their eggs' from Holland to the London markets. This 'wholesale trafficing' of breeding herons, spoonbills and bitterns was in such large numbers that Gould feared these species would be greatly reduced within a few years.

Today the Purple Heron is still widespread in Europe but decreasing in some areas. Lear's illustration, two-thirds lifesize, shows the heron's characteristic posture of standing on one leg, emphasized by the long shadow in the water.

BLACK STORK

CICONIA NIGRA

Ciconia nigra (Linnaeus)

PLATE 30

'Among the wading birds, there are few if any, which excel the Black Stork either in richness of plumage or stateliness of aspect.'

Unlike the White Storks which assembled near human habitation, the Black Storks were secretive and lived in secluded woods near marshlands. Gould added: 'Notwithstanding the length of its limbs and its semipalmated toes, it perches on trees, and builds its nest on the branches, choosing for that purpose some tall pine of ancient growth in the depths of the forest, whence its colour assimilates with the gloomy hue of the surrounding objects.'

At this time the Black Stork lived in central and northern Europe but today it is a much rarer bird there, though in other parts of its extensive range it is still reasonably common.

Lear's original stork, depicted half lifesize, was blackish with purple, green and bronze reflections; it had red legs and bill and a white belly.

GREATER (COMMON) FLAMINGO

PHOENICOPTERUS RUBER

Phoenicopterus ruber Linnaeus

PLATE 33

'Of all forms of ornithology, none is more extraordinary than that of the Flamingo, whose singularly shaped bill, long and slender neck, stilt-like legs, and brilliant colouring render it a most striking object.'

The Flamingo inhabited 'morasses, the sides of rivers, and the low muddy and sandy shores of the sea, creeks and inlets'.

FLAMINGO.

Phœnicopterus ruber; (Linn.)

33   Greater Flamingo (EL)

Its extremely long legs enabled it to wade through the water skimming the mud for food with its drooping bent neck. It collected small molluscs, marine larvae and algae by holding its top bill upside-down, a position which Gould described as 'quite contrary to that of any other bird . . . but for which the acute bend in the upper mandible is expressly adapted'.

In the wild flamingos develop their pink colour naturally from their diet; however, in captivity the birds lose the intensity of the red pigments unless artificial pigment is added to their food.

Originally Lear illustrated, about half life-size, a young grey bird and a rosy-pink adult to show the plumage change from youth to maturity. Gould described the Flamingo as abundant in the Mediterranean coasts of Greece, Sicily, and Sardinia. Today there are remaining colonies in southern France and Spain with large numbers of breeding birds, but these wetlands are now greatly threatened by drainage and tourist developments.

VOLUME V

BEAN GOOSE

ANSER SEGETUM

Anser fabalis (Latham)

PLATE 34

Gould wrote that in summer the Bean Geese bred in the Arctic Circle and northern Europe; they migrated south to southern Europe in autumn and a few flocks reached England in October and November. During the day they grazed on stubble lands, and fed on beans and other crops left in the fields after the harvest. At night they retired to the safety of lakes and marshy areas.

The Bean Goose could be confused with the more widespread Greylag Goose. However, the Bean Goose is darker especially on the head and neck and the legs are

orange-yellow, and not pink as they are in the Greylag.

Lear's adult male goose, originally drawn about two-thirds life-size, swims through pale water and there is a clear view of its large orange webbed feet. Geese and ducks were later some of Lear's favourite characters in his comic verse and animal alphabets. A lively sketch of a goose family illustrates the tongue twister: 'Flights of grey gregarious gaggling geese adorn the silver shining surfaces of the softly sounding sea.'

WHOOPER (WHISTLING OR HOOPER) SWAN

CYGNUS FERUS

Cygnus cygnus (Linnaeus)

PLATE 35

This species, now known as the Whooper Swan, was referred to by Gould as the Whistling or Hooper because its call-note

BEAN GOOSE.
Anser segetum *(Steph.)*

34 *Bean Goose* (EL)

35 *Whooper Swan* (EL)

resembled 'the sound of the word *hoop*, loudly and harshly uttered several times in succession'.

In summer the Whoopers lived in the Arctic Circle, Iceland, Scandinavia and northern countries of Europe; some pairs had been known to breed in the Shetlands, Orkneys and even in Sutherland, Scotland. They migrated south in autumn but their numbers in southern Europe and England depended on the severity of the winter, and in prolonged cold weather large flocks were common. A few semi-domesticated pinioned birds were residents in England, breeding on the lakes of country estates.

The adult male birds had entirely white plumage except for an occasional tinge of buff on their heads. They had black bills, with a long patch of yellowish-orange extending forwards from the base to a point beyond the nostrils.

Whooper Swans from Iceland are now an exciting winter sight when they reach wildfowl reserves in Britain. As in the past, their numbers depend largely on northern weather conditions from September to April.

SHOVELER (SHOVELLER DUCK)
ANAS CLYPEATA
Anas clypeata Linnaeus

PLATE 37

The Shovelers have distinctive broad spoon-shaped bills. Their bills are serrated at the sides for sifting or trapping food, and Gould wrote that they fed on 'larvae of insects, and freshwater vegetables such as grasses and chickweed'. Like many of the duck family, in late summer the striking male Shovelers went through a transition of plumage so that they looked similar to the sombre females. Gould puzzled over the reason for this colour change but suggested it gave the drakes protection in the critical period when they were fostering their young families.

In the breeding season the sexes greatly differed in their colours, the male had an iridescent green head, chestnut belly, white breast and blue on its wings, whereas the female was a general dull brown colour.

They breed throughout Europe, Asia and North America and most have extensive migrations southwards.

GARGANEY (GARGANY TEAL)
ANAS QUERQUEDULA
Anas querquedula Linnaeus

PLATE 38

'The feathers pendent from the back of this little Duck, together with its chaste and sombre plumage, render it one of the most interesting and graceful species of this family.'

The Garganey winters in Africa, and is one of the few ducks that migrates to Europe as a summer visitor. Gould wrote that it came in April and May to English small lakes and inland waters, where it fed on 'the tops and shoots of various aquatic plants, to which are added shelled snails, water insects and their larvae'.

The sexes in spring have different colouring. The male's head is dark brown and chestnut mottled with a striking broad white stripe extending over each eye; the female is a general speckled brown colour.

The Garganey breeds throughout much of central and western Europe, including small numbers in Britain, east through Asia as far as Sakhalin and Kamchatka.

36 Red-knecked Grebe

a rare visitor to England and was mainly found in eastern Europe.

This species is smaller than the familiar Great-crested Grebe, and its summer plumage is distinguishable by its light grey cheeks and deep chestnut neck. In winter the beautiful chestnut and grey colours disappear, leaving the grebe's neck and cheeks a whitish-grey colour.

The illustration shows an adult in summer plumage, and a young bird in its first year. Gould said that the fully grown young grebe was greyish brown and white, similar to other grebes, but its lower yellow bill was distinctive of its species.

This print is unusual for it bears no credit to any artist, lithographer, or printer. It was probably Elizabeth Gould's work and rushed to press before Gould had time to add the full inscription.

They migrate southwards to wintering grounds in southern Europe, Africa, India and South Asia.

Their preferred habitat of shallow, permanent or seasonal freshwater wetlands are in many parts of the world under threat from drainage and pollution, and like so many water birds Garganey are potentially at risk.

RED-NECKED GREBE
PODICEPS RUBICOLLIS

Podiceps grisegena (Boddaert)

PLATE 36

Gould wrote that the Red-necked Grebe lived on large inland lakes, rivers, estuaries, and the borders of the sea. It was

GREAT AUK
ALCA IMPENNIS

Pinguinus impennis (Linnaeus)

PLATE 39

'In this noble species of Auk we recognise a close approximation to the true Penguins . . . being, like them, destitute of

37 Shoveler (EG)

powers of flight, its narrow slender wing serves more as an oar for aquatic progression than for any other decided purpose.' Gould described the fish-eating Great Auk as 'found in abundance along the rugged coast of Labrador', Spitzbergen and throughout the Arctic Circle, 'where it may often be seen tranquilly reposing on masses of floating ice'. In its heyday the Great Auk swam in areas of the North Atlantic from the Gulf of St Lawrence across to Norway.

Agile in the water, the poor flightless auks were awkward on land when they scrambled clumsily on to the rocks to lay their eggs and rear their young. They were an easy target for ruthless sailors who herded them into pens, clubbed them to death, and threw them into vats of boiling water. They were eaten and their feathers collected. The Great Auk is thought to have become extinct in 1844, some ten years after Lear's illustration.

Gould described the auk's large, almost pointed egg laid on the bare rock as 'white tinged with buff, marked with spots and crooked lines of brownish black'. Later, at Victorian auctions, Great Auk eggs reached legendary astronomic prices.

The bird is depicted in its summer plumage of black back, white belly and a large oval white eye patch. Although the plate is signed on the lower right, 'E. Lear del', it was not credited to Lear, and bears the routine inscription 'Drawn from Nature & on Stone by J & E Gould'.

Atlantic Puffin (Puffin)

Mormon Fratercula

Fratercula arctica (Linnaeus)

PLATE 40

Gould remarked that after just a glance at a Puffin one was immediately struck by its unusual short, stubby body and odd-shaped bright beak. In the sea its rounded form and sharp bill were not a hindrance for it 'displayed great agility and arrow-like quickness of motion; its beak, deep, compressed, and pointed with a sharp ridge and keel, affords the beau ideal of an instrument for cutting through the water'. Its feathers were thick, close and smooth and able to throw off every particle of wetness.

The beak was also used to catch 'innumerable hordes of fry and smaller fishes which swim near the surface of the water'. During the breeding season the fish were held across the bill 'till a row of little pendent victims is arranged along each side, their heads firmly wedged in the beak, and their tails and bodies hanging outside'. Thus loaded, the Puffin flew off with its catch to its mate and offspring, which nested on cliff crevices or in holes of deserted rabbit burrows.

Gould wrote that breeding puffins had an extensive range on rocky coasts off the Isle of Wight, Wales, Scotland, the Orkneys and Hebrides, and also the northern coasts of Europe and America. Recently, possibly because of overfishing in the North Sea and climatic changes which have affected the quantity and distribution of small fish, they have been unable to raise their young and are becoming rarer.

GARGANY TEAL.
Anas querquedula. *(Linn)*
Querquedula circia. *(Steph.)*

38 *Garganey (EG)*

GREAT AUK.

39   *Great Auk* (EL)

was more amused in my life at seeing so many thousand Pelicans all together.' An illustrated description of this scene was published in Lear's *Journals of a Landscape Painter in Albania*, 1851. Lively pelicans from the Nile featured in Lear's music and comic lyrics in *The Pelican Chorus*, 1877. The plate is signed by E. Lear del.

NORTHERN (SOLAN) GANNET

SULA BASSANA

Morus (Sula) bassanus (Linnaeus)

PLATE 42

Gould wrote that countless multitudes of gannets bred in summer along the steep rocky coasts of Scotland, especially on the

DALMATIAN PELICAN (PELICAN)

PELECANUS ONOCROTALUS

Pelecanus crispus Bruch

PLATE 41

'Those of our readers who are desirous of seeing this noble bird in a state of nature need only pay a visit to the southern and eastern portions of Europe to gratify their laudable curiosity.' Today the Dalmatian Pelican is a very rare species in eastern Europe, and the total world population is possibly fewer than three or four thousand pairs.

The pelicans were renowned for their large size (about 5 feet, or 1.5 metres, in length with a 12 foot, or 3.5 metre, wing-span), their longevity, and for the long period of three to six years taken by the young brown birds to attain the adult plumage. The pelican was a voracious eater of fish, 'in the capture of which it displays considerable activity and cunning', for although its immense body and bill seemed very awkward, 'its movements were so quick that even young fry and eels can scarcely escape its vigilance'.

During his travels in Albania as a painter, Lear discovered immense flocks of pelicans at Avlona. He wrote to Lord Derby in January 1849, describing how he saw 'an innumerable multitude of odd looking white stones (as I thought) — I rode up to them, when lo! they were all pelicans! & away they flew . . . I never

40   *Atlantic Puffin* (EG)

Above: 41   Dalmatian Pelican (EL)

Below: 42   Northern Gannet (EL)

44

AUDOUIN'S GULL.
Larus Audouinii (*Temm*)

43   *Audouin's Gull* (EL)

Bass Rock and the isles of Ailsa and St Kilda. In autumn their great numbers dispersed and solitary gannets set out to sea southwards feeding on herrings, pilchards and other fishes. As their flight was extremely 'rapid, vigorous and capable of being sustained', they covered large distances with comparative ease.

The gannets take about four years to attain full adult plumage, each stage being recognizable from their colouring. Lear's illustration depicts a pure white adult bird with upper neck and head pale yellow, and black-tipped wings. Behind is a young bird of the first year with blackish and brownish-grey plumage.

Gould related that in northern Scotland young birds were protected and farmed for their feathers and food, 'their flesh being considered by some a delicacy, though to most persons it is extremely disagreeable'. Since Gould's day, this exploitation of gannets has ceased and numbers have increased with the formation of several new colonies.

AUDOUIN'S GULL

LARUS AUDOUINII

Larus audouinii Payraudeau

PLATE 43

Audouin's Gulls bred on islands in the Mediterranean, but are now one of Europe's rarest birds, with their largest colony in the Chafarinas Islands off the coast of Morocco.

They feed on small fish and fly low over the sea, picking up food without settling on the water. As such fish are becoming scarcer in the Mediterranean, these gulls have resorted to taking food from land and may have suffered from poisoning and contamination from debris. Attempts are being made to protect some of their island habitat among the grass and low bushes from interference, including disturbance caused by tourists and egg-collectors.

Gould had little knowledge of this white gull with small feet and a dark red bill with a black and yellow tip, except that it was found in the Mediterranean near Gibraltar. The plate is signed and dated 'Edward Lear del 1837', the year when Lear himself set off on his wanderings through Europe and the Mediterranean countries.

This gull was named in 1826 after a French zoologist, Jean Victor Audouin (1797–1841).

A MONOGRAPH OF THE RAMPASTIDAE OR FAMILY OF TOUCANS

First edition (1833–1835), one volume, 33 plates.
Second edition (1852–1854), one volume, 51 plates.

The *Monograph of the Toucans*, first edition, was Gould's first publication of all the known species of a single family of birds. Edward Lear had earlier pioneered the idea of illustrating all the birds in one family, but his book on parrots, commenced in parts a few years previously, was never completed, for he had been unable to organize a subscription list large enough to cover the costs of production. Gould greatly admired Lear's lithographs of birds and employed him to illustrate the flamboyant and gaudy toucans in the same life-size format as the parrots.

Toucans live in the tropical forests of America, and their curious name derives from the Tupi Indians of Brazil who call them 'tucano'. Toucan skins were first brought back to Europe by explorers in the sixteenth century, and the birds were illustrated by woodcuts in early zoological works emphasizing their enormous bills, which seem disproportionate to their bodies. Included in both Gould's editions is an article by Richard Owen on the anatomy of the toucan and engraved sections by G. Scharf which show that the bill is in reality very lightweight, for inside its horny sheath is a crisscross of cellular fibres that imparts strength with lightness.

Lear contributed ten illustrations and Elizabeth Gould twenty-three to the first edition. The plates by both artists are very similar in presentation, but Lear's toucans have more panache although some, disturbingly, appear almost menacing. A few captive toucans were successfully kept by Lord Derby and Nicholas Vigors in England, but the illustrations were all drawn from specimens as models. Gould found that classification of the rarer toucan species from skins brought from America posed many problems as soon after death the colours of their bills and the skin around their eyes changed and faded.

In the second edition Gould added new species discovered in South America by the explorers Natterer, Wallace and Schomburgk. All the plates were by H.C. Richter who worked closely from Gould's rough sketches, many of which are now in the Spencer Library, University of Kansas. Some of the species already included in the first edition were repeated with new information; for most of these the illustrations were completely redrawn, but a number slightly resembled the earlier plates, and one had only minor alterations. Richter depicted the toucans with authentic tropical plants, orchids and palms drawn from flower specimens or copied from botanical prints and drawings.

Both editions were dedicated to Professor C.J. Temminck, eminent Dutch ornithologist, director of Leyden Museum, author of a finely illustrated set of zoological books, and avid collector of bird skins.

44   Yellow-ridged Toucan (EL)

YELLOW-RIDGED (CULMINATED) TOUCAN

RAMPHASTOS CULMINATUS

Ramphastos culminatus Gould

PLATE 44

The Culminated Toucan belongs to the genus *Ramphastos*, a group of the larger, crow-sized toucans with distinctive black plumage, enormous multicoloured bills and short square tails. They also have contrasting yellow or white chests, and patches on top and under their tails of red, white or yellow. Their habitat is the lowland rain forests of South America from southern Mexico to north Argentina. Fruit is their main food but some are known to rob smaller birds' nests of eggs and fledglings.

The illustration was based on a specimen in the London Zoological Society Museum, which had a slightly incurved bill with a pale yellow band along its whole length. Its black body contrasts with the bright colours of its white throat and chest and the crimson of its chest band and under-tail coverts.

Lear's illustration is signed and dated 1833, a year after he had ceased producing his prints of parrots. Both the toucans and parrots are noisy, flamboyant birds and Lear emphasized their bold shapes and striking colours. This first edition plate was

45   *Red-billed Toucan* (EL)

copied and redrawn by H.C. Richter for the second edition, published after Lear had left England to work abroad. Lear's signature no longer appears and the later plate is inscribed 'Gould & Richter del et lith'. Gould had seen further specimens whose bills were not so curved, and in Richter's picture the front toucan's bill is straighter.

RED-BILLED TOUCAN

RAMPHASTOS ERYTHRORHYNCHUS

Ramphastos tucanus Linnaeus

PLATE 45

This species differed, as its name implies, from all other toucans by the bright red colouring of its bill. Gould found that these toucans were difficult to identify from museum specimens because the redness of their bills faded soon after death. Later, after he had seen captive birds, he added in the second edition that the brilliancy of their bills depended on their health and vigour, and during the breeding season the red colour was more intense than at any other period.

Gould wrote that this richly coloured toucan inhabited 'the deep forests which border the Amazon, and wooded districts of Cayenne [French Guiana] and Guiana [Guyana], being spread in considerable abundance over a wide extent of country'. He added: 'In its general habits and manners it resembles the rest of its congeners, leaping lightly from branch to branch among the topmost foliage of the highest trees, where it passes its existence.' Today Red-billed Toucans still live in these areas but they are much threatened by the destruction of their tropical habitat through deforestation.

Lear's watercolour of the Red-billed Toucan, an exact study for the plate, is in the Blacker-Wood Library, McGill University, Canada (see also plate 58).

46 Toco Toucan (EL)

TOCO TOUCAN

RAMPHASTOS TOCO

Ramphastos toco Müller

PLATE 46

The Toco Toucan, (see also plate 55), has achieved more fame as a well-known poster image than as an ornithological illustration. Between 1925 and 1960 the Toco Toucan designed by John Gilroy (1898–1985) for Guinness's advertisement campaign was a familiar sight in every bar parlour. Gilroy's pictures and sculptures caricatured the bird's large bill, which is almost 2½ inches (6 centimetres) wide, and some 8 inches (20 centimetres) long, just under a third of the bird's total length of about 26 inches (66 centimetres).

Gould described the colours of this toucan's bill as 'rich orange, with a basal band of black, and a broad oval spot on each side of the tip of the upper mandible'. Its plumage is deep black, except for its white throat, chest and upper-tail coverts, and a patch under its tail of scarlet. The Toco Toucan also has a very short, square tail, which makes its long bill seem particu-larly disproportionate. In spite of its clumsy appearance the toucan can leap agilely among the trees in the forests. In flight it is more awkward, and has an unmistakable silhouette as it undulates through the air with its large beak pointed slightly down-wards.

This illustration is dated 1833, and three years later in July 1836 Lear painted the same species at Knowsley menagerie. Although live toucans were kept in the Knowsley aviaries, Lear's watercolour was made from Lord Derby's valuable collection of specimens.

Toco Toucans are found in the woodlands of the Guianas through Amazonian Brazil, south-east Peru and Paraguay to north Argentina.

RAMPHASTOS SWAINSONII.
Swainson's Toucan.

47 Chestnut-mandibled Toucan (EG)

CHESTNUT-MANDIBLED (SWAINSON'S) TOUCAN

RAMPHASTOS SWAINSONII

Ramphastos swainsonii Gould

PLATE 47

Gould examined many specimens of this species and found that their bills varied from brown to black, probably due to seasonal changes. He believed this toucan differed from *Ramphastos ambiguus*, which had a black bill and was depicted in an illustration commissioned by Swainson. William Swainson, naturalist, taxidermist and artist, had travelled in South America from 1816 to 1818, and Gould dedicated this new species to him as a testimony of gratitude for his special study and scientific research of South American ornithology.

Apart from the brown or black on its large bill, this species also has bright yellow on the upper mandible. Like the other large black toucans the birds have contrasting yellow, white and red on their chests and tail coverts.

These toucans have a distinctive call heard at nightfall when they float down from the tree-tops, which has been described as 'dios te de, te de, te de', meaning 'God keep you'. It is one of the more melodious of the toucan noises, which are usually loud and raucous.

Now called the Chestnut-mandibled Toucan, this species lives in Central America and north-west South America from south-east Honduras to west Ecuador, including the Panama Canal Zone.

RAMPHASTOS VITELLINUS, (Illiger).
Sulphur-and-white-breasted Toucan.

48 *Channel-billed Toucan* (EL)

CHANNEL-BILLED (SULPHUR-AND-WHITE-BREASTED) TOUCAN

RAMPHASTOS VITELLINUS

Ramphastos vitellinus Lichtenstein

PLATE 48

Gould wrote that the beautiful yellow chest-feathers of this toucan were much prized by natives and used for decoration. This species also had distinctive white plumage on the side of its face and chest, and a cobalt-blue band at the base of its black bill. Like other large toucans it was mainly black, with contrasting scarlet on its lower chest, rump and under its tail.

These toucans gather in small flocks on tree-tops of tropical forests, and are sometimes very playful, chasing each other in and out of the branches, clapping their bills, and uttering strange rattling noises. They live in Trinidad, Venezuela, the Guianas and Brazil. The plate is signed 'E. LEAR April 1833'.

ARIEL TOUCAN

RAMPHASTOS ARIEL

Ramphastos vitellinus ariel Vigors

PLATE 49

Nicholas Aylward Vigors, Secretary of the Zoological Society, who wrote the text for Gould's *Century of Birds*, kept a caged Ariel Toucan for eight years. He published a

RAMPHASTOS ARIEL, (Vig.).
TUCANUS, (Linn?)
Ariel Toucan.

Drawn from Nature & on Stone by J. & E. Gould.   Printed by C. Hullmandel.

49   Ariel Toucan (EG)

lively account of his pet in the second volume of the *Zoological Journal*, from which Gould quoted extensively in his second edition.

Vigors's, toucan, which fed from the hand, was a tolerant and playful bird. Although it looked very clumsy, it was on the contrary extremely graceful, and glided from perch to perch in 'light and sylph-like' movements. Its glossy black and lighter coloured plumage were kept in beautiful condition by a daily bath, which it enjoyed greatly, immersing itself in cold water even in severe weather. The toucan had a regular daily routine, and at dusk, after its evening meal of fruit and vegetables, took a few turns round the perches of its cage for exercise, and then settled down 'with his head drawn in between its shoulders, and his tail drawn almost vertically over his back'. For about two hours the toucan remained 'in a state between sleeping and waking; his eyes for the most part closed, but opening on the slightest interruption'.

Elizabeth Gould's picture of the toucan half-asleep, with its head under its wing and tail cocked up, aptly illustrates Vigors's narration.

The Ariel Toucan, which is now considered to be a subspecies of the Channel-billed Toucan, is found in east and south-east Brazil.

SAFFRON TOUCANET (SAFFRON-COLOURED ARAÇARI)

PTEROGLOSSUS BAILLONI

Baillonius bailloni (Vieillot)

PLATE 50

The araçaris and toucanets are smaller and more slender than the large toucans of the *Ramphastos* genus. Their bills are shorter and their tails are not square but composed of graduated shaped feathers. Araçari is a Portuguese word derived from 'arassaris', the name for small toucans in the Tupi Indian language.

Gould described the Saffron-coloured Araçari as exceptionally beautiful, 'particularly in the sweeping breadth of rich golden yellow which pervades the breast and all the underparts'. This toucan has not only saffron yellow on its breast, but also olive green on its back and tail, and a rump of bright scarlet. Gould thought that these

50 *Saffron Toucanet* (EL)

colours were very conspicuous; however, in the wild the toucan's greens, reds, and yellows do not stand out, but harmonize with their tropical surroundings. This species, which inhabits the humid forests of the lowlands of east and south-east Brazil, was named after L.A.F. Baillon (1778–1851), a French zoologist from Abbeville. The plate is signed 'E. LEAR 1833'.

GREEN ARAÇARI

PTEROGLOSSUS VIRIDIS

Pteroglossus viridis (Linnaeus)

PLATE 52

Gould thought that the name *viridis* or 'green' was not very appropriate for a bird which had so many different colours. This toucan's plumage is indeed a gaudy mix-

PTEROGLOSSUS MACULIROSTRIS. (Cuv et Lichtenst.)
Spotted-bill Araçari.

ture, for it has a dusky green back, scarlet rump and bright yellow underparts. The bill is black below, yellow on the top and red along the sides. The two sexes vary slightly in colour, for the female's head and neck are rich chestnut and the male's are glossy black. In the wild these bright aracaris are not easily seen except when they are moving, for at rest their colours blend perfectly with the fruits and flowers of the rain forest.

In the first edition Gould used an illustration from Swainson as a guide to the bill colours which faded so quickly in specimens. Later, in 1844, when Green Araçaris lived in London Zoo, Gould was able to study the live birds, and the colours are more exact in the second edition.

The plate is signed 'E. LEAR 1833'. These birds live in the humid forests of Guianas, south Venezuela and north-east Brazil.

52 Green Araçari (EL)

SPOT-BILLED (SPOTTED-BILL) ARAÇARI
PTEROGLOSSUS MACULIROSTRIS
Selenidera maculirostris (Lichtenstein)

PLATE 51

Gould wrote that this species from Brazil was one of the commonest of the small toucans. It had an appropriate name *maculirostris* (meaning marks on the bill), because it had irregular spots of black on the upper mandible.

Unlike the large *Ramphastos* toucans, the sexes of the smaller toucans sometimes have different colouring. In this species the male has a glossy black head and breast whereas the female's is rich chestnut coloured. Both sexes are mainly dusky green, and at the back of their necks is a crescent-shaped golden collar.

This species lives in the humid tropical forests of south-east Brazil and north-east Argentina.

EMERALD TOUCANET (GOLDEN-GREEN ARAÇARI)
PTEROGLOSSUS PRASINUS
Aulacorhynchus prasinus (Gould)

PLATE 53

Gould wrote in the first edition that specimens of this small toucan were exceedingly rare. 'I know but of one museum in Europe possessing specimens, namely, that of Berlin; and I am indebted to the kindness and liberality of Professor Lichtenstein, who made it known to science, for permission to examine and make drawings of the unique examples under his immediate care.'

Lear accompanied Gould on a visit to

53 Emerald Toucanet (EL)

Rotterdam, Berne, Berlin and Amsterdam, in 1831 or 1832, to gain material for *The Birds of Europe* and *The Toucans*; probably during this rushed tour Lear made studies of the specimen for this illustration. Martin Lichtenstein (1780–1857), appointed in 1815, was the first Director of the Berlin Zoological Museum.

The picture shows an adult and an immature bird and the changes in size and colouring of the grooved beak from youth to maturity. The younger bird's bill was 'clouded at its base with reddish' and had not attained the strong yellow and black colours of the adult.

This species inhabits the mountain forests of Mexico through central America to Nicaragua and into Colombia, west Venezuela to east Ecuador and Peru to north-east Bolivia.

54   *Keel-billed Toucan* (HCR)

TOCO TOUCAN

RAMPHASTOS TOCO

Ramphastos toco Müller

PLATE 55

'Although other members of the family equal the present species in the size of the body and relative proportions of the wings and tail, none of them have so large or so gaily-coloured a bill; in this respect it far exceeds all the other known species, and is rendered not only one of the most striking and singular members of the group to which it belongs, but one of the most *outré* birds yet discovered.'

Toco Toucans (see also plate 46) bred in the Earl of Derby's menagerie at Knowsley and lived in the Zoological Gardens, London. Gould observed that the toucan's beak was not cumbersome, but 'carried with the greatest ease, the lightness of its structure enabling the bird to feed and to plume its feathers with as much facility as other birds do with their shorter and more manageable bills'.

Included in both editions of Gould's monograph is Professor Richard Owen's article *Observations on the Anatomy of the Toucan* with detailed engravings by George Scharf of this bird's cranium, bill, tongue and foot. A section through the beak shows that enclosed within a horny sheath

55   *Toco Toucan* (HCR)

is a crisscross of thin bony rods, or meshes of 'beautiful osseus network'. Despite their strong internal structure, toucans' bills get damaged, and experiments have been made with replacements in metal and plastic. Nevertheless, the birds have been known to survive a long time with parts of their bills missing.

Richter's Toco Toucan, like Lear's, faces forwards, but Richter has turned the bill sideways to gain a better view of its large size in relation to the rest of the body. A tropical flowering plant and a second bird in a tree hole are also added.

KEEL-BILLED TOUCAN

RAMPHASTOS CARINATUS

Ramphastos sulfuratus Lesson

PLATE 54

This species, also known as the Rainbow-billed Toucan, has a beak delicately tinted with all the colours of the rainbow except violet. The upper bill which is largely yellow-green is tipped with dark red and has a large wedge of orange above the serrated cutting edges. The lower bill, also yellow-green and red-tipped, has a middle area of light blue. These tints blend delicately into each other, ending at the base of the bill with a black margin.

Gould wrote that these bills had great colour variations: 'some individuals having the lower mandible blue and the upper green, while in others both mandibles are of the latter colour; in some the orange spot on the sides of the bill is almost wanting; in others it is divided into a succession of small ones, or dilated into a broad band occupying nearly the whole length of the mandible.' The toucan in the illustration had correct colouring, as it was drawn from a bird that lived 'during part of the years 1849 and 1850 in the Gardens of the Zoological Society'.

These toucans live in densely wooded areas from south-east Mexico throughout central America to north Colombia and Venezuela.

56   *Keel-billed Toucan* (HCR)

Keel-billed (Short-billed) Toucan

Ramphastos brevicarinatus

Ramphastos sulfuratus brevicarinatus Gould

PLATE 56

Gould wrote that this toucan was similar to the Keel-billed Toucan but its broad bill was about a third shorter, and the scarlet band on its chest was much wider.

During his researches for his first monograph, Gould saw examples of this toucan in Paris, among the Prince of Massena's large collection of specimens, which in 1845 were sold to the Museum of the Academy of Natural Sciences, Philadelphia. He suggested that American ornithologists should take the opportunity to see these birds and determine whether the Short-billed Toucan was a distinct species or 'only a local variety'. Now considered to be a subspecies of the Keel-billed Toucan, this bird is found from south-east Guatemala to Colombia and Venezuela.

Black-mandibled (Doubtful) Toucan

Ramphastos ambiguus

Ramphastos ambiguus Swainson

PLATE 57

The Doubtful Toucan was appropriately named, for the *Ramphastos* toucans were difficult to identify. Gould found that this Colombian species was even more perplexing than the Keel-billed Toucans from Mexico.

Gould and Richter worked closely together in preparing the illustrations for the second monograph of toucans. Gould painted preparatory sketches showing the placing of the birds on the page and Rich-

RAMPHASTOS AMBIGUUS, *Swains.*

57   *Black-mandibled Toucan* (HCR)

RAMPHASTOS ERYTHRORHYNCHOS, *Gmel.*

Gould & Richter, del.
Hullmandel & Walton, Imp.

58   Red-billed Toucan (HCR)

ter did the finished detailed drawing on the lithographic stone. Some of Gould's lively toucan sketches have survived and are now in the Spencer Library, University of Kansas. A lively sketch in pencil and watercolour shows these two Doubtful Toucans emerging from a tree hole, prominently displaying their splendid large bills.

In his preliminary sketches Gould quickly indicated the colours with broad watercolour washes. Later, further colour instructions were given to the colourists on important details such as the toucan's bill and the bare skin round the eye. The finished plate of the Doubtful Toucan shows that additional blues and greens were painted round the eye and on the black and yellow upper-bill.

This species, now called the Black-mandibled Toucan, lives in humid forests from Colombia and north and west Venezuela through east Ecuador to north Peru.

RED-BILLED TOUCAN

RAMPHASTOS ERYTHRORHYNCHOS

Ramphastos tucanus Linnaeus

PLATE 58

Gould stated that the Red-billed Toucan was one of the oldest known species of toucan, and a drawing of it, with a small bird in its mouth, by Maria Merian (1647–1717) was in the British Museum.

The naturalist Charles Waterton (later known as the eccentric squire of Walton Hall, Wakefield) saw this species during his travels in Demerara, British Guiana (now Guyana) from 1804 to 1824, which he described in *Wanderings in South America*. Waterton stated that these toucans lived in the forest eating only fruit, and their native Indian name was 'bouradi' meaning 'nose'. They made noises 'like the clear yelping of a puppy dog', which the South American Spaniards described as 'pia-po-o-co', and called them 'piapoco'.

Gould included an account written in 1825 by William John Broderip (a magistrate and founder member of London Zoo) of a living bird at a dealer's in St Martin's Lane. This toucan liked fruit and vegetables but also showed 'the utmost partiality for animal food'. A small bird was added every second or third day to its food, which the toucan decidedly preferred, 'picking

out all morsels of that description, and not resorting to the vegetable diet until all the former is digested':

In Richter's plate a second bird is added, and Lear's deciduous foliage is replaced by palm trees (see also plate 45).

59 *Cuvier's Toucan* (HCR)

CUVIER'S (INCA) TOUCAN

RAMPHASTOS INCA

Ramphastos cuvieri Wagler

PLATE 59

Gould based his knowledge of the Inca Toucan on a single specimen from Bolivia. Thomas Bridges, the botanical collector, procured it 'in the elevated and dense forests at Chimoree in the country of the Yuracaras Indians'.

This toucan was very similar to the Red-billed Toucan, but had deeper, richer colours. Part of its bill was black, and it had a triangular mark of scarlet each side of the upper mandible. It had a broad blood-red band on its breast, its white throat was tinged with yellow, and its upper-tail coverts were fiery orange.

It was believed that Bridges's specimen was a female, and as the male *Ramphastos* toucans were often slightly larger and brighter, Gould added: 'the male, when discovered, will prove to be one of the most richly coloured species of the genus.'

Now, however, the Inca Toucan is not considered to be a valid species, and is thought to be merely a specimen of Cuvier's Toucan, *Ramphastos cuvieri*.

OSCULANT OR OSCULATED TOUCAN

RAMPHASTOS OSCULANS

Ramphastos vitellinus × *R. culminatus*

PLATE 60

'It may be regarded as, without exception, one of the loveliest of the *Ramphasti* vieing as it does in the variety of its colours with all the other members of the group. The white feathers at the side of the neck are dense, and of a pure white; the orange-yellow wash on the centre of the breast is of the most lovely tint imaginable; the tail coverts too are of an equally beautiful orange . . . and the general plumage is of the blackest jet.' Gould also mentioned the scarlet on its chest, which in some birds formed a band, and in others covered a larger area.

When Gould published the first edition he knew of only one specimen in Europe, at the Imperial Museum in Vienna. Afterwards he saw three more examples from the remote parts of South America; one procured by John Natterer from the River Madeira, another sent by Alfred Russel Wallace from the River Negro, and the third brought from the interior of Guiana by Sir Robert Schomburgk.

Osculant Toucans are not now thought to be a separate species, but are considered to be hybrids. They have been found in one area only, and that is where the ranges of at least two other species meet – the Channel-billed Toucan *Ramphastos vitellinus* (and its subspecies the Ariel Toucan (*R. v. ariel*) and the Yellow-ridged Toucan *R. culminatus*; Osculant Toucans appear to represent a population with unstable characters, the result of hybridization between these species.

60   *Osculant or Osculated Toucan* (HCR)

61   Green-billed or Red-breasted Toucan (HCR)

GREEN-BILLED OR RED-BREASTED TOUCAN

RAMPHASTOS DICOLORUS

Ramphastos dicolorus Linnaeus

PLATE 61

'The two lower figures represent young birds in a state in which they are barely capable of providing for their own wants; the bill at this stage is extremely delicate in texture, and is so soft and yielding as apparently to require the most soft and pulpy fruits, to which in all probability insects and larvae are added.' Gould said that the toucans had nesting habits similar to kingfishers and woodpeckers for they laid white eggs in tree holes and dark recesses.

Young *Ramphastos* toucans are very slow developers and remain for about fifty days in the nest. At first they do not look like toucans at all, for they are blind and naked when hatched and have no trace of down. Their beaks are broad and flat, with the lower bill projecting beyond the tip of the other. Even month-old nestlings are un-feathered, but gradually the bill grows bulky and their bodies assume adult proportions. The Green-billed Toucans are found in south-east Brazil, Paraguay and north-east Argentina.

62 *Collared Araçari* (HCR)

63 *Lettered Araçari* (HCR)

COLLARED ARAÇARI

PTEROGLOSSUS TORQUATUS

Pteroglossus torquatus (Gmelin)

PLATE 62

Gould wrote that these small toucans lived in southern Mexico, but their range extended further 'into the forests on the shores of both the Atlantic and of the Pacific'. He had received specimens from Guatemala, Nicaragua, Costa Rica and other parts of central America. We now know that their range extends into north Colombia and Venezuela.

Although there was 'scarcely a more ornamental or better defined species', Gould noted that the black chest spot varied in size: 'in some it is nearly obsolete, in others a large round patch, and in others it assumes a triangular shape.' Its broad, flattened bill was particularly impressive, 'presenting an appearance of massiveness and strength'.

Field observations of the Collared or Spot-chested toucans reveal that they roost and nest in old woodpecker holes or cavities in trees. They can crowd into a very small space, for they turn their heads backwards and bring their tails forwards so that they seem like balls of feathers. Some fifty years ago, in a Panamanian forest, six Collared Araçaris were seen to squeeze with difficulty through a narrow hole under a thick branch 100 feet (30 metres) up a great tree. Several weeks passed and the roosting birds left, leaving one remaining toucan nesting. When the eggs hatched the five original birds returned to sleep in the hole, and brought insects and fruit to the nestlings. After about forty-three days the first fledgling flew from the tree, but at nightfall as it returned to enter the hole, a hawk carried it off and was pursued by all the adults.

No detailed studies in the wild of the Collared Araçari's nesting habits have been made since, and it is not clear whether co-operative breeding among these toucans is widespread. In the illustration the toucan is perched beside the orchid, *Maxillaria leptosepala*.

Lettered Araçari

Pteroglossus inscriptus

Pteroglossus inscriptus Swainson

PLATE 63

'A glance at the accompanying Plate will indicate to the reader why this bird has been named *Inscriptus*, as it will be seen that the markings of the bill offer a considerable resemblance to Hebrew characters, which circumstance has obtained for it the trivial name of the Lettered Araçari.'

Gould added that the letter-like bill markings varied on individual toucans. The sexes also slightly differed, for the female had a brown and the male a black throat. The illustration was drawn from specimens sent by Alfred Russel Wallace from Para, Brazil and the species was found throughout the Amazon basin.

This species or subspecies of the Green Araçari *P. viridis*, is one of the smallest of the toucans, and is only about 13 inches (35 centimetres) long. It lives in humid forests and palm groves, often near water, from south-east Colombia, south through

PTEROGLOSSUS BEAUHARNAISI, *Wagl.*

64 *Curl-crested Araçari* (HCR)

Ecuador and Peru to north Bolivia and Amazonian east Brazil.

An appropriate plant, *Bilbergia iridifolia*, was copied by Richter from 'a drawing made by Miss Hamilton Smith, whose talents as an artist are only equalled by her other many acquirements and amiable disposition'.

Curl-crested Araçari

Pteroglossus beauharnaisi

Pteroglossus beauharnaesii Wagler

PLATE 64

Gould considered this species was one of the finest and most remarkable of the toucan family. This aracari had unusual curled glossy feathers on its crown, which

PTEROGLOSSUS BITORQUATUS. ½

65 *Red-knecked Araçari* (HCR)

River Madeira, Upper Amazon. The two naturalists had noted the colours of the bills and parts of the toucan which faded, and Gould had used their information for the illustration.

We now know that the Curl-crested Araçari is found not only in west Brazil, but also in east Peru and north Bolivia. The aracaris are shown with the plant *Sida integerrima*.

RED-NECKED (DOUBLE-COLLARED) ARAÇARI

PTEROGLOSSUS BITORQUATUS

Pteroglossus bitorquatus Vigors

PLATE 65

The Red-necked Araçari was also called the double-collared because it has two narrow bands of yellow and black surrounding its chest. The first specimen in England belonged to Nicholas Vigors, who gave it to the London Zoological Society. Afterwards examples were sent by Alfred Russel Wallace from Para, on the Lower Amazon.

Gould wrote: 'The Plate represents the species in the state of excitement at the sight of a snake; it must not, however, be understood that the bird feeds on these animals; they are merely so represented to show how readily (as mentioned by Prince Maximilian of Wied) they are excited by the sudden appearance of an unwonted object.'

These aracaris are found in the humid forests of Amazonian Brazil and extreme east Bolivia. Both sexes are illustrated, and two toucans are shown flying in the background.

Gould found 'impossible to do justice' in the illustration. These curious feathers have since been described as resembling 'curled horny shavings'.

Several specimens of this attractive bird reached Europe in the 1830s, causing much excitement among ornithologists, and various names were given to it. The German naturalist Dr Joannes G. Wagler named it in honour of Max J. Beauharnais (1817–1852), Duke of Leuchtenburg, a prince distinguished for his love of natural history. The duke died prematurely in 1852 and Gould hoped that this commemorative name would be retained permanently.

Gould wrote that these aracaris were found in Brazil; they had been seen by the naturalist Johann Natterer near the mouth of the River Negro, and were sent to England by Alfred Russel Wallace from the

GOULD'S TOUCANET

SELENIDERA GOULDI

Selenidera gouldii (Natterer)

PLATE 68

This toucan was first illustrated by Elizabeth Gould for *Icones Avium*, 1837–1838, a series of plates showing newly discovered species. Gould abandoned this project when he set off to Australia, and only two parts in one volume containing eighteen plates were issued.

The Viennese naturalist Johann Natterer found these toucans on the banks of the River Madeira, Brazil, and presented specimens to the Zoological Society, London. At a meeting there on 11 April 1837, he returned Gould's compliment of calling a toucan species *nattereri* by naming these new discoveries *gouldi*.

Gould described these birds as similar to the small Spot-billed Toucanets, but pointed out that their differences were a single large black patch on the upper mandible, and stronger orange colouring on the sides of the body. Some authorities, however, consider it to be a race of the Spot-billed Toucanet.

Gould's Toucanet lives in the humid forests of north-east Brazil and in extreme north-east Bolivia.

TAWNY-TUFTED (NATTERER'S) TOUCANET

SELENIDERA NATTERERI

Selenidera nattereri (Gould)

PLATE 66

Gould wrote: 'although I have at all times endeavoured to avoid imposing a specific title on a new species, which did not convey some idea connected with its form and colouring, I have been induced to deviate from this rule in the present instance.' He wished to pay tribute to the naturalist Johann Natterer, who was commissioned by the government in Vienna to collect flora and fauna and had spent eighteen years in Brazil making valuable discoveries. Natterer died in 1843, eight years after his return to Europe, and Gould was gratified to know that the name of his friend had been perpetuated.

In his first edition the illustration had been made from the only specimens in Europe, housed at the Imperial Museum, Vienna, and collected by Natterer at the River Madeira, Brazil. Afterwards Sir Robert Schomburgk brought examples from the interior of British Guiana (Guyana) and Alfred Russel Wallace saw them in the forests by the River Negro, in the Upper Amazon.

This small toucanet, now called the Tawny-tufted Toucanet, has a reddish-brown bill striped with black, and lives in the lowland forests of east and south Venezuela, the Guianas and north-west Brazil.

SELENIDERA NATTERERI, *Gould*

SELENIDERA REINWARDTI.

66   *Tawny-tufted Toucanet* (HCR)

67   *Golden-collared Toucanet* (HCR)

68   Gould's Toucanet (HCR)

GOLDEN-COLLARED (REINWARDT'S) TOUCANET

SELENIDERA REINWARDTI

Selenidera reinwardtii (Wagler)

PLATE 67

Gould described this species as one of the rarest of the toucanets. The first edition illustration was made from the only known example in Munich, but during the twenty years which followed specimens had been sent from the eastern foothills of the Andes, Peru, and the banks of the River Napo, Ecuador.

Richter illustrated the male and female with a plant sent to Gould by Thomas Reeves of Rio de Janeiro. Reeves supplied Gould with drawings of South American plants for his hummingbird illustrations, including a Brazilian orchid portrayed with the Tufted Coquette, and a *Bilbergia* with the Phaon Comet.

This species, named after J.T. Reinwardt, Professor of Ornithology in Copenhagen, lives in south-east Colombia, east Ecuador and north-east Peru.

ANDIGENA NIGRIROSTRIS.

70 *Black-billed Mountain-Toucan (HCR)*

SK. SKLKKIDEKA FIFKRIVORS.

69 *Guianan Toucanet (HCR)*

GUIANAN (CULIK'S) TOUCANET

SELENIDERA PIPERIVORA

Selenidera culik (Wagler)

PLATE 69

Gould wrote that this toucanet lived in Cayenne (French Guiana) and the lowland forests by the Amazon. It was known locally by the name of Culik, after its unusual cry, which sounded like 'koo-lik'. It was said to feed principally on peppers, which was the reason why Linnaeus gave it the name *piperivora*.

The illustration shows that the male and female have colour differences. The male has a black head and throat, and a yellow crescent between the shoulders. The female is duller, she has a grey breast and underparts, and on her back is a band of chestnut.

The male is shown stretching forward to pluck fruit or berries, for with its long bill it can reach food which is normally inaccessi-

71 *Saffron Toucanet* (HCR)

72 *Emerald Toucanet* (HCR)

ble. The toucans eat fruit by seizing chunks with the tip of the bill, throwing their heads back and tossing the morsels back into their throats. As slighter bills could serve the same purpose it is not clear why the toucans' bills are so large and cumbersome. However, their bright bold colours may be used aggressively to seize chicks from other birds' nests or frighten away other creatures. They also may serve as recognition marks between different species with similar body colours.

BLACK-BILLED MOUNTAIN- (HILL) TOUCAN

ANDIGENA NIGRIROSTRIS

Andigena nigrirostris (Waterhouse)

PLATE 70

The Black-billed Hill Toucan inhabits the humid forests and thickets of the Andes from north-west Venezuela, Colombia and north-east Ecuador, and moves seasonally up and down the mountainsides as various fruits and berries ripen.

Gould described this species as having unusual and interesting colouring; it differed from other toucans 'in the black colouring of its bill, which is beautifully contrasted with the snowy whiteness of its throat, while the blue of its undersurface is even more delicate'.

The colours for the finished toucan plates were carefully indicated on 'pattern' plates, or prints specially hand-coloured as a guide for the colourists. A pattern plate for the *Andigena nigrirostris* has survived and is now owned by Henry Sotherans Ltd, London. Gould has added in pencil extra instructions for Bayfield the colourist, including 'blue round the eye very delicate like the breast' and 'keep this blue sky a little higher'.

SAFFRON TOUCANET (SAFFRON-COLOURED HILL TOUCAN)

ANDIGENA BAILLONI

Baillonius bailloni (Vieillot)

PLATE 71

'For a knowledge of the colouring of the soft parts [bill, legs and feet, and skin round the eye] I am indebted to Mr. John Natterer, who, when passing through on his return to Vienna, after a residence of eighteen years in the Brazils, obligingly furnished me with drawings and full particulars as to the colouring of this and other species of the *Ramphastidae*.'

The second edition illustration was based on a specimen collected by Natterer in November 1822, from among the dense woods in southern Brazil. From Natterer's information a more accurate picture of the bill could be given than in Lear's earlier illustration, which was based on a faded specimen. The bill's sides have a broad red pointed mark, and the surrounding pale greenish-blue colours merge into white at the serrated edges. The feet are greyish-green and have yellow soles.

73 *Wagler's Toucanet* (HCR)

EMERALD TOUCANET (GOLDEN-GREEN GROOVEBILL)

AULACORAMPHUS PRASINUS

Aulacorhynchus prasinus (Gould)

PLATE 72

When Gould described this species in the first edition it was very rare, but afterwards he received several specimens, including some from his collector and friend, Lorenzo Floresi, who travelled in Mexico.

The illustration shows two young birds in a tree hole and their parents. Recent research has shown that these groovebills, now called Emerald Toucanets, use the old holes of woodpeckers, or even evict smaller birds by force from their holes and then enlarge the entrances. Their nesting locations can be found between 7 and 90 feet (2–28 metres) from the ground; and the three or four white eggs are laid on the floor of the hole without any nest lining. Both parents help in the incubation, but are very restless parents, often spending a short time on the eggs, and leaving before the return of their mate. They keep the nest very clean and clear away all waste matter. The blind, naked chicks develop very slowly and take over forty days to fledge and leave the nest. Juvenile birds are like adults with smaller bills and duller throat patches.

The Emerald Toucanets live in the highland mountain forests between 3,300 and 10,000 feet (1,000–3,000 metres) in southern Mexico through Central America to Nicaragua, Costa Rica and Panama and into South America from Colombia and west Venezuela through east Ecuador and east Peru to north and east Bolivia.

WAGLER'S (GROOVEBILL) TOUCANET

AULACORAMPHUS WAGLERI

Aulacorhynchus prasinus wagleri (Sturm)

PLATE 73

This species was named after Dr Johannes G. Wagler (1800–1832), Professor of Zoology at Munich University from 1827 to 1832. Wagler died accidentally during a shooting excursion near Munich. Gould related that Wagler was 'passing through a hedge with a loaded gun, the muzzle of which was directed towards his body', when the gun unfortunately discharged and 'deprived natural history of the service of one of her more talented and enthusiastic professors.'

Gould wrote that this species was similar to the Golden-green Groovebill in its longer bill and 'the larger amount of black at the base of the upper mandible'. The Golden-green Groovebills are now called Emerald Toucanets, and Wagler's Toucanet is considered to be one of their subspecies and lives in south-west Mexico. They are similar, but Wagler's Toucanet has a forehead much lighter than the crown and a different bill pattern.

A Monograph of the Trogonidae or Family of Trogons

First edition (1835–1838), one volume, 36 plates.
Second edition (1858–1875), one volume, 47 plates.

PHARODMACKUS PAVONINUS.

Gould's second monograph described all the known species of the family of trogons which, like the toucans, were brightly coloured and lived in the tropical forests. In contrast to the active and strident toucans, trogons are mysterious, reclusive and sedentary birds, spending much of their day perched on high branches, their gay colours concealed among dense foliage. They feed mainly on insects, which they spot from their perches and catch on the wing while making short forays into the forest.

The most striking of all the trogons is the Quetzal, which has a long streamer-like tail and lives in the American rainforests. This bird, sacred to the ancient Mayas, was worshipped as a god of the air, and its plumes were used in ceremonial costume. It was considered a crime to kill the Quetzal, and the feathers were taken from the living bird which was released to grow more. The Quetzal has been the symbol of liberty for thousands of years, as it was believed that it died of a broken heart when kept in captivity. Today it is the national bird of Guatemala, and a picture of a flying bird with its long plumes trailing behind it appears on all their currency.

Elizabeth Gould's illustration of the Quetzal is unique among Gould's plates for it needed a double page folded upwards to accommodate the extra long tail. Her sensitive draughtsmanship and delicate line was especially appropriate for the delineation of the graceful trogons. She contributed all the plates in the first edition except the *Trogon gigas*, which was copied by Lear from an illustration in a book by Levaillant.

Gould described the classification of trogons as a 'labyrinth of confusion', due to differences in plumage between the males and females, young and adults. He studied the skins in European museums and private collections, for few observations had been made of the birds in the wild as they lived in very remote regions. In the first edition he listed thirty-four species; twenty-three were American, ten Indian and one African.

In the second edition, begun twenty years later, Gould updated the descriptions, the plates were redrawn, and newly discovered species were added to make a total of forty-seven – thirty-three from America, eleven from India and two from Africa. The majority of plates were by H.C. Richter, who depicted appropriate tropical plants, some copied from *Curtis's Botanical Magazine*. The last plates were by William Hart who contributed some elaborate backgrounds; perhaps his extensive tropical landscape setting for the plate showing the Quetzal is his most sophisticated.

The dedication of the first edition was made to the Reverend Joseph Goodall, Provost of Eton College, who had encouraged Gould's youthful natural history interests when he lived at Eton, near Windsor. The second edition was dedicated to the Duke of Argyll, an eminent statesman with a keen interest in ornithology.

74 Blue-crowned Trogon (EG)

MOUNTAIN (MEXICAN) TROGON

TROGON MEXICANUS

Trogon mexicanus Swainson

PLATE 75

From his examination of various specimens, Gould found that the Mexican Trogon's plumage changed between adolescence and maturity. In this illustration the adult male is shown with its mature colours of a green chest circled with a band of white, scarlet breast and belly, and a striking square-ended tail with black feathers terminating in white tips. A second illustration depicted a young male with changing plumage, and showed a single adult white-tipped black plume emerging among its adolescent barred tail-feathers.

The Mexican Trogon was first described in 1827 by William Swainson, a versatile naturalist, traveller, artist and writer, whose picture of a young male appeared in the second series of his *Zoological Illustrations*, published in 1829–1833. Swainson pioneered the use of lithography for bird illustration, and his prints in this new technique, although smaller in scale, probably served as models for Elizabeth Gould's work. Both artists adopted the traditional style of depicting the bird as a silhouette on a perch with no background. But whereas Swainson's trogon looked very flat through his use of repetitive shading, Elizabeth Gould achieved a more rounded effect by emphasizing strong shadows on the bird's chest and belly.

Both Swainson and Gould employed Gabriel Bayfield and his assistants to hand colour their prints expertly with watercol-

TROGON MEXICANUS, *(Swain.)*
Mexican Trogon.
Adult Male.

75   *Mountain Trogon* (EG)

ours. A pattern print of Swainson's Mexican Trogon with written colour notes has survived. Swainson's instructions to Bayfield were as follows: bill 'carmine and saffron', 'breast and belly to be very brilliant' and the chest 'clear prussian green, bright as possible and smooth'.

This species, now known as the Mountain Trogon, lives in open pine woodland, pine-oak and humid forest in Mexico and Central America.

ELEGANT OR COPPERY-TAILED (GRACEFUL) TROGON

TROGON ELEGANS

Trogon elegans Gould

PLATE 76

The Graceful Trogon, now called the Elegant Trogon or Coppery-tailed Trogon, was first described by Gould in 1834 from a specimen collected in Guatemala. It is also found in Mexico and in the southern U.S.A.. Small numbers spend the summer in the southern parts of Texas and Arizona. They breed in forest canyons among pine, oak, sycamore, ash, walnut and juniper trees, and feed on grasshoppers, caterpillars, small beetles, and fruit pulp.

In Elizabeth Gould's illustration the male bird gracefully displays its long tail,

76 *Elegant or Coppery-tailed Trogon* (EG)

77 *Elegant Trogon* (EG)

while stretching downwards towards a beetle. The two middle tail-feathers, described by Gould as 'green with bronzy reflections', are painted with brown and green watercolour with a little added gum to give a glossy effect, and heightened with a few strokes of gold paint.

The female is depicted in duller shades of brown, grey and scarlet.

ELEGANT (DOUBTFUL) TROGON

TROGON AMBIGUUS

Trogon elegans ambiguus (Gould)

PLATE 77

Gould was at first uncertain about this trogon's species, so he called it the Doubtful Trogon. It was similar to the *Trogon elegans*, but Gould found a few slight differences in its markings. One difference

was that its outer tail-feathers had fine speckles, whereas those of the Elegant Trogon were barred. Gould decided that this trogon was a different species only after an examination of many specimens of various ages.

Elizabeth Gould's picture shows the male stretching upwards towards a caterpillar. Some twenty years later, the species was illustrated by Richter in the second edition; the male bird shown preening and the female peering into the cavity of a tree. Little new information was added except that their tails were 'fully an inch shorter' than the *Trogon elegans*.

The Doubtful Trogon, now classified as a subspecies of the Elegant Trogon, is found in South Texas, and east and central Mexico.

BLUE-CROWNED (PURPLE-BREASTED) TROGON

TROGON VARIEGATUS

Trogon curucui Linnaeus

PLATE 74

It was unusual for three birds to be depicted on one plate but Gould was anxious to show variations in the Purple-breasted Trogon's plumage. He examined many specimens and found that 'although they all bear the usual characteristics of the species, still scarcely two examples are to be found possessing strictly similar markings of the three lateral tail feathers: in some specimens the black bars predominate, and in others the white'.

Gould was indebted to William Swainson for the loan of three specimens. The lower bird with the black tail-bars partially obliterated was an old male, the central

78 *Gartered Trogon* (EG)

Gould's illustration is of the Gartered Trogon, now considered to be a subspecies of the Violaceus Trogon.

BLACK-THROATED OR GRACEFUL TROGON

TROGON ATRICOLLIS

Trogon rufus Gmelin

PLATE 79

Gould remarked that both sexes of this trogon had already been illustrated in many ornithological books but each time the species had been given a different name. Also the female, due to her dull colouring, had sometimes been described as a different species from the more striking male.

During the previous century George Edwards called the male the 'Yellow-billed Green Cuckoo', and the Comte de Buffon described the female as 'Courucou à queue rousse'. Both sexes had been called the 'Courucou arranga' in the splendid works of François Levaillant. The title of *Trogon atricollis* had been ascribed to them by the French zoologist L.J.P. Vieillot in 1817. Gould decided that because of the confusion, it was best to follow the scholarly authority of Vieillot and use the scientific name of *Trogon atricollis*. Now, however, most authorities give precedence to the 1788 description by J.F. Gmelin and his scientific name *Trogon rufus*.

Gould stated that this trogon came from Guiana, Surinam and the banks of the Amazon, but we now know the species has a wide distribution from Honduras to central Paraguay and north-east Argentina.

one, which had not yet acquired the mature bright-green back plumage, was possibly a young male, and the upper figure with brown, grey and scarlet plumage was undoubtedly an adult female.

This species comes from the humid forests of South Colombia, Brazil through to Equador, Peru, Bolivia, Paraguay and north-west Argentina.

GARTERED (BOOTED) TROGON

TROGON CALIGATUS

Trogon violaceus caligatus Gould

PLATE 78

Gould had little information about this small trogon, which was illustrated from a specimen bought in Paris. He was especially interested in its thick, unscaled or 'booted' legs, and gave a detailed diagram of its tarsus and claw. The legs and claws of all trogons are remarkably small, and weak in relation to the size of their bodies. Their claws are 'yoke-toed', having two toes in front and two behind, and the two front toes are joined together at the base.

On Gould's personal copy of this print he noted in pencil on the top left-hand corner: 'The crown of the bird is wrongly coloured, it should be *black* except the nape which alone should be blue.' Later, in the second edition, Gould apologized profoundly for this mistake in colouring.

79 *Black-throated or Graceful Trogon* (EG)

RESPLENDENT (TROGON) QUETZAL

TROGON RESPLENDENS

Pharomachrus mocinno de la Llave

PLATE 80

'It is scarcely possible for the imagination to conceive anything more rich and gorgeous than the golden-green colour which adorns the principal part of the plumage of this splendid bird; or more elegant and graceful than the flowing plumes which sweep pendent from the lower part of the back, forming a train of metallic brilliancy.' Gould continued: 'Nature appears to have ordained that birds possessing unusual brilliancy of plumage should be inhabitants of retired and obscure situations; and in strict conformity with this law the Resplendent Trogon, by far the most beautiful of its tribe, is only to be found in the dense and gloomy forests of the southern states of Mexico, remote from the haunts of civilised man.'

This beautiful bird, called the Quetzal (see also plate 87), was revered and protected by the Aztec Indians, and only members of their royal family were allowed to wear its plumes in their head-dresses. The male Quetzals' tails are around 3 feet (just under 1 metre) long, and during spring and summer they make spectacular display flights over the forest canopy. They fly and swoop in graceful arcs with their tails streaming out behind them.

Gould said that it was only possible to give a faint idea of the brilliant colours of the Quetzal. In order to accommodate the male's long tail, Elizabeth Gould illustrated it on a double page folding upwards. Gould believed he was the first to publish a plate of both the male and female.

The Quetzal is now a protected species in the cloud-forest habitat of Mexico, Guatemala, Honduras, El Salvador, Nicaragua, Costa Rica and Panama.

NARINA TROGON

TROGON NARINA

Apaloderma narina (Stephens)

PLATE 82

The Narina Trogon (see also plate 100) comes from Africa, and was named after a Hottentot girl called Narina who lived in the Knysna District of Cape Province

80   Resplendent Quetzal (EG)

about the years 1765 to 1782. Little is known about her, but she seems to have been very beautiful, to have led a sad life, and to have died young.

This trogon was first illustrated by Levaillant in his book on African birds. It was described as living in the densest parts of the forests, where it sat motionless on low branches during the middle of the day. In the morning and evening it was active in catching locusts, beetles and caterpillars. Its flight was short and rapid; it darted from its favourite perch at passing insects and returned to the same place again.

The male is glossy green with a red belly, whereas the female has a duller red belly and a brown and grey chest.

(GIANT TROGON)

TROGON GIGAS

Unknown Species

PLATE 83

Gould commented that this trogon was so rare that he had been unable to obtain a specimen for illustration. Instead he made a copy of Barraband's illustration 'Le Grand Couroucou à ventre blanc de java, ou le Couroucou géant' in Levaillant's *Histoire Naturelle des Couroucous et des Touracos* (1816). Gould's comments on the bird's rarity are not surprising for this bird has never been seen, and is somewhat euphemistically stated to be a 'doubtful species' (*Catalogue of the Birds of the British Museum*, 1892, vol. XVII). The bird is based perhaps on a faded specimen of a trogon from Asia, but is more likely to be another example of Levaillant's vivid imagination which has sadly tarnished his reputation.

This picture is of special interest because a watercolour drawing by Edward Lear has survived of the 'Trogon gigas', a study for this plate. The trogon is carefully painted and the branch quickly sketched in pencil. The bird faces left, in the opposite direction to the finished plate, for the drawing would be traced on to the lithographic stone and thus appeared reversed in the process of printing.

Edward Lear was not known to have contributed to the *Monograph of the Trogons*, as the other thirty-five prints of the first edition are inscribed 'Drawn from Nature and on Stone by J & E Gould'. The Giant Trogon is unusual among Gould's plates as it bears only the Latin title of the bird and no credit to any artist, lithographer or printer.

This plate shows Lear's broad and sweeping pencil line, which differed from Elizabeth Gould's more delicate and precise style of draughtsmanship. It is not clear how much Lear assisted Elizabeth Gould in the drawing of the trogon prints. Although some of the supporting foliage has Lear's mannerisms, the birds themselves show Elizabeth Gould's careful precision.

Gould issued this plate of the *Trogon gigas* in the last part of the monograph on trogons in March 1838, some eight months after Edward Lear had set off from England to pursue the career of a landscape painter in Italy.

TROGON ERYTHROCEPHALUS.
Red-headed Trogon.

Drawn from Nature & on Stone by J.& E. Gould.

Printed by C. Hullmandel.

TROGON NARINA. (Shaw).
Narina Trogon.

82 Narina Trogon (EG)

83 Giant Trogon (EL)

RED-HEADED TROGON

TROGON ERYTHROCEPHALUS

Harpactes erythrocephalus (Gould)

PLATE 81

The Red-headed Trogon inhabits the forests of the Himalayas of north-east India, Burma, south-east China, Indochina and Sumatra. The male has a red head,

chest and belly, short rounded wings with vermicular markings, and a long square-tipped tail. The female is similar but her head is brownish. Compared to most trogons they are large, measuring in length 13 inches (33 centimetres). Like other trogons they have short weak legs and small feet with two toes pointing forwards and two backwards.

Gould wrote that this trogon was com-

mon near Rangoon, Burma. 'Like the rest of its genus, it gives preference to the thickest jungles; hence in that luxuriant country it finds a retreat at once congenial with its habits and mode of life.'

RED-HEADED (HODGSON'S) TROGON

TROGON HODGSONII

Harpactes erythrocephalus (Gould)

PLATE 84

Gould named this trogon from the Himalayas as a compliment to Brian Houghton Hodgson (1800–1894) who lived for over twenty-three years in Katmandu, Nepal, where he played an ambassadorial role as British Resident. Hodgson also lived for fifteen years in Darjeeling, and compiled detailed observations on Nepalese bird life. His collection of over 9,500 bird specimens was one of the largest ever made in Asia.

Gould wrote that Hodgson's 'forthcoming work, on the Zoology of those regions, cannot fail to be of the highest interest'. Unfortunately, Hodgson's collection of superb bird and mammal watercolours by Nepalese artists working under his direction was never published.

Hodgson's Trogon (see also plate 101) is the nominate subspecies of the Red-headed Trogon found in the forests from Nepal eastward to Burma and north-west Thai-

84 Red-headed Trogon (EG)

land. Elizabeth Gould was particularly skilled in capturing the characteristically upright perching position of the trogon, with
its tail hanging almost vertically below it.

PHILIPPINE (ROSY-BREASTED) TROGON

TROGON ARDENS

Harpactes ardens (Temminck)

PLATE 85

Gould wrote that this male trogon could be
distinguished from the other red-headed
Asian species 'by the beautiful band of
delicate rose-colour which crosses the
breast'. This species, now called the Philippine Trogon, lives in the forests of the
main Philippine islands. In spite of their
brilliant plumage these trogons are not very
conspicuous, for they perch on trees among
dense vegetation where the light is very
gloomy.

   Elizabeth Gould's illustration was drawn
from specimens 'recently transmitted to the
Museum of the Zoological Society,
together with many other rarities, which
were collected in the Manillas'.

TROGON ARDENS, *(Temm)*
Rosy-breasted Trogon

85   Philippine Trogon (EG)

SECOND EDITION
(1858–1875)

RESPLENDENT QUETZAL (QUETZAL)

PHAROMACRUS MOCINNO

Pharomachrus mocinno de la Llare

PLATE 87

The Quetzal illustrated by Elizabeth Gould in the first edition (see also plate 80) needed a double-folded page to accommodate its very long tail. In the second edition, William Hart restricted his life-size depiction of the bird to one page by showing its tail curving up and over its back, but in the distant forest background he showed male quetzals perched on branches, with their long tails trailing.

William Hart's Quetzal was drawn some thirty years after Elizabeth Gould's picture and indicates the difference in presentation between the early and later Gould illustrations. The first, with its long sinuous outline, is a simple silhouette, a clear contrast to Hart's more crowded page with its curved shapes and detailed background.

Gould quoted from an account by Osbert Salvin in 1860 of watching the quetzals in the Guatemala forests. Salvin wrote that unlike the hummingbirds, whose iridescence could only be seen at certain angles, the Quetzal's metallic green was brilliant in every light and its vivid colours surpassed all the other birds of the tropics.

Recent reports reveal that these birds,

although protected in Mexico, Costa Rica and Guatemala, are severely threatened by the destruction of their forest habitat. They eat insects, and wild avocados (the fruits of a type of laurel tree, *Persea americana*), which they swallow whole but regurgitating the seeds; they nest in holes excavated in old trees some 10 to 60 feet (3 to 18 metres) from the ground. The young have enormous mouths and when only a few days old can eat whole avocados.

In Guatemala the Quetzal, traditionally a sacred bird, and a symbol of life and freedom, still plays a part in modern culture. It is the national bird, and is the name of Guatemala's currency.

CRESTED QUETZAL (BEAUTIFUL TRAIN-BEARER)

PHAROMACRUS ANTISIANUS

Pharomachrus antisianus (d'Orbigny)

PLATE 88

This species was discovered by Professor Alcide d'Orbigny (1803–1887), the French zoologist, during his travels in the hot and humid forests of the Bolivian Andes. There it was rare, and usually found near torrents in the thickest parts of the woods. In the morning and evening its monotonous cry

'Couroucou' could often be heard, but explorers usually found the source of the call was difficult to trace among the dense vegetation.

Gould saw and sketched d'Orbigny's male specimen during a visit to Paris in 1837, and it was illustrated in the first edition of the *Trogonidae*. By 1858 both sexes had been discovered; in the second edition Gould showed the dullish female as well as the 'truly beautiful male' with its raised crested tuft of bright green feathers.

Now called the Crested Quetzal, it is found in Venezuela, Colombia, Ecuador, Peru, Bolivia and Brazil.

PAVONINE QUETZAL (RED-TAILED TRAIN-BEARER)

PHAROMACRUS PAVONINUS

Pharomachrus pavoninus (Spix)

PLATE 89

'The bird here represented is the only species of the form that has yet to be discovered with a red bill; if then, this peculiarity be kept in view, and the uniform brownish-black of the tail be remembered, the bird will be readily recognised.'

Gould's illustration in the first edition was based on a pair of specimens brought to London by John Natterer, who was return-

87 *Resplendent Quetzal* (WH)

88 *Crested Quetzal* (HCR)

quietly among the branches until hunger impels it to dash out, whirl round the tree and seize its food in its passage; it likewise feeds on insects, which are also taken on the wing, the bird darting after them and returning to the same branch in the manner of a Flycatcher.'

The species is found in Upper Amazonia and is now called the Pavonine Quetzal. The male and female are perched on a spray of *Eugenia brasiliensis*, a plant which Richter also illustrated in his plate of the Blue-chinned Sapphire in the *Monograph of the Humming Birds*.

EARED (WELCOME) TROGON

EUPTILOTIS NEOXENUS

Euptilotis neoxenus (Gould)

PLATE 90

'I first became acquainted with this species in the year 1836, when an immature specimen came into my possession, an examination of which satisfied me that it was the young of a very splendid bird, which could not fail of being welcomed with feelings of gratification by every ornithologist, I therefore gave it the name of *Trogon neoxenus* (Welcome Trogon).'

When Gould later received a full-grown pair from Mexico, he was able to describe the species with more accuracy. The adult birds had fine hair-like tufts on their heads, which looked like feathered ears, and their bills were less robust and serrated but longer than those of other trogons. Gould added that, as specimens of these trogons continued to be rare, examples would still be most 'welcome to collectors both in this country and on the continent of Europe'.

Now called the Eared Trogon, this bird inhabits central Mexico and in the summer and autumn south-eastern Arizona.

MASKED (BLACK-FACED) TROGON

TROGON PERSONATUS

Trogon personatus Gould

PLATE 86

The illustration shows two gaily coloured males and a brownish female looking down from a creeping plant. These birds, now called Masked Trogons, live in western Guyana, Venezuela, Colombia, Ecuador,

89 *Pavonine Quetzal* (HCR)

eastern Peru and Bolivia.

Gould quoted from an account by Claude Wyatt from the journal the *Ibis*, 1871, who described seeing the birds in the Andean forests at about 8,500 feet (2,500 metres). 'They are very tame, and generally sit motionless up in the trees (where the cock bird, should his back be turned to you, is very difficult to see), and allow one to ride by within a few yards.'

Wyatt added: 'The skin of these birds is

90 *Eared Trogon* (HCR)

ing to Vienna after eighteen years' residence in Brazil. Natterer had seen these birds on high branches in forests on the upper parts of the Amazon and the river Negro.

Further specimens from Brazil were brought to England by the naturalist Alfred Russel Wallace. Gould quoted Wallace's account of watching them eat berries, fruit and insects in the high forests and plantations of Amazonia: 'The bird usually sits

91 *Gartered Trogon* (HCR)

92 *Jalapa or Bar-tailed Trogon* (HCR)

93 *Orange-bellied Trogon* (HCR)

exceedingly delicate, and the feathers come out in handfuls when they are shot, should they fall even a short distance before reaching the ground.' Trogons are known to have soft, fluffy plumage delicately attached to their skins, so that taxidermists need to be exceptionally skilled to be able to prepare their skins as museum specimens. Gould wrote in his introduction that their feathers were 'so feebly implanted that they fall at the slightest agitation, and their skin is so delicate that it will tear at the slightest tension'.

Jalapa or Bar-tailed (Rayed-tailed) Trogon

Trogon puella

Trogon collaris puella Gould

PLATE 92

The male trogon is depicted with similar green upper-parts, white chest band and red belly to those of other American trogons but it differs by the markings on its

tail. These consist of 'a series of narrow cross-bars of white on a jet-black ground'. The female differs from the male in having brown instead of green plumage and her three outer tail-feathers are not barred but 'clouded or sprinkled with extremely small dots of brown on a light greyish white ground.'

The trogons were illustrated against tropical green palm trees. Pictorial settings and appropriate backgrounds replaced the isolated branches of the first edition. These trogons, now considered to be a subspecies of the Collared Trogon, live in areas ranging from central Mexico to west Panama.

Orange-bellied (-breasted) Trogon

Trogon aurantiiventris

Trogon aurantiiventris Gould

PLATE 93

This trogon with black bars on its tail was rarer and smaller, but very similar to the

Rayed-tailed Trogon. The only difference is that the colouring of its chest and belly is deep orange instead of scarlet. Gould at first wondered whether its plumage went through a change of colouring from orange to scarlet or scarlet to orange, but eventually decided that its bright breast colours were 'assumed from the beginning'.

The female like the male has a bright orange breast and belly, but brown instead of bronze-green upper-parts.

This species, now called the Orange-bellied Trogon, lives in Costa Rica and Panama.

Gartered Trogon

Trogon caligatus

Trogon violaceus caligatus Gould

PLATE 91

In the second edition, Gould took the opportunity to write a long apology about a colouring mistake which had occurred in the first edition for the picture of *Trogon caligatus*, then called the Booted Trogon: 'To commit an error, though unintentionally, leads to unpleasant reflection; to acknowledge and admit it is becoming to everyone; but this should more particularly be done by the man of Science; I must therefore confess that I certainly did make a mistake in my former illustration of this species, when I coloured the entire head blue instead of black, and thereby sadly puzzled every ornithologist who has had occasion to study this group of birds.'

Gould did not know how this error arose, but fortunately he still had the original specimen, and Richter was able to show the correct colours in the second edition. The male's face, head and throat were black, banded on the back by a collar, and on the breast by a gorget, of bluishgreen. The female also had a black head but slaty-gray instead of bronzy-green upper-parts.

Gould added: 'The *Trogon caligatus* is a neat and compact little bird, the bright orange of its breast must form a very effective contrast to the dense foliage of the gloomy forest which this and other members of the genus are known to inhabit.'

The Gartered Trogon, a subspecies of the Violaceus Trogon, lives in Central America and northern South America. Pairs often make a nest out of the large paper nests built in the cavities of high trees by tropical wasps. The trogons first eat all the wasps (to whose stings they appear to be immune), and then feast on the larvae while they are digging their own nest.

BLUE-CROWNED (PURPLE-BREASTED) TROGON

TROGON VARIEGATUS

Trogon curucui Linnaeus

PLATE 94

As in the first edition, this species was illustrated by three birds, two males below and a female above, but in the later picture tropical flowers were added and the plate was more brightly coloured.

A change in taste had occurred in the thirty years between Elizabeth Gould's and Hart's illustrations. Gould favoured ornate backgrounds and strong colouring in his late publications, and the soft washes of the earlier period gave way to heavier brushwork. The 'bronzy-green' backs of the male trogons, indicated by flecks of gold paint on a broad green wash in the early prints, were painted with small streaks of yellow, orange and green set side by side in the later pictures.

Gould commented that Swainson first found these trogons in Brazil, in the humid Bahai forests, and Natterer also saw them along the Madeira and Negro Rivers of Amazonia.

The name *variegatus* was very appropriate, for the markings of their black and white tails varied greatly, especially in the Bahai specimens. This bird is now called the Blue-crowned Trogon.

94 *Blue-crowned Trogon* (WH)

95 *Blue-crowned Trogon* (HCR)

96 *White-tailed Trogon* (WH)

White-tailed (Snow-tailed) Trogon

Trogon Chionurus

Trogon viridis chionurus (Sclater and Salvin)

PLATE 96

The first specimens of both sexes of this species were sent from the area opened up by the Panama Railway to the New York ornithologist George Lawrence, but remained with him for some time before they were described and named in 1870.

The male has a black-tipped purple tail with distinctive outer tail-feathers of pure white, except for a narrow black patch at the base which is concealed when the tail is closed. Its back is 'purplish-blue glossed here and there with coppery-green, shading off to rich purple on the rump and upper tail-coverts'. The female lacks the male's glossy plumage and is grey with white outer tail-feathers barred with black.

These trogons, a subspecies of *Trogon viridis*, are found in east Panama, west Colombia and Ecuador.

Blue-crowned (Behn's) Trogon

Trogon Behmi

Trogon curucui behni Gould

PLATE 95

When Gould first examined specimens of this species, left with him by Professor Behn of Kiel, who was visiting London on the way from South America, he discovered that they had some red feathers in their crowns. He soon realized these had been surreptitiously added, 'for nature would never have acted so inharmoniously as to have decorated any one of these green Trogons, all of them so perfectly of one type, with such an anomaly as a red crown!'

Although the skins had been tampered with by deceitful traders, Gould recognized that they were a new species, and decided to name them after Professor Behn who had discovered them.

Later, Gould received further specimens from Thomas Bridges in Bolivia. The male's head, neck and breast were shining bluish-green with a golden gloss. Its back was bright coppery-green with a golden gloss, shading off to a metallic grass green on the rump and upper tail-coverts.

These trogons, a subspecies of *Trogon curucui*, are found in Bolivia, Brazil, Paraguay and Argentina. Gould regretted that by a misprint the title *Trogon behni* had been written *Trogon behmi*.

97 *Baird's Trogon* (WH)

98 *Black-headed Trogon* (HCR)

BAIRD'S TROGON

TROGON BAIRDI

Trogon bairdii Lawrence

PLATE 97

The birds of Costa Rica were little known to ornithologists until 1868, when George Lawrence compiled a list based on specimens sent by various collectors to the Smithsonian Institution, Washington. Among the skins were two male specimens of this beautifully coloured trogon which Lawrence named in honour of Professor Spencer Fullerton Baird, ornithologist and secretary of the Smithsonian.

Since then these birds have also been found on the slopes of the volcano Chiriqui and in the forests of Panama. They are very similar to the Snow-tailed Trogon but have red instead of yellow breasts.

The female is shown looking out of a tree-hole. Most trogons nest in cavities of tree-trunks and stumps which they enlarge by gnawing. As their beaks are small and are not particularly suited for digging or chiselling they prefer to work in dead or rotting wood. They do not add any lining to their nesting hole and lay two to four eggs at the bottom of the cavity.

These birds, considered by some authorities to be a subspecies of *Trogon viridis*, live in humid lowland and foothill forests in Costa Rica and west Panama.

BLACK-HEADED TROGON

TROGON MELANOCEPHALUS

Trogon melanocephalus Gould

PLATE 98

In the first edition Elizabeth Gould illustrated a lone male with a black head and chest which came from Tamaulipas, Mexico. Gould thought its dull black colouring was so unusual for an American trogon that he decided to call it *Trogon melanocephalus*.

Gould added in this edition: 'When fully adult, the male is a really fine bird, the greenish blue of the back being very beautiful, and the three outer tail-feathers, with their bold and squarely-formed white tips, showing very conspicuously.'

The lower bird in the plate is a young male about six weeks old. It has beautiful markings, but its outer tail-feathers are narrower, more pointed and without the definite white bars of the adult. In the background a female is depicted; her smaller scale in the distant tropical forest gives the scene an almost three-dimensional feeling.

NARINA TROGON

HAPALODERMA NARINA

Apaloderma narina (Stephens)

PLATE 99

Gould thought it was remarkable that so many trogons inhabited the tropical regions of South America and India whereas Africa could claim only one or two species. Today three African species are listed, the Narina, Bar-tailed and Bare-cheeked Trogons. The Narina Trogon is the commonest and most widespread, its range extending in lowland and montane forests south of the Sahara from Sudan to Cape Province.

In the second edition, Hart's illustration is an adaptation of Elizabeth Gould's picture from some thirty years earlier (see also plate 82). The line of the birds is altered to move from left to right, a forked branch with lichen is introduced and the birds are placed closer together. Much of Elizabeth Gould's sinuous line is lost; in the earlier picture the male trogon gracefully offers his mate a succulent mantis, but in the later print the pair appear to be involved in a

100   *Narina Trogon* (WH)

tussle with their insect.

A wider range of colours is used in the later plate, but the watercolour washes are less smooth and delicate. The two prints of the Narina are interesting examples of the difference in style and colouring technique between Gould's early and late publications.

NARINA (WEST AFRICAN) TROGON

HAPALODERMA CONSTANTIA

Apaloderma narina constantia Sharpe and Ussher

PLATE 100

Gould wrote that the West African Trogon had close similarities to the Narina Trogon, and came from the Gold Coast (Ghana). There, specimens were obtained by 'Mr. St. Thomas D. Aubinn, a native hunter in the employ of Governor Ussher, after whose daughter Constance this species is named'. H.T. Ussher, an English naturalist, was in the Gold Coast from 1866 and Governor from 1879 to 1880.

Gould's protégé R.B. Sharpe, who was particularly interested in African birds, gave Gould the specimen which Hart drew for the illustration. These trogons, a subspecies of the Narina Trogon, are found in West Africa from Sierra Leone and Liberia, eastwards to Ghana.

101 *Red-headed Trogon* (HCR)

102   Reinwardt's Blue-tailed Trogon (HCR)

HARPACTES DIARDI.

103 *Diard's Trogon* (HCR)

are shown with the plant *Hoya coriacea*, and are found in Malaysia, Borneo and Sumatra.

RED-HEADED (HODGSON'S) TROGON

TROGON HODGSONI

Harpactes erythrocephalus (Gould)

PLATE 101

This race of the Red-headed Trogon, named by Gould in honour of Brian Houghton Hodgson, British Resident in Nepal and naturalist, was illustrated by a single bird in the first edition (see also plate 84).

Gould added in the second volume an account by T.C. Jerdon, collector and author of *The Birds of India*, 1862–1864. Jerdon wrote that these trogons were found in the Himalayas at altitudes of 2,000 to 4,500 feet (600 to 1,400 metres). They liked darkly shaded valleys, and flew from tree to tree 'making sallies every now and then and seizing insects on the wing'.

The male has a blood-red head, neck and breast 'separated from the rich scarlet of the undersurface by a crescentic mark of white'. Gould also included Jerdon's detailed description of the trogon's bill which was 'deep smalt-blue', the skin round the eyes 'deep lavender-blue', and its legs and feet which were 'pale lavender'. The plant is *Benthamia fragifera*.

REINWARDT'S BLUE-TAILED (REINWARDT'S) TROGON

HARPACTES REINWARDTI

Harpactes reinwardtii (Temminck)

PLATE 102

A young bird and an adult male were illustrated to show the species' change in plumage between youth and maturity. The young bird is similar to the adult in the colours on its back and tail, but different in the markings on the wings, and the rufous brown tint of the breast.

The species was rare in bird collections, having been discovered in Java by J.T. Reinwardt, Professor of Ornithology in Copenhagen. It is shown with the plant *Medinilla javensis*. This trogon is found in the highland forests of Java and Sumatra.

DIARD'S TROGON

HARPACTES DIARDI

Harpactes diardii (Temminck)

PLATE 103

'Of this beautiful trogon I have seen a large number of specimens in the course of my life, and after a very careful comparison I have not been able to separate examples from Malacca from others of Bornean origin.' Gould decided these birds from different areas were all one species. Richter's illustration of both sexes was also included in *The Birds of Asia*.

These trogons were richly coloured like other Asiatic species, but differed in having freckled markings on the outer tail-feathers, a feature of some of the South American trogons.

The species was dedicated 'to the memory of an intelligent French naturalist, who in the flower of his youth fell a sacrifice to the unhealthy climate of the east'. They

THE BIRDS OF AUSTRALIA

Seven volumes (1840–1848), approximately 600 plates.
Supplement (1851–1869), one volume, 81 plates.

The Birds of Australia was Gould's greatest achievement. This series was the first attempt at a fully comprehensive account of Australian birds with illustrations and doubled the number of known birds. Some 600 species were included, of which about 200 were described for the first time. These volumes stand apart from Gould's other work, for the descriptions were not based solely on specimens but on extensive field research and observation too. The accounts by Gould and his assistant Gilbert of the lyrebird, bowerbirds or mound-builders convey the immediacy and excitement of discovery. The illustrations by Elizabeth Gould were some of the first and most delightful pictures of flowers and birds of Australia.

Gould's interest in Australian birds was first aroused by the many unusual specimens which were arriving in London from the new colony, and also by skins and strange accounts of birds sent by his two brothers-in-law Stephen and Charles Coxen, who had settled in New South Wales. Before embarking on his momentous visit to Australia, Gould hoped to stimulate interest in his forthcoming series and published two preparatory works on Australian birds. He issued a small volume entitled *A synopsis of the birds of Australia* containing a list of 168 species with tiny prints of life-size birds' heads, and twenty plates (two

parts) of *The Birds of Australia*. The latter are now called the 'Cancelled Plates', because on his return from Australia Gould asked subscribers to send back these prints in exchange for the first parts of his new edition. He forecast correctly that these cancelled plates might not always be returned and could thus become very valuable to book collectors.

His travels kept Gould away for two years, but once back in London he quickly set to work on his new series, aided by a vast number of specimens and his wife's *ad vivum* drawings. Unfortunately Elizabeth Gould died just a year after their return and Gould was faced with the problem of searching for a new illustrator. Eventually he found in Henry Constantine Richter the ideal interpreter of his requirements, and was satisfied that his subscribers would find that the high standards set by Elizabeth were maintained.

Gould often hoped to return to Australia and frequently felt nostalgic about his early adventures. A *Supplement to the Birds of Australia* illustrated additional species and further discoveries. In the introduction Gould wrote that this continuation of his work was 'as much a labour of love . . . as when ardour and youth went hand in hand during my visit to the distant country whose natural productions I trust I have not in vain attempted to illustrate'.

104 *Wedge-tailed Eagle* (HCR)

VOLUME I

WEDGE-TAILED EAGLE

AQUILA FUCOSA

Aquila audax (Latham)

PLATE 104

Gould compared this majestic Australian bird to the Golden Eagle of the northern hemisphere. 'All that has been said representing the courage, power and rapacity of the one applies with equal force to the other; in size they are also nearly alike, but the lengthened and wedge-shaped form of its tail gives the Australian bird a more pleasing and elegant contour.'

The eagle could be seen soaring high over open plains and circling in the air looking out for such prey as small kangaroos. Once spotted, its victim had little hope of escape from its tremendous swoop and powerful grasp. Breeders of sheep concerned for their lambs regarded the eagle as an enemy and in Tasmania considerable sums of money were offered for its capture.

The eagle's nests were made of a platform of sticks and placed in the most inaccessible trees. The eggs could be procured only by the Aborigines who were able to scale trees which had branchless trunks over 100 feet (30 metres) high.

AUSTRALIAN HOBBY OR LITTLE FALCON (WHITE-FRONTED FALCON)

FALCO FRONTATUS

Falco longipennis Swainson

PLATE 105

This species is the smallest of the Australian falcons. Gould watched it during his travels into the interior and was impressed by its speed and determination. 'As its pointed wings clearly indicate, it possesses great and rapid powers of flight; and I have frequently been amused by pairs of this bird following my course over the plains for days together, in order to pounce down on the Quails as they rose before me.' Gould also noted that occasionally the fast flying quails escaped by dropping suddenly to the ground among the grasses. The original illustration by Elizabeth Gould was of a life-size adult and young falcon.

105 *Australian Hobby or Little Falcon* (EG)

SOUTHERN BOOBOOK OWL (BOOBOOK OWL)

ATHENE BOOBOOK

Ninox novaeseelandiae boobook (Latham)

PLATE 106

Reports of this common owl reached Gould from all the Australian colonies, and he was told that its nightly hoot had earned it the Aboriginal name of 'Buck-Buck'. But the colonists, according to the botanist George Cayley, thought it sounded more like a cuckoo, and wryly remarked that as everything was in reverse in Australia, this 'cuckoo' sang by night instead of by day.

Gould wrote that the owl 'breeds in the holes of large gum-trees during the months of November and December, and lays three eggs on the rotten surface of wood, without any kind of nest. Three eggs procured by my useful companion Natty were in a forward state of incubation . . . They were perfectly white as is ever the case with eggs of owls.' Natty was an Aboriginal servant, much valued for his bird knowledge and expertise in climbing trees, who accompanied Gould on his explorations in New South Wales.

This new owl is said by some authorities to be a distinct species *Ninox boobook* rather than a subspecies of the more widely distributed *Ninox novaeseelandiae*.

SPOTTED BOOBOOK (SPOTTED) OWL

ATHENE MACULATA

Ninox novaeseelandiae leucopsis (Gould)

PLATE 107

Elizabeth Gould drew these little Tasmanian owls, a subspecies of the Boobook Owl, from a pair of living birds which Gould kept in a cage at Hobart, during her ten-month stay from September 1838 to July 1839. According to Gould they 'bore confinement so contentedly, that had an opportunity presented itself, I might easily have sent them alive to England.'

These little owls like their European counterparts spent the whole day 'in a state of drowsiness, bordering on sleep' but could be easily aroused to action. 'Its visual powers are sufficiently strong to enable it to face the light, and even to hunt for its food in the daytime.'

106 *Southern Boobook Owl* (HCR)

107 *Spotted Boobook Owl*

108 *Tawny Frogmouth* (EG)

VOLUME II

TAWNY FROGMOUTH
(TAWNY-SHOULDERED PODARGUS)

PODARGUS HUMERALIS

Podargus strigoides (Latham)

PLATE 108

This strange bird, known as the Tawny Frogmouth because of its broad bill used for seizing moving insects, is found throughout Australia and Tasmania.

Gould described it as 'strictly nocturnal, sleeping throughout the day on the dead branch of a tree, in an upright position across, and never parallel to, the branch, and which it so nearly resembles as scarcely to be distinguishable from it'. He saw the birds mostly in pairs, perched near each

other on the branches of the gum trees. During the day they were so sleepy and lethargic, that it was possible to lift them up by hand or knock them down with a stick. When roused they flew lazily off with heavy flapping wings to a neighbouring tree to resume their slumbers until the approach of evening. Then, there would be a remarkable change, and the birds would become as animated and active as they had been dull and stupid.

Elizabeth Gould's illustration shows the bird asleep, 'in the position it is usually seen during the day'.

SPOTTED NIGHTJAR (GOATSUCKER)

EUROSTOPODUS GUTTATUS

Caprimulgus guttatus Vigors and Horsfield

PLATE 109

The Goatsucker's name was derived from an ancient belief that it sucked the milk of goats and other animals and probably originated from the Nightjar's habit of seeking insects on pasture land. This species is now called the Spotted Nightjar, and is found throughout the drier parts of mainland Australia, except the eastern and south-eastern coastal areas.

Nightjars have beautiful variegated patterns of greys and browns that look like dead foliage. The Spotted Nightjar has finely freckled markings, but also cream-buff spots and a white patch on its wing. Gould saw the adult birds breeding on the bare earth, and a downy chick 'of reddish brown colour, not very dissimilar from the surface of the ground where it had hatched'.

Gould was greatly interested in the nightjar family and before leaving for Australia began a project on the *Caprimulgidae*, which was published in 1837–1838 as Part 2 of *Icones Avium or Figures and Descriptions of New and Interesting Species*. It contained eight plates by Elizabeth Gould illustrating nightjars throughout the world.

According to some authors the scientific name for the Spotted Nightjar should be *Eurostopodus argus* Hartert, as the original name *Eurostopodus (Caprimulgus) guttatus* was based on a misidentification of a closely related species, the White-throated Nightjar.

WELCOME SWALLOW
HIRUNDO NEOXENA
Hirundo neoxena Gould

PLATE 110

Gould considered that the Welcome Swallow was very appropriately named, for in southern Australia as in Europe it was welcomed as an indication of the approach of spring. Gould reported that 'it arrives in Van Diemen's Land about the middle or end of September, and after rearing at least two broods departs again northwards in March.' The English botanist George Cayley, who lived in New South Wales from 1800 to 1810, noted during his stay that the earliest swallows arrived on 12 July

110   *Welcome Swallow* (HCR)

1803 and the latest left on 30 May 1806.

Although a few stragglers remained in New South Wales for the whole winter, a great many more 'wended their way to a warmer and more congenial climate, where insect life is sufficiently abundant for the support of so great a multitude'.

In the wild these swallows nested in clefts of rocks or caverns. Their sites in colonized areas were 'the smoky chimneys, the chambers of mills and out-houses or the corner of a shady verandah'.

FAIRY MARTIN
CHELIDON ARIEL
Hirundo (Cecropis) ariel (Gould)

PLATE 112

Gould did not even know about the existence of the Fairy Martin until his stay at Cohan's Inn, Maitland, New South Wales, when he was awakened by twittering noises and found that hundreds of martins were nesting under the verandahs and corners of the windows. On 27 September 1838 Elizabeth Gould noted in her journal: 'A species of martin builds under the eaves of the inn in which we are, their curious nests are placed close together in great numbers.'

109   *Spotted Nightjar* (HCR)

The martins' mud or clay nests were described as 'bottle-shaped with a long neck'. The birds appeared to work together 'six or seven assisting in the formation of each nest, one remaining within and receiving the mud brought by others in their mouths'.

111 *Rainbow Bee-eater* (HCR)

RAINBOW (AUSTRALIAN) BEE-EATER

MEROPS ORNATUS

Merops ornatus Latham

PLATE 111

The Bee-eater, also known as the Rainbow Bird, was a favourite with Australians because of its beautiful colours. Gould wrote that like the European cuckoo or swallow it was associated with the return of spring, arriving in New South Wales in August and departing in March.

During the evenings the birds would congregate by the banks of the rivers; they perched upright on dead branches like kingfishers, and darted to and fro to capture flying insects.

Gould recorded that he had seen the holes and tunnels in sandy banks by the river where the bee-eaters reared their young. An entrance the size of a mouse-hole led to a yard-long tunnel, and a room at the end was large enough to hold the female and four or five chicks. The Rainbow Bee-eaters are seen throughout mainland Austalia.

LAUGHING KOOKABURRA (GREAT BROWN KINGFISHER)

DACELO GIGANTEA

Dacelo novaeguineae (Hermann)

PLATE 113

The *Dacelo gigantea*, now called the Kookaburra, was a familiar bird for every New South Wales resident and traveller. Gould described it as an inquisitive bird which often perched on the dead branch of a tree to watch 'a party traversing the bush or pitching their tent'. When its 'extraordinary gurgling, laughing note' was heard, the bushman would say, 'There is our old friend the Laughing Jackass'—or in another mood some words of a less pleasant nature! The Kookaburra could sometimes pay dearly for its temerity by being roasted for food on the traveller's fire.

Reptiles, insects and crabs were the Kookaburra's diet, but it also devoured 'lizards with great avidity' or carried off snakes 'in its bill to be eaten at leisure'.

By the year 1843 a Kookaburra had been

CHELIDON ARIEL: *Gould*

112 *Fairy Martin* (HCR)

113 *Laughing Kookaburra* (HCR)

kept in captivity for several years at the Zoological Gardens, London. Another at Blackdown, Sussex, attracted 'the attention of everyone by its singular actions and extraordinary notes, which are poured forth as freely as in its native wilds'.

Sacred Kingfisher (Halcyon)

Halcyon sanctus

Halcyon (Todirhamphus) sancta
Vigors and Horsfield

PLATE 116

In the bush the Sacred Kingfisher soon betrayed its presence; its plumage of 'brilliant and metallic lustre' was easily seen, and its loud, piercing cry of a continuous 'pee-pee' could be heard especially during the nesting season.

The diet of this kingfisher depended on its locality; and in some areas it ate mantises, grasshoppers, caterpillars, even lizards and small snakes which it knocked dead against a stone. In the mangroves it fed on crabs left by the receding tide. On the banks of the River Hunter the kingfishers excavated holes around the boles and dead branches of the eucalyptuses. Gould thought they were searching for the larvae of ants but they were probably burrowing to make nests rather than looking for food.

116 Sacred Kingfisher (EG)

115 Mistletoebird (EG)

Mistletoebird (Swallow Dicaeum)

Dicaeum hirundinaceum

Dicaeum hirondinaceum (Shaw and Nodder)

PLATE 115

In spite of its rich, scarlet breast, this little bird, now called the Mistletoebird, was very difficult to see as it darted among the thick foliage of lofty trees. It could be recognized more easily by its pretty, warbling song.

Elizabeth Gould depicted a pair among the 'branches of a beautiful parasite . . . *Loranthus* . . . gathered at Dartbrook, on the Upper Hunter, where it is very common on the Casaurinae'.

Gould was puzzled by the Mistletoebird's feeding activities. 'Whether the bird is attracted to this misseltoe-parasite (*sic*), like many others, for the purpose of feeding upon the sweet and juicy berries, I could not make out. Its chief food is insects, but in all probability it may partially feed on these fruits also.' It is now known that the Mistletoebird swallows large quantities of

J&E Gould del et lith. CHLAMYDE[F

CULATA. *Gould.*   *C Hullmandel Imp.*

GRALLINA AUSTRALIS.

J. Gould and H.C. Richter del et lith.

C. Hullmandel Imp.

118   Magpie Lark (HCR)

berries whole; these pass quickly through its body and land on the branches to make new plants.

Suspended from a twig is the Mistletoebird's purse-shaped nest, which resembles a baby's bootee. It was made of a 'white cotton-like substance found in the seed-vessels of many plants'.

PIED BUTCHERBIRD (BLACK-THROATED CROW-SHRIKE)

CRACTICUS NIGROGULARIS

Cracticus nigrogularis (Gould)

PLATE 114

Gould observed these birds, now called Pied Butcherbirds, usually in pairs, and wrote that their 'active habits and conspicuous pied plumage' made them striking objects among the trees. Often they flew down to search for insects and small lizards on the ground, but their prey was also

'young birds, mice, and other small quadrupeds'. With their powerful and strongly hooked bills they could kill, tear, devour and inflict severe blows and lacerations on their victims.

The Butcherbird is now widespread in mainland Australia. Gould wrote that their habitat in New South Wales was in areas 'of rich land known as apple-tree flats, and low open undulating hills studded with large trees'.

MAGPIE LARK (PIED GRALLINA)

GRALLINA AUSTRALIS

Grallina cyanoleuca (Latham)

PLATE 118

Gould described the Pied Grallina, now called the Magpie Lark, as similar in its actions to the Pied Wagtail in England, for it was a graceful and friendly bird and would be seen running along the house-

tops and verandahs of settlers' homes.

The pudding-basin-shaped nest of the Magpie Lark is very unusual and Gould called it 'one of the anomalies of Australia'. He described it as like 'a massive clay-coloured earthenware vessel' formed of soft mud which hardened upon exposure to the air. It is often plastered on to a bare horizontal branch overlooking the water, so that the young 'mudlarks' when fledged are able to feed on a plentiful supply of water snails and insects.

GILBERT'S WHISTLER (PACHYCEPHALA)

PACHYCEPHALA GILBERTII

Pachycephala inornata Gould

PLATE 119

Gould wrote that the names of many eminent scientists were perpetuated by the 'complimentary' titles given to birds, but it was a practice of which he did not

wholeheartedly approve. However, in assigning the name of this species to its discoverer, his assistant John Gilbert, he was paying 'a just compliment to one who has most assiduously assisted me in the laborious investigations required for the present work'.

Gilbert had hoped that Gould would give the name *Gilbertii* to his discovery of a beautiful new parrot (the Paradise Parrot, now believed extinct), but this request was not granted. However, this species, Gilbert's Whistler *Pachycephala inornata* still bears his name, although the scientific name *gilbertii* is now only used for a subspecies. Gilbert described it to Gould as an early breeder living in the thick brushes of the interior of Western Australia. Today it is an uncommon bird, and is famed for its rich, far-carrying, whistle-like and haunting calls.

CRESTED (FRONTAL) SHRIKE-TIT

FALCUNCULUS FRONTATUS

Falcunculus frontatus (Latham)

PLATE 120

'I had many opportunities of observing this bird, both in New South Wales and South Australia . . . It alike inhabits the thick brushes as well as the trees of the open plains.' Gould described this tit-like bird as pert and lively, and it often erected its crest whilst clinging and climbing on branches.

These birds had very strong beaks and could inflict severe wounds. Gould commented from experience: 'No bird of its size with which I am acquainted possesses greater strength in its mandibles . . . as I experienced on handling one I had previously winged, and which fastened on to me in a most ferocious manner.'

Elizabeth Gould depicted the male and female with a branch of a shrub gathered in the district of Illawarra, New South Wales.

VOLUME III

121   Eastern Yellow Robin (HCR)

EASTERN YELLOW (YELLOW-BREASTED) ROBIN

EOPSALTRIA AUSTRALIS

Eopsaltria australis (White)

PLATE 121

Gould saw the Eastern Yellow Robin in many gardens of settlers near Sydney and in the interior of New South Wales. 'It is by no means shy, and may often be seen crossing the garden walks, perching on some stump or railing, regardless of one's presence, at which time the fine yellow mark on its rump is very conspicuous.' Its sprightliness was like an English robin, also its 'habit of raising its tail at the moment of perching'. It flitted from bush to bush and tree to tree in search of insects.

The robin's compact, cup-shaped nest of narrow strips of bark was so well camouflaged that it was almost impossible to detect. Gould believed this demonstrated the bird's inherent 'instinctive power of imitation'.

SUPERB LYREBIRD (LYRE BIRD)

MENURA SUPERBA

Menura novaehollandiae Latham

PLATE 123

'Were I requested to suggest an emblem for Australia among its birds, I should without the slightest hesitation select the *Menura* as the most appropriate, being not only strictly peculiar to Australia, but, as far as is yet known, to the colony of New South Wales.'

Gould's search for the elusive Lyrebird, now called Superb Lyrebird, was a hazardous experience, creeping and crawling through 'inaccessible and precipitous sides of gullies and ravines, covered with tangled creepers and umbrageous trees'. Although the birds could be heard on all sides 'pouring forth their loud and liquid calls, for days together', the slightest sound, 'the cracking of a stick, or rolling of a small stone', would alarm them and they would vanish from sight as if by magic.

Gould was amazed by the Lyrebird's habit 'of forming small hillocks . . . upon which the male is continually trampling, at the same time erecting and spreading out its tail in the most graceful manner, and uttering various cries, sometimes pouring out its natural notes, at other mocking those of other birds, and even the howling of the native dog or Dingo'.

122   Eastern Whipbird (EG)

123 *Superb Lyrebird* (EG)

EASTERN (COACH) WHIPBIRD

PSOPHODES CREPITANS

Psophodes olivaceus (Latham)

PLATE 122

Gould described this bird as usually shy and reclusive; it inhabited the same areas of dense foliage and undergrowth in New South Wales as the Lyrebird. It was renowned for its call, and the woods constantly reverberated with its loud drawn-out note which ended like the cracking of a whip. In spring, 'the males may often be seen chasing each other, frequently stopping to pour out their notes with great volubility, making the brushes ring for a considerable distance around them.' They also raised their crests and spread out their tails in display. Elizabeth Gould illustrated the male and female on the branch of a variety of cherry growing on the brushes of the Hunter River.

conceal itself and creep mouse-like through the dense grass beds. As it had small wings its flight was feeble, but in low cover it would move nimbly, bouncing and running over the ground.

Gould thought that the colonists' name of Emu Wren was most appropriate, as the bird's tail-feathers with their loose structure resembled those of an Emu. The tail was usually held erect but occasionally it drooped over the wren's back.

These wrens inhabit restricted areas of south-east and south-west Australia and Tasmania. They are an uncommon and possibly endangered species as their habitat is threatened by clearing, land-development and sand-mining.

RIGHT: *126 Superb Fairy-wren* (EG)

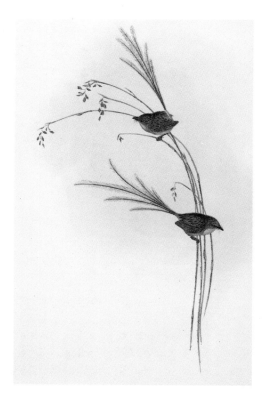

124 Southern Emu-wren (EG)

SOUTHERN EMU-WREN (EMU WREN)

STIPITURUS MALACHURUS

Stipiturus malachurus (Shaw)

PLATE 124

This reclusive little bird, was especially fond of low marshy areas covered with high grasses and rushes. In danger it would

125 Noisy Scrub-bird (HCR)

127 Gouldian Finch (HCR)

His attention was drawn by its peculiar and noisy note, but it was only after many days of patient watching that he succeeded in obtaining a specimen. Gould commented that as so little was known of the bird 'future research will doubtless furnish us with some highly interesting information'.

After 1889 this bird was unseen for seventy years and believed extinct, but in 1961 it was located again near Two People Bay, east of Albany, West Australia.

After some local controversy the area was declared a nature reserve and the dense scrub, low forests and overgrown swamp that Noisy Scrub-birds prefer was created. Since 1970 effective fire exclusion has allowed the vegetation to mature, and the population has increased and spread. In 1989 a census, based on the number of singing males, estimated there were around 500 individuals present in the reserve. Since 1983 birds have been translocated to other sites, and at least one small colony has been successfully established. Equally encouraging has been the appearance of Noisy Scrub-birds outside the reserve and translocation sites. The Noisy Scrub-bird is no longer one of the rarest of all birds, though it still requires careful management.

SUPERB FAIRY-WREN (BLUE WREN)
MALURUS CYANEUS

Malurus cyaneus (Latham)

PLATE 126

During the winter months the male of this species of wren was tame and friendly, hopping about the gardens and shrubberies of the New South Wales colonists, 'as if to court, rather than shun, the presence of man'. In summer, when its plumage changed from dull brown to glossy blue, it became more shy and retiring, and appeared 'to have an instinctive consciousness of the danger to which his beauty subjects him'.

The dome-shaped nest, constructed with grasses and lined with feathers or hair, had a small entrance hole at the side. Several broods were reared annually in the Botanic Gardens in Sydney, and Gould saw a pair busily making a nest in a tree close to the Colonial Secretary's Office in the town.

NOISY (BRUSH-BIRD) SCRUB-BIRD
ATRICHIA CLAMOSA

Atrichornis clamosus (Gould)

PLATE 125

This rare bird was discovered in 1842 by Gould's explorer John Gilbert, who found it in the dense scrubs of West Australia.

GOULDIAN FINCH
AMADINA GOULDIAE

Chloebia (Erythrura) gouldiae (Gould)

PLATE 127

Gould thought this little finch had such beautiful rainbow colours of lilac, green and golden yellow that it could not fail to be a general favourite. He dedicated it to the memory of his wife Elizabeth, who died tragically a year after their return to England, and who had been of immeasurable help to him in Australia because of her interest in his work and her remarkable drawing skills.

These finches were discovered in 1840 by John Gilbert on Greenhill Island near the head of Van Dieman's Gulf, where he saw small groups feeding among the high grasses. Dr Benjamin Bynoe, surgeon of HMS *Beagle*, who sent specimens to Gould from the ship's third surveying trip round the world, also collected some of the first

Gouldian Finches that Gould ever saw including an adult male in full breeding plumage. They inhabited the edges of the mangroves and thickets and when disturbed flew to the uppermost branches of the lofty gum trees.

The illustration shows two adults and a young bird. The Gouldian or Painted Finch is now scarce in the wild, and is much better known as a cage and aviary bird. This species, which comes from northern Australia, used to be seen in flocks of thousands but in recent decades has declined alarmingly. One theory is that the birds may be suffering from a mite which infects the lungs.

VOLUME IV

SPOTTED BOWERBIRD

CHLAMYDERA MACULATA

Chlamydera maculata (Gould)

PLATE 117

Gould was fascinated by the Spotted Bowerbird, a species he previously illustrated from a specimen in the *Cancelled Parts*. During his visit to Australia Gould was determined to see for himself this shy bird and its strange tunnel of woven branches which he named a 'bower'.

On his journey north of Liverpool Plains into the interior Gould was guided by a native to a remote water-hole in a rock which had probably never been visited before by a white man. While Gould lay motionless on the ground, the Spotted Bowerbirds would dash past to drink, even though 'an enormous black snake was lying coiled upon a piece of wood near the edge of the pool'. Gould later found their 'artificial bower, or playing-ground' at some distance from the water, and he commented that the male birds had 'a task of great labour' to carry almost 'half a bushel' of shells, bleached bones and pebbles which they used to make paths and to decorate the entrances. The bower itself was 'outwardly built of twigs, and beautifully lined with tall grasses', these being placed so that the tops of the branches almost met to form an archway.

128   Green Catbird (HCR)

A carefully preserved bower was brought back to England and exhibited at the British Museum. In 1840 at the Zoological Society Gould gave the first scientific description of bowerbirds' habits, explaining that the bowers were courtship grounds decorated by males to lure and attract females. This account caught the fancy of the Victorian public, and the 'bower' became an amusing conversational talking-point.

GREEN CATBIRD (CAT BIRD)

PTILONORHYNCHUS SMITHII

Ailuroedus crassirostris (Paykull)

PLATE 128

The Cat Bird, now known as the Green Catbird was neither shy nor wary, and when approached 'its loud, harsh and extraordinary voice' could be heard, 'a note that differs so much from that of all other

River, where they were considered a serious garden pest, causing great damage to the summer fruit crops.

The males attain their full adult plumage of yellow and deep velvety black after many years, and Gould reckoned that only about one bird in fifty sported these beautiful colours.

These birds, now called Regent Bowerbirds, make secluded avenue bowers with walls and platforms constructed from twigs, and with leaves, shells and brightly coloured berries displayed at the entrance.

The male and female are shown on the branch of a wild fig tree.

129   *Regent Bowerbird* (HCR)

HUIA (GOULD'S NEOMORPHA)

NEOMORPHA GOULDII

Heteralocha acutirostris (Gould)

PLATE 130

This species, now called the Huia, was described by Gould as 'highly curious' because the male and female had such different shaped beaks. The male's beak was stout, straight, and chisel-like, whereas the female's was longer, thin, and curved down gracefully. Unfortunately these birds were excessively hunted, for European collectors prized their skins as curiosities and Maoris their tail-feathers as ceremonial headdresses. They are now considered extinct and living Huias have not been reliably reported since 1907.

Gould first saw two specimens which were without wings or legs in the Zoological Society's collection, and because of their different beaks described them in 1836 as two distinct species. In 1841 he was corrected by Dr Robert Gray, compiler of *A Genera of Birds*, who decided that as they were one species, and neither of Gould's names seemed appropriate, they should both be given the new name of *Neomorpha gouldii*. Gould appreciated the compliment but added that he hoped this change would not lead to further confusion.

The male and female Huias may have used their different beaks to co-operate in food gathering. Possibly the male attacked wood with its powerful beak and the female extracted the grubs and insects.

Elizabeth Gould's illustration was drawn from a pair of birds brought from New Zealand by Dr Dieffenbach for the collec-

REGENT BOWERBIRD (REGENT BIRD)

SERICULUS CHRYSOCEPHALUS

Sericulus chrysocephalus (Lewin)

PLATE 129

Gould saw these beautiful birds in the brushes at Maitland, New South Wales, 'feeding on the same trees with the Satin and Cat Birds'. They were also abundant on the islands at the mouth of the Hunter

birds, that having once been heard it can never be mistaken'. Gould commented the cries of several of these birds resembled 'the nightly concerts of the domestic cat', likening their performance to 'London grimalkins of house-top celebrity'.

These catbirds inhabited the forests of New South Wales and fed on fruit, particularly 'the wild fig, and the native cherry'.

130 Huia (EG)

tion of the New Zealand Company, London. Dr Dieffenbach described the birds as belonging to a limited area in the south of North Island. The Maoris collected their tail-feathers for gifts and trade and as tokens of friendship; they would lure the birds by imitating their calls and when they came near would kill them with sticks. He believed that the species was becoming scarce and foretold that it would probably soon become exterminated.

Many other causes may have led to extinction, including the loss of habitat and the introduction of other birds with avian diseases to which native birds had no natural immunity.

131 *New Holland Honeyeater* (HCR)

New Holland Honeyeater

Meliphaga novae-hollandiae

Phylidonyris novaehollandiae (Latham)

PLATE 131

Gould described this little honeyeater as one of the most abundant and familiar birds of New South Wales, Tasmania and South Australia, for 'all the gardens of the settlers are visited by it, and among the shrubs and flowering plants it annually breeds'. A nest which he had was taken from a pea row in the kitchen garden of Government House, Sydney.

These birds flitted among low foliage from bush to bush. The illustration shows a male and female on a 'Banksia of Van Diemen's Land'.

Crescent (Tasmanian) Honeyeater

Meliphaga australasiana

Phylidonyris pyrrhoptera (Latham)

PLATE 132

This species lives in south-east Australia and the Bass Strait islands, but it is most common in Tasmania.

Gould described how the 'loud, shrill and liquid notes' of the honeyeaters broke the extreme silence of the 'almost impenetrable' Tasmanian forests, where they lived among 'a thick brush of dwarf shrubby trees growing beneath more lofty gums'.

The honeyeaters were also seen on more open hills at the foot of Mount Wellington, and the thick beds of the red and white heath-like *Epacris impressa*, which grew to the north side of the Derwent between Kangaroo Point and Clarence Plains. There they were often so intent on feeding that they could be watched without disturbance; they would cling to the stems

132 *Crescent Honeyeater* (EG)

at every possible angle and insert their 'slender brush-like tongue up the tube of every floret with amazing rapidity'.

The male and female had such different colouring that Gould believed before his visit to Tasmania that they were two different species. The male had 'a black stripe passing from the base of the bill through the eye, and a black lunar-shaped mark down each side of the breast, nearly meeting in the centre.' The female was a uniform dusky brown. Elizabeth Gould's illustration depicts the male and female with the plant *Epacris impressa*.

Regent (Warty-faced) Honeyeater

Zanthomyza phrygia

Xanthomyza phrygia (Shaw)

PLATE 133

'This is not only one of the handsomest of all the Honey-eaters, but is also one of the most beautiful birds inhabiting Australia, the strongly contrasted tints of black and yellow plumage rendering it a most conspicuous and pleasing object, particularly in flight.'

These birds are distributed from South Australia and Victoria northwards to southern Queensland. Their presence depends on the blossoming of the eucalyptuses; and Gould observed that they are 'consequently only to be found in any particular locality during the season that those trees are in full bloom'. Recent studies have shown that the Regent Honeyeater, which once occurred in large flocks, has dramatically declined in the last few decades. This decline is probably due to the fragmentation of the eucalyptus woodlands, which has resulted in other more aggressive honeyeater species colonizing the area.

Brush or Little Wattlebird

Anthochaera mellivora

Anthochaera chrysoptera (Latham)

PLATE 134

Gould described the Brush or Little Wattlebird as spirited and pugnacious, often to be seen fearlessly attacking and driving

133 *Regent Honeyeater* (HCR)

134 *Brush or Little Wattlebird* (EG)

away all other birds from the trees on which it was feeding.

From a top perch the male would scream 'its harsh and peculiar notes', which had 'not unaptly been said to resemble a person in the act of vomiting, whence the native name of *Goo-gwak-ruck*'. The birds forced out these gutteral sounds by throwing back their heads, jerking up their tails and distending their throats with great exertion. As the banksias were in bloom during much of the year, each blossom was diligently examined by the wattlebird, which inserted 'its long feathery tongue into the interstices of every part of the flower, extracting the pollen and insects, in searching for which it clings and hangs about the flowers in every variety of position'.

This little wattlebird is sometimes nicknamed 'Mock Wattlebird', as unlike other wattlebirds it has no 'wattles', or pieces of flesh hanging from below the eyes.

NOISY FRIARBIRD (FRIAR BIRD)
TROPIDORHYNCHUS CORNICULATUS
Philemon corniculatus (Latham)

PLATE 135

Friarbirds were often perched on the topmost dead branches of trees, where their 'garrulus and singular notes' usually attracted more attention than their dull colouring. Their nosiy calls often resembled the phrases used by colonists, and thus they were given nicknames such as 'Poor Soldier', 'Pimlico' and 'Four o'clock'. Their strange unfeathered bare heads and necks also earned them the names 'Friar Bird', 'Monk' and 'Leather Head'.

Among the branches the Friarbird adopted many strange positions, 'its curved and singular claws enabling it to cling in every variety of attitude, frequently hanging by one foot with its head downwards, etc.' During the breeding season it became

135 *Noisy Friarbird* (EG)

aggressive, 'readily attacking hawks, crows, magpies . . . or any other large birds that may venture within the precincts of its nest'.

Elizabeth Gould recorded that she heard 'the curious note of the coul bird or bald-headed friar' at Maitland, New South Wales on 26 September 1839. Her illustration shows an old and a young bird on a wild fig tree of the Upper Hunter River.

BLUE-FACED HONEYEATER (ENTOMYZA)

ENTOMYZA CYANOTIS

Entomyzon cyanotis (Lantham)

PLATE 136

Gould watched these honeyeaters in groups of eight or ten among the eucalyptus flowers in New South Wales, 'searching among the blossoms and smaller lofty branches for its food, which is of a mixed character, consisting partly of insects and partly of honey, and probably, judging from others of its family, berries and fruit'. They were very agile birds and often clung to the ends of the thickly flowered branches, bending them down with their weight.

Although they mixed with other honeyeaters and parrakeets, they could easily be identified by their large size, brilliant blue face, and the contrasting colours of their plumage. They were also conspicuous for their bold character, and would aggressively chase away other birds.

Gould found that these honeyeaters had unusual nesting habits, for they frequently laid their eggs in deserted dome-shaped babblers' nests. He wondered if they built their own nests in other localities or lived only where these nests were available. Today, the honeyeaters are known to lay eggs in the old nests of the babblers, the Magpie Lark or the Apostlebird. They line the abandoned nests with roots and grasses, and only occasionally build the whole structure themselves.

Elizabeth Gould's illustration shows a male and female 'on a branch of the lofty Eucalypti of the river Hunter'.

CHANNEL-BILLED CUCKOO (CHANNEL-BILL)

SCYTHROPS NOVAE-HOLLANDIAE

Scythrops novaehollandiae Latham

PLATE 137

'This remarkable bird, which has been considered a Hornbill by some naturalists, and as nearly allied to the Toucans by others, is in reality a member of the family *Cuculidae* or Cuckoos; an examination of its structure and a comparison of it with that of other species of the family will render this very apparent.'

Gould saw this large grey cuckoo in New South Wales, where it was a migratory bird, arriving in October and departing in January. In northern Australia it is sometimes called the 'Storm Bird' because it comes at the beginning of the wet season and is regarded as a portent of rain. It leaves Australia and travels as far as Sulawesi and the Bismarck Archipelago.

136 *Blue-faced Honeyeater* (EG)

137 *Channel-billed Cuckoo* (HCR)

larly interesting to me as being one of the birds procured by poor Gilbert on the day of his lamented death, the 28th June 1845.'

Gilbert was killed by Aborigines in a night attack during the Leichhardt expedition from Moreton Bay to Port Essington. His pocket diary and specimens were saved by Leichhardt and eventually sent back to Gould in England. Gilbert recorded that he collected treecreepers on the ninth, eleventh, and thirteenth of June, but strangely, no mention was made of them on the twenty-eighth, the day of his death.

Several specimens of this type have been kept in museum collections. One beautifully preserved and labelled is in Liverpool Museum, another in the Royal Albert Museum, Exeter, and two at the Academy of Natural Sciences, Philadelphia.

As Gilbert left no notes Gould could not add any more information about this bird. It is now called the Black Tree-creeper which is a subspecies of the Brown Tree-creeper, common in East Australia in a habitat of dry forest and woodland.

138 *Black Tree-creeper* (HCR)

Gould was not able to discover if this cuckoo was parasitic, but it is now known that it lays eggs in the nests of crows and currawongs. It lives among tall trees in wooded areas, and feeds on figs, fruit and insects. Richter's dramatic illustration shows the cuckoo's downward hawk-like flight, with its tail and pointed wings prominent. It utters raucous screeches during the evenings, especially when harassed by other birds.

Black (Black-backed) Tree-creeper
Climacteris melanotus

Climacteris picumnus melanota Gould

PLATE 138

This little bird is a poignant reminder of the death of Gould's explorer John Gilbert. Gould recorded: 'It was killed in latitude 15°57' South, on the eastern side of the Gulf of Carpentaria, and is rendered particu-

CACATUA LEADBEATERI: Wagl

139   Leadbetter's Pink or Major Mitchell's Cockatoo (HCR)

VOLUME V

LEADBEATER'S, PINK OR MAJOR MITCHELL'S COCKATOO

CACATUA LEADBEATERI

Cacatua leadbeateri (Vigors)

PLATE 139

'Few birds tend more to enliven the monotonous hues of the Australian forests than this beautiful species.' Gould described this pink cockatoo as ranging widely over southern Australia in 'belts of lofty gums and scrubs clothing the sides of rivers in the interior of the country'.

In 1835, four years before Gould's visit, Sir Thomas Mitchell (1772–1853) explored the plains of the Darling and wrote of the cockatoo: 'The pink-coloured wings and glowing crest of this beautiful bird might have embellished the air of a more voluptuous region.'

The gorgeously coloured cockatoo was much prized in England as an aviary bird. Two birds kept in Lord Derby's menagerie were less animated but also a good deal less noisy than those in the wild.

This species was first named Leadbeater's Cockatoo in 1831 after Benjamin Leadbeater, founder of a London firm of skin-dealers, but it is now also known as Major Mitchell's Cockatoo or Pink Cockatoo.

GALAH (ROSE-BREASTED COCKATOO)

CACATUA EOS

Cacatua (Eolophus) roseicapilla (Vieillot)

PLATE 140

In New South Wales Gould saw this bird, known as the Galah, on the plains bordering the Namoi River. 'The Rose-breasted Cockatoo . . . frequently passes in flocks . . . with long sweeping flight, the group at one minute displaying their beautiful silvery-grey backs . . . and the next, by a simultaneous change of position, bringing their rich, rosy breasts into view.'

During the years of Gould's visit from 1838 to 1840 large numbers bred in the boles of the eucalyptus trees. Many of the

140   *Galah* (HCR)

young were captured and taken to Sydney for transport to England, where this cockatoo was a popular cage bird.

In Australia the Galah was very tame, and could be seen in farmyards 'enjoying perfect liberty, and coming round the door to receive food in company with pigeons and poultry'.

RED-TAILED BLACK (BANKSIAN) COCKATOO

CALYPTORHYNCHUS BANKSII

Calyptorhynchus magnificus (Shaw)

PLATE 141

This black cockatoo was named after Sir Joseph Banks, the famous botanist who travelled with Cook on the *Endeavour*, which landed at Botany Bay in 1770. Among the birds he listed were: 'Parrots and Paraquets most Beautiful, White and black Cocatoes'. It is now called the Red-tailed Black Cockatoo.

Gould said that this bird could be seen in the 'immediate neighbourhood of Sydney and other large towns' and also 'in the brushes and more open parts of the colony, where it feeds on the seeds of the Banksiae and the Casuarinae'.

Glossy Black (Leach's) Cockatoo

Calyptorhynchus leachii

Calyptorhynchus lathami (Temminck)

PLATE 142

This black cockatoo was distinctive for the 'swollen and gibbose form of its bill'. Gould obtained specimens in the interior of New South Wales at the Lower Namoi, the cedar brushes of the Liverpool range,

Charles Throsby's park at Bong-bong, and the creeks of the Upper Hunter. 'So invariably did I see it among the Casuarinae, that those trees appeared to be as essential to its existence as the Banksiae to some species of Honeyeater.'

Captive black cockatoos had not reached England, as only Aborigines could find the young and eggs in holes of the highest trees in remote parts of the forest.

Gould found that some birds had yellow feathers on their cheeks and head, but this variation followed no precise rule. This species is now called the Glossy Black Cockatoo, and the yellow markings occur on most but not all females.

143 *Port Lincoln Ringneck or Twenty-eight Parrot* (HCR)

141 *Red-tailed Black Cockatoo* (HCR)

142 *Glossy Black Cockatoo* (HCR)

PORT LINCOLN RINGNECK OR TWENTY-EIGHT PARROT (YELLOW-COLLARED PARRAKEET)

PLATYCERCUS SEMITORQUATUS

Platycercus (Barnardius) zonarius (Shaw)

PLATE 143

This parrot was widely spread throughout West Australia and called the Twenty-eight Parrot by the colonists, a reference to its distinctive repetitive call. It fed on the ground or among the trees, eating grass-seed or fruit. As an aviary bird it was much valued for its large size and richly coloured plumage.

The Twenty-eight Parrot made no nest but deposited its eggs on soft debris in a hole of a gum tree.

MALLEE RINGNECK (BARNARD'S PARRAKEET)

PLATYCERCUS BARNARDI

Platycercus (Barnardius) barnardi (Vigors and Horsfield)

PLATE 144

Gould described this species, now called the Mallee Ringneck, as one of the beautiful parrots, 'the brilliant hues of its expanded wings and tails appearing like a meteor as it passes from tree to tree amidst the dark glades of the forest'. Its range extended 'through the great basin of the interior from South Australia to New South Wales'. It was seen on the ground among the tall grasses, and among the high trees, particularly the eucalyptuses. A pair of birds brought by Gould from Australia were believed to be the first live examples of this species in England.

CRIMSON ROSELLA (PENNANT'S PARRAKEET)

PLATYCERCUS PENNANTII

Platycercus elegans (Gmelin)

PLATE 146

This showy parrot, now called the Crimson Rosella, was seen on the grassy hills and brushes of New South Wales. In flight the beautiful pale blue of its outspread wings contrasted strongly with the rich scarlet colours of its body.

In England as a captive bird it was the most common of the Australian parrots. 'In disposition it is tame and destitute of distrust, and as a pet for the aviary or cage, few birds can exceed it in interest or beauty.'

The illustration shows an immature bird in the background and an adult in the foreground.

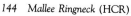

144 *Mallee Ringneck (HCR)*

145 *Eastern Rosella (HCR)*

146 *Crimson Rosella* (HCR)

Green Rosella
(Yellow-bellied Parrakeet)

Platycercus flaviventris

Platycercus caledonicus (Gmelin)

PLATE 147

This parrot, now called the Green Rosella, was widely spread over Tasmania, and could be seen running on the ground in small flocks, searching for seeds among the tall grass. On one occasion Gould saw hundreds of parrots feeding among some newly threshed corn like English sparrows or pigeons in a farmyard. These parrots were the staple diet of the early Tasmanian colonists, and pies of the birds were frequently made. Soon after he arrived, Gould 'tested the goodness of the flesh of this bird as a viand' and found it so excellent that he partook of it whenever an opportunity arose.

It nests in hollow trunks or branches and is confined to Tasmania and Bass Strait.

Eastern Rosella
(Rose-hill Parrakeet)

Platycercus eximius

Platycercus eximius (Shaw)

PLATE 145

Gould was amazed to find that these rich scarlet and yellow birds seemed as common

in Tasmania as sparrows in England. They were even seen on public roads and when disturbed merely flew off to the nearest tree or railing. The colonists no longer thought of these beautiful birds as a novelty, and they were unsparing in destroying them for causing harm to their crops of ripe corn.

These parrots are now called Eastern Rosellas. The early settlers saw large numbers at Rose Hill, near Parramatta, west of Sydney, and it is thought that 'rosella' may be derived from the district where they were first found.

Paradise Parrot
(Beautiful Parrakeet)

Psephotus pulcherrimus

Psephotus pulcherrimus (Gould)

PLATE 148

This beautiful small long-tailed parrot is now possibly extinct; it was last reliably sighted near Gayndah, Queensland, in November 1927.

John Gilbert was the first to record the parrots on the Darling Downs, Queens-

147 *Green Rosella* (HCR)

land, in 1844, when he saw them in small groups feeding on the grasses and plants of the plains. Delighted with his find, Gilbert hoped that Gould would give the species his own name *Gilbertii*, but sadly his wish was not granted, and the bird was called *pulcherrimus*, meaning 'very beautiful'. The following year while on the Leichhardt expedition, Gilbert saw the 'new green parrot of the Darling Downs' in several parts of eastern Queensland, and commented on its pleasant song. Its unusual method of nesting, by burrowing a tunnel and making a nest-chamber in a termite mound, was a much later discovery.

149   Scarlet-chested Parrot (HCR)

probably the first to bring to England two live budgies from Australia. They were given to him by his brother-in-law Charles Coxen, who had reared them in New South Wales. Even while he wrote, Gould had the budgies beside him 'in exuberant health after having braved the severities of a passage . . . by way of Cape Horn in the midst of winter'. They became ideal pets, for they sang with animation, and were 'constantly billing, cooing and feeding each other, and assuming every possible variety of graceful position'.

Gould saw the nomadic wild budgerigars in New South Wales, in 1839, 'breeding in all the hollow spouts of the large *Eucalypti*

148   Paradise Parrot (HCR)

SCARLET-CHESTED PARROT (SPLENDID GRASS PARRAKEET)

EUPHEMA SPLENDIDA

Neophema splendida (Gould)

PLATE 149

Gould regretted that he was unable to give more than a brief notice of this beautiful grass parrot, now called the Scarlet-chested Parrot. Several fine specimens were collected for him near Moore's River, West Australia, by Johnston Drummond, son of the botanist James Drummond. Tragically Johnston Drummond suffered the same fate as Gould's other collector John Gilbert. He

was killed by Aborigines in July 1845, within two weeks of Gilbert's death on the opposite side of the continent.

These nomadic little parrots are scarce and inhabit arid and inaccessible areas. The illustration shows two males and a female on a brnach of *Beaufortia decussata*, a West Australian plant.

A very small number of prints have survived by Elizabeth Gould showing a single male bird on a spray of the same plant. This earlier illustration was issued by Gould at the beginning of his main series and was drawn from a specimen he had in 1840. Later, when Gould received more specimens, he cancelled the earlier plate and replaced it with Richter's more elaborate composition.

BUDGERIGAR (WARBLING GRASS PARRAKEET)

MELOPSITTACUS UNDULATUS

Melopsittacus undulatus (Shaw)

PLATE 150

These little parrots, now known by their Aboriginal name 'Budgerigar', are in all likelihood the world's most popular cage birds. Gould was delighted that he was

150   Budgerigar (EG)

bordering the Mokai'. They had flown further east than was usual, and when Gould camped near a waterhole he was surrounded by large numbers 'arriving in flocks varying from twenty to a hundred or more'. During flight they made a screeching noise, but in the heat of the day they settled motionless on the trees and could hardly be detected among the gum leaves.

NYMPHICUS NOVÆ-HOLLANDIÆ, (Wagl)

COCKATIEL (COCKATOO PARRAKEET)

NYMPHICUS NOVAE-HOLLANDIAE

Nymphicus hollandicus (Kerr)

PLATE 151

Gould saw the Cockatiel in the summer of 1839 in New South Wales 'on the apple tree flats on the Upper Hunter, as well as similar districts on the Peel, and other rivers northwards'. The Cockatiels congregated in great numbers near waterholes, where some hundreds would feed on the ground and perch on the dead branches of gum trees.

Gould found that the Cockatiels adapted well to captivity and were playful and amusing. He brought some back to England, and an oil portrait of Elizabeth Gould shows one perched on her hand which lived for many years as a favouite pet in the Gould family.

This illustration was adapted by Elizabeth Gould from a picture by Edward Lear of two living birds owned by the Countess

152 *Swift Parrot* (EG)

of Mountcharles. Lear's plate, the first depiction of a male and female Cockatiel, was originally made for his *Illustrations of the Family of Parrots*, published in 1832.

SWIFT PARROT (LORIKEET)

LATHAMUS DISCOLOR

Lathamus discolor (White)

PLATE 152

The drawing of the Swift Lorikeet among thick clusters of eucalyptus blossom was made by Elizabeth Gould during her stay in Tasmania, as a guest of Sir John and Lady Franklin at Government House. The Franklins were greatly interested in the natural history of the island, and gave the Goulds every encouragement.

The Lorikeet was migratory and appeared during spring in the shrubberies and gardens of Hobart. So intent were the birds on feeding on the nectar of the

153 *Flock Bronzewing* (EG)

154 *Orange-footed Scrubfowl* (HCR)

full-blown blossom that they even appeared on gum trees bordering the streets 'within a few feet of the heads of the passing inhabitants'. Small flocks of Lorikeets would frequently be seen 'passing over the town, chasing each other with the quickness of thought, and uttering at the same time a shrill screaming noise, like the Swift of Europe'.

companion Natty called out 'Look! Massa,' and 'in an instance the air before us seemed literally filled with a dense mass of these birds, which had suddenly risen from under the trees at his exclamation.'

Recordings of the huge numbers of Flock Pigeon declined following settlement, and by the early 1900s it was feared extinct. Since the 1950s it has again been frequently observed, at times in flocks of thousands.

other islands; at least ten subspecies have been described but the validity of most is open to doubt. With its powerful legs it scoops up earth, vegetation and sand to make an immense mound for the incubation of its eggs.

John Gilbert gave Gould a lengthy account of the huge piles of earth he found near Port Essington, north of Port Darwin, Northern Territory, in 1842. He was told by the natives that these were nest-mounds of birds, and in one mound about 5 feet (1.5 metres) high he found a young bird in a hole 2 feet (60 centimetres) under the surface. Other mounds were excavated, and in one measuring about 15 feet (4.5 metres) high and 60 feet (18 metres) round the base, the natives found holes where large eggs were buried at a depth of 5 to 6 feet (1.5 to 1.8 metres).

FLOCK (HARLEQUIN) BRONZEWING

PERISTERA HISTRONICA

Phaps histronica (Gould)

PLATE 153

'I first met with this new and beautiful pigeon on the 2nd December, 1839, while encamped on the banks of the Mokai, a river which rises in the Liverpool range, and falls into the Namoi.' On the plains some three weeks later, Gould's Aborigine

ORANGE-FOOTED SCRUBFOWL (MOUND-RAISING MEGAPODE)

MEGAPODIUS TUMULUS

Megapodius reinwardt Dumont

PLATE 154

The Orange-footed Scrub Fowl inhabits the rain-forests and scrubs of the northern coast of Australia, the south and west coasts of New Guinea and a number of

155 *Brown Kiwi* (HCR)

DROMAIUS NOVÆ-HOLLANDIÆ.

156 *Emu* (WH)

VOLUME VI

EMU

DROMAIUS NOVAE-HOLLANDIAE

Dromaius novaehollandiae (Latham)

PLATE 156

'This find bird, which is only exceeded in size by the Ostrich of Africa; was first described and figured under the name of the New Holland Cassowary in Governor Phillip's *Voyage to Botany Bay* published in 1789.' Gould wrote that since then it had been found throughout Australia, especially in the north regions, but due to the encroachments of colonization it was becoming rare in many areas of New South Wales, Tasmania and the Bass Strait islands, although 'a few still range over the western part of Van Diemen's Land, and it may yet be met with on the Liverpool Plains, in New South Wales, and probably on some of the low islands at the mouth of the Hunter, where I observed its recent foot-marks.'

The members of the Leichhardt expedition from Moreton Bay to Port Essington (which included Gould's assistant Gilbert) saw many Emu flocks. At the later stages of the journey near the Gulf of Carpentaria the bird was invaluable as food and at least a hundred would be seen in the space of eight miles. Leichhardt named one area in eastern Northern Territory '7-Emu Creek' after a successful hunting expedition.

This robust illustration of the Emu and its chicks was drawn and lithographed by Benjamin Waterhouse Hawkins, and is the only example of his work in Gould's imperial folio volumes.

BROWN KIWI (KIWI-KIWI)

APTERYX AUSTRALIS

Apteryx australis Shaw

PLATE 155

The first knowledge of the Kiwi in England came from a specimen brought from New Zealand in 1812, but Gould's picture was drawn from a later skin presented to the Zoological Society by the New Zealand Company.

According to Gould the nocturnal Kiwis were avidly hunted by Maoris, often by torchlight, because their skins were greatly prized for chieftains' cloaks. When attacked the birds would conceal themselves in dense beds of fern or crevices of hollow trees and defend themselves by striking with their powerful feet and sharp spurs.

The birds feed on worms, snails and insects, thrusting their bills deep in the soil. Their name is derived from a Maori word imitating their cry. They have suffered considerably since European settlement began, but as they are a national emblem, measures are being taken for their protection.

The illustration of the Kiwi initially appeared in the *Cancelled Parts*, drawn and lithographed by Elizabeth Gould.

AUSTRALIAN BUSTARD

OTIS AUSTRALASIANUS

Ardeotis australis (Gray)

PLATE 157

'It was not until I personally visited the *terra Australis* that I ascertained that the present species was one of the most abundant, and one of the widely dispersed of the larger birds inhabiting that country.'

Gould was impressed by the grandeur of this large bird: 'when seen at freedom slowly stalking on its native plains, no Australian bird, except the Emu, is so majestic or assumes in its carriage so great an air of independence.'

Although formerly common, the numbers of bustards have declined due to colonization and shooting.

BLACK-WINGED, PIED OR WHITE-HEADED STILT

HIMANTOPUS LEUCOPCEPHALUS

Himantopus himantopus leucocephalus Gould

PLATE 159

Gould watched the elegant movements of these long-legged pied stilts 'near Mr. Edward Uhr's station on the banks of the river Mokai' in December 1839. 'This part of the Mokai was one of the most beautiful, and to me, one of the most interesting localities I had seen in New South Wales, and therefore I encamped on its banks for some time.'

The stilts fed in shallow water on insects and small snails, and 'ran about with great celerity, displaying many graceful, lively actions'. Their flight, in contrast, 'was heavy and inelegant, and their long legs streaming out behind them gave them a very grotesque appearance'.

157 Australian Bustard (HCR)

STRAW-NECKED IBIS

GERONTICUS SPINICOLLIS

Threskiornis spinicollis (Jameson)

PLATE 160

These ibises are distributed throughout Australia but are highly nomadic or migratory and breed in areas where water and food are assured. After the severe drought of 1839, Gould saw them in such abundance on the Liverpool Plains and by the Lower Naomi 'that to compute the number in a single flock was impossible'. They waded knee-high among the shallow lagoons in closely packed groups, perpetually searching for molluscs, frogs and newts, but were also known to eat grasshoppers and other insects. Gould was informed by the Aborigines that sometimes many seasons passed without the ibises being seen. He suggested that there might be a vast oasis in the centre of Australia to which the birds migrated.

In flight these striking birds wheeled over the plains in great flocks, 'at one moment showing their white breasts, and at the next, by a change in their position, exhibiting their dark-coloured backs and snow-white tails'.

BROLGA (AUSTRALIAN CRANE)

GRUS AUSTRALASIANUS

Grus rubicundus (Perry)

PLATE 158

Gould saw great numbers of the Brolga or 'native companion' in December 1839, near the Naomi River and on the Brezi Plains in New South Wales. Like the European Crane it was stately and elegant and made a picturesque addition to the scenery. It could be easily tamed, and at Parramatta Gould saw a fine-looking crane, perfectly at its ease, 'walking about the streets in the midst of the inhabitants'.

The Brolga fed on lizards, bulbous roots and other vegetables tearing up the earth with its powerful bill. In flight it could soar and circle at great height, gyrating gracefully and uttering hoarse, croaking cries.

PURPLE SWAMPHEN (BLACK-BACKED PORPHYRIO)

PORPHYRIO MELANOTUS

Porphyrio porphyrio melanotus Temminck

PLATE 162

Gould saw the Purple Swamphen in Tasmania, where it was plentiful on the Derwent and Tamar Rivers and on the lagoons between Kangaroo Point and the Clarence Plains. Early in the morning and at dusk it would run about in search of snails, insects, grain and vegetable substances, threading through the coverts with amazing speed at the approach of any intruder.

The Purple Swamphen could be easily domesticated, and Gould saw two roaming

GRUS AUSTRALASIANUS; *Gould*

159   *Black-winged, Pied or White-headed Stilt* (EG)

160   *Straw-necked Ibis* (HCR)

freely in the Government Gardens at Hobart. It was observed that the bird could use its foot as a hand, and a tame example known to Gould's friend George Bennet of Sydney always seized 'maize, or any other vegetable in the palm of the foot, holding it in that manner until it be devoured'.

COMB-CRESTED JACANA OR LOTUSBIRD (GALLINACEOUS PARRA)

PARRA GALLINACEA

Irediparra gallinacea (Temminck)

PLATE 161

The Comb-crested Jacana or Lotusbird has extremely long toes and claws which are especially adapted for walking on leaves that float in the water. Gilbert, Gould's explorer, saw them in the middle of a lake near Point Smith, Northern Territory, in December 1840, when the water was so low that he could wade across to watch them feeding and running among the aquatic plants. At the slightest alarm they would expertly dive down and submerge under water, or fly weakly away.

Lotusbirds can stay beneath the water for some time with only the nostrils in their bills protruding. In contrast their flight appears awkward, with their long legs and toes trailing behind them.

VOLUME VII

CAPE BARREN OR CEREOPSIS GOOSE

CEREOPSIS NOVAE-HOLLANDIAE

Cereopsis novaehollandiae Latham

PLATE 163

Gould saw the Cereopsis or Cape Barren Goose on Isabella Island, near Flinder's Island, on 12 January 1839. He remarked

ABOVE: *161   Comb-crested Jacana or Lotusbird* (HCR)
CENTRE: *162   Purple Swamphen* (HCR)
BOTTOM: *163   Cape Barren or Cereopsis Goose* (HCR)
OPPOSITE: *164   Black Swan* (HCR)

that, although previously it had been a common bird on the islands in Bass Strait and described by many travellers, it was rapidly becoming rare through hunting by colonists for its much prized delicate flesh.

This goose spent most of its time grazing and seldom took to water. Although it could be domesticated, it was a menace in the farmyard, for it readily attacked pigs or dogs, 'often inflicting severe wounds with its hard and sharp bill'. Now found breeding on islands off South Australia, Bass Strait and Tasmania.

BLACK SWAN

CYGNUS ATRATUS

Cygnus atratus (Latham)

PLATE 164

Gould wrote that, although the Black Swan had been reported by the Dutch East India Company from as far back as about

1698, two live swans had been brought to Batavia from West Australia in 1726, and Captain Cook had seen it on several parts of the coast, there was still only limited knowledge of its range and habits. He believed that it had not been sighted on the north coast but was widely distributed on rivers, estuaries and pools over south, west and east Australia, the Bass Strait islands, and Tasmania, where sometimes flocks of many hundreds could be seen.

Unfortunately in colonized parts of the country, particularly on the large Tasmanian rivers, such as the Derwent, the Black Swan was becoming 'almost extirpated' by the white man, its deadly enemy. It was hunted often wantonly, but especially during the moulting period when the flightless parent birds were cruelly attacked for their beautiful downy breast feathers.

When the Black Swan was not intruded upon, it was in Gould's words 'as tame, gentle and harmless as it was graceful and ornamental in appearance'.

PLUMED WHISTLING (EYTON'S DUCK)

LEPTOTARSIS EYTONI

Dendrocygna eytoni (Eyton)

PLATE 166

A single specimen of this duck was presented to Gould by Dr Benjamin Bynoe (Surgeon on HMS *Beagle*) who obtained it from the north coast of Australia. Gould saw at once that it differed in structure from any other members of its family and gave it a new name as a tribute to the naturalist Thomas Campbell Eyton, of Donnerville, Shropshire, who a few years previously in 1838 had written *A Monograph of the Anatidae, or Duck tribe*.

This duck, common in the lowlands of north and east Australia, was described as making a peculiar whistling sound on flight, which could be heard at a great distance. It is now called the Plumed Whistling Duck.

165 *Musk Duck* (HCR)

166 *Plumed Whistling Duck* (HCR)

MUSK DUCK

BIZIURA LOBATA

Biziura lobata (Shaw)

PLATE 165

This strange and often solitary duck is seen in lakes, secluded pools, bays and inlets of the sea in south-east, east and west Australia and Tasmania. The male, almost twice the size of the female, had a curious lobe under its bill. In the mating season the male emitted 'a strong musky odour', which according to Gould lingered in the skins of specimens for some years.

The Musk Duck's call was also unusual. Gould described it as resembling 'the sound caused by a large drop of water falling into a deep well' and said that it could be imitated 'by the sudden parting of the lips'.

The Musk Duck is now well known for its curious courtship display. It sails out into a clear pool, kicking the water and throwing jets of spray. Then it raises its head, blows its cheeks and expands the bladder under its bill. It raises its tail-feathers and spreads them fan-like over its body and revolves in the water, uttering a grunt and piercing noise with each kick.

GREAT SKUA (SKUA GULL)

LESTRIS CATARRHACTES

Stercorarius skua (Brunnich)

PLATE 167

'Every voyager to and from Australia, whether by the Cape of Good Hope or Cape Horn will observe that in all the higher latitudes the ship will be frequently visited by solitary examples of this Gull, which may be distinguished from the Albatross and Petrels by its more flapping and heavier mode of flight, and by the white mark on its wing, which shows conspicuously when underneath.'

Gould often saw this Skua 'a thousand miles from land', passing two or three times round the ship, then winging its way over the expansive ocean until lost to sight. He puzzled as to where the birds could find rest so far from land, but the problem was solved when he saw them settle on the scattered masses of seaweed floating in the sea. As a predator it obtained food by chasing petrels and albatrosses and compelling them to disgorge their food.

This skua is sometimes called a 'sea-hawk' because of its hooked bill and strong feet with talon-like nails. The widespread subspecies *lonnbergi* is the usual form seen on Australian coasts: during summer it breeds in Antarctica and sub-Antarctic islands but in winter is seen off the south-western, south-eastern and southern coasts of Australia and Tasmania.

LESSER NODDY

ANOUS MELANOPS

Anous tenuirostris (Temminck)

PLATE 168

The Lesser Noddy's only breeding place in Australia is at the Houtman's Abrolhos

167 *Great Skua* (HCR)

before the most furious gale'.

Richter's lithograph is based on Elizabeth Gould's watercolour painted on board the *Parsee* in the South Indian Ocean and dated 26 August 1838.

The Wandering Albatross changes colour as it ages, from dark chocolate brown in the young to the white of older birds. It will be more than ten years before the full adult plumage is attained. The illustration shows an adult bird and one of about two years.

SOUTHERN FULMAR (SILVERY-GREY PETREL)

PROCELLARIA GLACIALOIDES

Fulmarus glacialoides (Smith)

PLATE 170

Gould saw numerous examples of this fulmar in the Atlantic and Pacific Oceans, during his voyages to and from Australia. He first observed it off the Cape of Good Hope, and then frequently across the South Indian Ocean, while on the return trip there were many near the Falkland Islands. Gould described how Elizabeth made a beautiful watercolour on board ship of a fulmar that he had captured with a baited hook and line. From this specimen Gould could study in detail the great breadth of its wings and its unusual tube-like bill and nostrils.

Islands off the Western Australian coast. Gilbert visited these almost unknown islands in 1843 and was amazed at the tremendous noisy gatherings of seabirds. On the South Island, closely packed Lesser Noddys nested on mangrove branches some 4 to 10 feet (1.2 to 3 metres) above ground. The female noddy laid a single egg on an untidy mass of hanging seaweed cemented by excrement, 'the disagreeable and sickly odour of which is perceptible at a considerable distance'.

For Gilbert the tremendous clouds of birds congregating in the evening were reminiscent of Audubon's earlier description of the astonishing flights of the passenger pigeons of America.

sailed before the wind at more than 200 miles in a day, until the end of the voyage in Storm Bay, Hobart, Tasmania. Gould admired the bird's remarkable powers of flight, observing how 'it performs circles of many miles in extent, and returns again to hunt up the wake of the vessel for any substances thrown overboard.' It was almost constantly on the wing, with little rest, scanning the surface of the ocean for food, and was 'equally at ease while passing over the glassy surface during the stillest calm, or sweeping with arrow-like swiftness

WANDERING ALBATROSS

DIOMEDEA EXULANS

Diomedea exulans Linnaeus

PLATE 169

Gould's first sight of the most legendary of all sea birds, 'the largest and most powerful species of its tribe . . . held in terror by every other bird with which it is surrounded', took place on 24 July 1838 in the middle of the South Atlantic.

For two months the great bird was constantly around the ship, which often

168 *Lesser Noddy* (HCR)

Richter, who completed the illustrations after Mrs Gould's sudden death, used her work to make the finished lithograph, which is credited to 'J. Gould and H.C. Richter'.

Short-tailed Shearwater (Petrel)

Puffinus brevicaudus

Puffinus tenuirostris (Temminck)

PLATE 173

The astonishing habits of the Short-tailed Shearwater or Tasmanian Muttonbird have been widely investigated since Gould visited a breeding colony in Green Island during January 1839. It is now known that they leave the islands off Tasmania, South Australia and Bass Strait about May, migrate north across the equator to the oceans near Japan and Siberia, then return via Alaska and the west coast of America in late September.

Gould had heard much of the 'great nursery of Petrels' but was amazed by the countless numbers of eggs and young. Numerous sealers, natives and settlers came to the island to collect eggs, feathers and the young birds, which were considered excellent food when fresh or salted. They are still sought for their flesh and oil but the thriving Muttonbird industry is well controlled and the numbers of birds appear to be on the increase.

170 *Southern Fulmar* (HCR)

Black-bellied Storm-Petrel

Thalassidroma melanogaster

Fregetta tropica (Gould)

PLATE 171

During his voyage to Australia Gould first viewed the storm-petrels about 12 August 1839 off Cape Agulhas, Cape of Good Hope. They were observed almost daily across the South Indian Ocean until his arrival at Tasmania on 19 September. On the journey back to England the birds were seen between the eastern coast of Australia and New Zealand.

This species of petrel could be distinguished from others by the broad black mark down the centre of the abdomen, which contrasted with the snowy whiteness of its flanks. Its flight was powerful and it often patted along the surface of the rising waves. Gould illustrated it 'breasting one of those tempestuous seas which so frequently occur in high southern latitudes'.

Grey-backed Storm-Petrel

Thalassidroma nereis

Garrodia (Oceanites) nereis (Gould)

PLATE 172

During his four-month voyage to Australia Gould was not idle on board ship, as he was able to make a special study of oceanic birds and particularly petrels. In favourable weather, with the permission of Captain Robert McKellar and Robert Gordon, the owner of the *Parsee*, he was lowered in a small dinghy from the ship's side and caught nearly thirty different species with a baited hook and line.

Gould obtained four Grey-backed Storm-petrels during a calm while sailing between Hobart and Sydney in May 1839; he also saw them in Bass Strait and, during the passage home in April 1840, between New South Wales and the north coast of New Zealand. This species could be identified from other storm-petrels by the absence of any white mark on the rump.

169 *Wandering Albatross* (HCR)

171   Black-bellied Storm-petrel (HCR)

172   Grey-backed Storm-petrel (HCR)

SPOTTED SHAG (CORMORANT)

PHALACROCORAX PUNCTATUS

Phalacrocorax punctatus (Sparrman)

PLATE 174

Gould wrote, 'This beautiful species of Cormorant is a native of New Zealand; but although numbers of Europeans have now for many years visited those islands, it is still so extremely rare that I have never been able to discover more than two specimens.' The British Museum owned one example and the other (on loan to Gould) was presented to the United Service Museum by Captain Lambert of HMS *Alligator*.

This illustration was drawn and lithographed by Edward Lear, and is the only signed example of his work in *The Birds of Australia*. It appeared first as Plate 10 in the *Cancelled Parts*, issued in August 1837, and was repeated in the major series. As Lear left England to work abroad at the end of July 1837 he did not make any further contributions to Gould's books.

The bird is now called the Spotted Shag; and among Lear's doodles of comic birds drawn to amuse children and adults are various shag-like creatures.

173   Short-tailed Shearwater (HCR)

174 *Spotted Shag* (EL)

RED-FOOTED BOOBY (RED-LEGGED GANNET)

SULA PISCATOR

Sula sula (Linnaeus)

PLATE 175

The Red-legged Gannet, or Red-footed Booby, could be found on the northern shores of Australia. Gould received several fine specimens from Raine Island, on the northernmost tip of the Great Barrier Reef, collected by Lieut. J.M.R. Ince, who supervised the erection of a stone tower beacon on the islet in 1844 and studied the zoology of the area during his spare time.

Notes and diagrams from the naturalist John MacGillivray, who visited the island at this time with the surveying ship HMS *Rattleship*, enabled Gould to illustrate the accurate shades of the gannet's bill and its red feet, for these soft parts completely change colour after death. In the foreground the adult bird is shown with the correct colours of bluish and bright-pink bill, crimson legs and white plumage. Behind is a young bird with brown feather-

175 *Red-footed Booby* (HCR)

176 *Rockhopper Penguin* (HCR)

ing, dull-blue bill and greyish legs.

The Australian gannets were known as 'boobies' because they were apparently so stupid that they could be easily captured. Gould found that one species of gannet *Sula australis* 'out-boobied' all the rest, for he was able to catch five by hand before the others thought to escape. However he suggested that it may not have been their natural stupidity that made them so vulnerable but the fact that they seldom saw man.

ROCKHOPPER (CRESTED) PENGUIN

EUDYPTES CHRYSOCOME

Eudyptes chrysocome (Forster)

PLATE 176

Crested or Rockhopper Penguins were occasionally seen on the Tasmanian and southern Australian coasts but their strongholds were on the islands of the Antarctic seas. Gould did not see the Crested Penguin alive and he was indebted to his friend the botanist Ronald Gunn of Launceston, Tasmania, for a body which had been washed ashore on the north part of the island after a heavy gale.

This penguin was called 'Hopping Pen-

guin and Jumping Jack' by the earlier naturalist John Latham, due to its habit of leaping out of the water over obstacles. Captain Cook's naturalist George Forster reported the aggressive nature of the birds, for when provoked 'they ran at the sailors in flocks, pecked their legs and spoiled their clothes.'

LITTLE PENGUIN

SPHENISCUS MINOR

Eudyptula minor (Forster)

PLATE 177

The Little Penguin was very abundant in the deep bays and harbours of Tasmania and southern Australia, and in the Bass Strait. It frequented the waters around the islands which had low beaches where it could land and breed.

It swam very deep in the water, bounding like a porpoise, with only its head, neck and upper back above the surface. Gould was astonished by its swimming powers: 'it stems the waves of the most turbulent seas with the utmost facility, and during the severest gale descends to the bottom, where, among . . . forests of sea-

weed, it paddles in search of crustaceans, small fish, and marine vegetables.'

SUPPLEMENT

ALBERT'S (ALBERT) LYREBIRD

MENURA ALBERTI

Menura alberti Bonaparte

PLATE 178

After the completion of *The Birds of Australia* in 1848, Gould was fascinated to learn of a second remarkable species of lyre bird found in New South Wales, a colony he had explored himself. However, as some parts of 'the dense, luxuriant and almost impenetrable brushes' in the colony were still only partially known he realized that 'novelties' were still to be discovered.

The Albert Lyre Bird differed from the previously known lyrebird by its rufous-coloured plumage and absence of brown barrings on the shorter lyre-shaped feath-

177 Little Penguin (HCR)

ers. A fine specimen was lent to Gould for illustration from Sydney Museum, and was forwarded by his friend Dr George Bennett. Gould quoted an account about its habits written by Dr Stephenson, York Station, Richmond River, September 1849, which described the lyre birds' 'corroboring places', or holes scratched in the sandy ground where they strutted, jumped about, and mimicked any other bird that they happened to hear—'the note of the Dacelo gigantea (Kookaburra) it imitates to perfection; its own whistle is exceedingly beautiful and varied.'

Gould named this new species in honour of the Prince Consort, His Royal Highness Prince Albert, 'as a slight token of respect for his personal virtues, and the liberal support he has rendered to my many publications'.

178   Albert's Lyrebird (HCR)

VICTORIA'S (VICTORIA) RIFLEBIRD
PTILORIS VICTORIAE
Ptiloris victoriae Gould

PLATE 179

Gould dedicates this Riflebird to Queen Victoria, as a 'tribute to her many virtues' and also as an acknowledgement for her permission to allow him to dedicate to her

his great work on the birds of Australia.

The male had magnificent colours: its plumage was velvety-black glossed on the upper surface, sides and chin with plum colour, while its crown, throat and upper breast had small scale-like feathers of shiny metallic bronzy-green. The female, in contrast, had drab colours of greyish-brown.

The Victoria Riflebird, which is often considered to be a race of the Paradise Riflebird, lives in a limited area of coastal north Queensland. In Gould's main series the similar but larger Paradise Riflebird is illustrated, which lives further south in Queensland and New South Wales.

The riflebird is usually shy, behaving like a treecreeper by climbing trunks and probing for insects with its long bill. During its courtship display the ecstatic male fans its raised wings into a circle until the tips reach over its head, and sways its body backwards and forwards.

Its name may derive from the resemblance of its plumage to the dark uniforms of the nineteenth-century British riflemen. Another explanation is that its high pitched call was like the whine or whistle of a rifle bullet.

STANDARDWING
SEMIOPTERA WALLACEII
Semioptera wallacii Gould

PLATE 181

'How much gratified Mr. Wallace must have been when this remarkable form first met his gaze! and how enthusiastically does he write on this and other objects with which he is surrounded!'

Although the Standardwing was not an Australian bird but was found in Batjan, one of the Moluccan Islands, Gould could not bear to miss the chance of including this new discovery.

Alfred Russel Wallace, British naturalist and explorer (who with Darwin put forward the theory of evolution), travelled to Malaysia and the islands of the East Indies. He wrote to England from Batjan, in October 1858, that he had found 'the *finest and most wonderful* bird in the island', which he considered his *greatest* discovery. He sent to G.R. Gray, British Museum, London, a specimen of this thrush-sized brownish bird which had a shiny emerald-

green breast shield and two 6 inch (15 centimetre) long white pennant feathers extending from the bend of each wing.

It is now known that the Standardwing has extraordinary communal courtship displays in specially cleared areas. The males puff out their metallic green breast shields, and rustle their wings so that their long white pennants form a great V-shape over their backs.

The illustration shows two males and a duller brown female.

179   Victoria Riflebird (HCR)

KAKAPO
STRIGOPS HABROPTILUS
Strigops habroptilus Gray

PLATE 182

Gould included this strange owl-like parrot from New Zealand in the *Supplement*, as he had already illustrated several other New Zealand species in his main series.

Evidence of the Kakapo's existence was first known from the feathered costumes worn by Maoris, but it was not until 1845 that a specimen reached Europe. Gould believed that the Kakapo could no longer be found on North Island, although not long previously it had inhabited all the islands of New Zealand. The introduction since Captain Cook's visit of the pig, dog, cat and above all the brown rat, had helped

J. Gould and H. C. Richter del. et lith.

NOTORNIS MANTELLI: *Owen.*

Hullmandel & Walton Imp.

SEMIOPTERA WALLACEII, *Gray*

181 *Standardwing* (HCR)

STRIGOPS HABROPTILUS, *G R Gray*

182 *Kakapo* (HCR)

to cause a large reduction in numbers of this helpless bird.

The Kakapo, with its rounded wings and small breast-bone, is virtually flightless, but can run very fast through dense undergrowth. It is nocturnal and hides in burrows during the day. During courtship the males follow winding tracks leading to bowl-shaped areas where they make booming noises.

In 1991 the world population was thought to be just forty-nine individuals of which only about fourteen were females. These are managed and monitored, relocated populations on Little Barrier, Maud and Codfish Islands. Reduction or elimination of the mammal predators, and supplementary, virtually rat-proof feeding stations have brought results, for in April 1991 two chicks were raised in probably the first successful breeding since 1981.

NOTORNIS OR TAKAHE

NOTORNIS MANTELLI

Porphyrio (Notornis) mantelli (Owen)

PLATE 180

The Notornis or Takahe was thought to be extinct, and knowledge of this large flightless rail was based on some bones found by New Zealand settlers in 1848 among the fossilized remains of the large ostrich-like Moas.

In 1849 some sealers camping on the south-western tip of South Island followed the trail of a large heavy bird and eventually captured it. They ate the body but preserved the skin, perhaps attracted by its bright indigo plumage. This skin, acquired by the New Zealand naturalist Dr Walter Mantell, was new evidence of the reality of the Takahe. It was described in the *Pro-*

ceedings of the Zoological Society, London, in 1850.

By 1898 there were several more instances of the Takahe being captured, but during the next forty years it was not seen and again presumed extinct. In 1948 an expedition to a fiordland valley high above Lake Te Anau returned with some photographs of living Takahes. Today, it is legally protected and a small dwindling population of about two hundred survives in one or two remote valleys of the Murchison Mountains on South Island.

There is a management programme which includes control of the introduced deer (food competitors) and a captive breeding (thirty-eight birds raised up to 1991) and reintroduction project.

OPPOSITE: 180 *Takahe* (HCR)

A Monograph of
the Odontophorinae or
Partridges of America

One volume (1844–1850), 32 plates.

Gould became interested in American partridges when some beautiful live California Partridges were presented to the Zoological Gardens, London, in 1830. Four years afterwards, he learnt of another species which inhabited California, the striking Plumed Partridge. Specimens and information on this bird were found with the possessions of David Douglas, the botanist, after his tragic death in Hawaii, during his return journey from California to England. Hoping that his monograph would be of value to both the sportsman and the ornithologist, Gould described his aims as threefold: first, to show the differences between the partridges of America and those of Europe; secondly, to describe their attractive variations in markings and colours; and thirdly, to point out that as in Europe, some species could be preserved by law as game, and used as a table delicacy.

In 1843, in order to find specimens of as many species as possible, Gould travelled not to America, where few comprehensive collections existed, but extensively throughout Europe, visiting museums and private collectors in Paris, Brussels, Frankfurt,

Nuremburg, Leipzig, Berlin, Hannover, Amsterdam and Leyden. By 1850, he was able to extend the number of known American partridges from eleven to thirty-five species.

The partridges were depicted life-size with appropriate scenery. Gould made vigorous full-scale sketches in pencil and coloured crayons of the birds in their landscape settings, some of which, signed and dated in December 1842, are still preserved at Knowsley Hall. H.C. Richter closely based the finished lithographs on Gould's working drawings and added the refined details of plumage and markings. The monograph was published in three parts, two with ten plates and the last containing twelve.

The *Partridges of America* was dedicated to the eminent naturalist Prince Charles Lucien Bonaparte (1803–1857), Prince of Canino and Musignano and a nephew of Napoleon. Bonaparte lived in Philadelphia from 1822 to about 1840. He published a sequel to Alexander Wilson's pioneer work on the birds of America under the title *American Ornithology not given by Wilson* (1825–1833).

ORTYX VIRGINIANTS.

183   *Northern Bobwhite* (HCR)

NORTHERN BOBWHITE (VIRGINIAN PARTRIDGE)

ORTYX VIRGINIANUS

Colinus virginianus (Linnaeus)

PLATE 183

Gould wrote that this species ranged from the northern parts of Canada and Nova Scotia through North America to Mexico, but attempts to naturalize it in England had been unsuccessful. It is a popular sporting bird, familiar throughout eastern and central U.S.A. in woodland edge habitats, fields and scrublands.

Gould quoted from Audubon's colourful text an account of the Bobwhite. The male's whistle or 'love-call' in spring was compared to the words 'Ah Bob White', the first note being 'a kind of aspiration' and the last 'loud and clear'. Several challenging males would be heard calling from different perches, and if they encountered each other would fight courageously and obstinately. The female laid ten to eighteen eggs in a nest among stalks of corn or tufts of grass. The young ran about soon after birth, and throughout spring followed their parents. Towards autumn the young attained their full size.

BLACK-THROATED BOBWHITE (PARTRIDGE)

ORTYX NIGROGULARIS

Colinus nigrogularis (Gould)

PLATE 184

At the time when Gould was writing, these partridges had recently been brought to England and some pairs had bred in the Earl of Derby's aviaries at Knowsley.

Gould quoted from an account by Samuel Cabot Jnr in the *Boston Journal of Natural History*, who had observed them in Yucatan during a six-month residence there. He said that they moved in coveys, fed, roosted and sometimes alighted on trees like the Virginian Partridges; they had a similar covey call in the autumn and winter, while in spring they whistled notes which sounded like the words 'Bob-white'. Indian boys trapped great numbers of these quail and took them alive to the large towns of Yucatan.

Now called the Black-throated Bobwhite, in the wild this species inhabits the Yucatan Peninsula of Mexico, Belize, northern Guatemala, north-eastern Honduras and northern Nicaragua.

MONTEZUMA QUAIL· (MASSENA'S PARTRIDGE)

CYRTONYX MASSENA

Cyrtonyx montezumae (Vigors)

PLATE 185

This species was named after the Prince of Massena (Victor, Duc de Rivoli and Prince D'Essling, *c.* 1795–1863) who had one of the largest private ornithological collections in Europe, which in 1845 was sold to the Academy of Natural Sciences in Philadelphia.

The unusual patterning on the male partridge's face reminded Gould of 'the painted face of the clown in a pantomime'. (He was perhaps thinking of the brightly coloured mask-like make-up introduced by the clown Grimaldi.) In contrast, the female had duller colours and markings similar to the Common Quail of Europe. Their full plumage and short tails gave both birds a plump, rounded appearance. They had short toes with very long claws for scratching in the earth as they searched for seeds and berries. This species now occurs mainly in the pine-oak woodlands of central Mexico and the oak-grasslands of south-western United States. Their diet is

184   Black-throated Bobwhite (HCR)

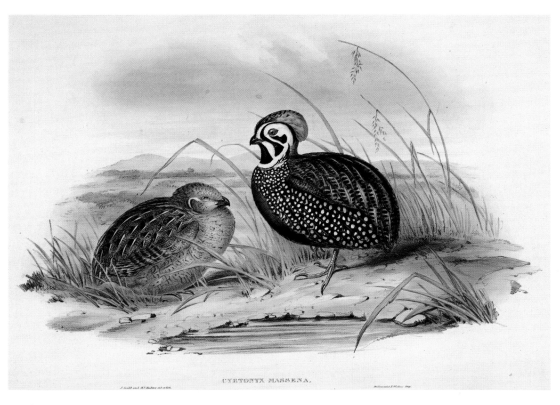

185 *Montezuma Quail* (HCR)

tically depicts a quizzical mouse in the foreground between a sleepy female and a more alert male Short-crested Partridge.

These birds have short straight crests, minutely freckled moth-like patterns on their back and tail feathers, and flanks with bold spotted markings. Although there were many specimens in museum collections Gould could not find any record of their habitat or habits.

While in London, J.J. Audubon drew a young crested quail from a specimen at the Zoological Society, and although a tropical bird, included it in *The Birds of America*.

These quail, now called the Crested Bobwhite, live among bushes and grass on the foothills of the Andes, in savannahs and woodland edge habitats from Panama to western Colombia and east to Guianas. There are up to fourteen subspecies, including. *C. cristatus parvicristatus* Gould.

chiefly bulbs, tubers, seeds, fruits and invertebrates.

* Also known as Harlequin or Massena or Mearn's Quail

OCELLATED QUAIL (PARTRIDGE)

CYRTONYX OCELLATUS

Cyrtonyx ocellatus (Gould)

PLATE 186

Gould knew of only two specimens of this partridge: one was drawn in the Zoological Society, London, and another was in the Jardin des Plantes, Paris. Gould noted that they were similar to the *Cyrtonyx massena* but had larger black marks on their faces, a brighter chestnut colour on their abdomens, and the stripes on their backs were chestnut instead of buff. Their longer wings almost covered their tails when folded close to their bodies.

In fact, this species is possibly a subspecies of the Montezuma Quail, *Cyrtonyx massena*, which occurs just north of the range of the Ocellated Quail; though separated geographically, the differences between them may not warrant specific separation. Today the Ocellated Quail live in the woodlands of south-west Mexico, south through to eastern Guatemala, El Salvador and Honduras to northern Nicaragua. They feed on seeds, vegetation and

186 *Ocellated Quail* (HCR)

roots which they scratch out of the ground with their strong claws.

CRESTED BOBWHITE (SHORT-CRESTED PARTRIDGE)

EUPSYCHORTYX PARVICRISTATUS

Colinus cristatus (Linnaeus)

PLATE 188

Gould's illustrations rarely have a touch of humour and this illustration uncharacteris-

MOUNTAIN QUAIL (PLUMED PARTRIDGE)

CALLIPEPLA PICTA

Oreortyx picta (Douglas)

PLATE 187

'For the discovery of this highly ornate species we are indebted to the researches of the late Mr David Douglas, in whose baggage three specimens were found after his lamented and untimely death.' In 1834,

CALLIPEPLA PICTA.

187   *Mountain Quail* (HCR)

Douglas, botanist and explorer (whose name is perpetuated by the Douglas Fir Tree), was tragically killed in Hawaii on his return from California. He fell into a pit where a wild bull was trapped and was trampled to death by the enraged creature.

Douglas said that these partridges congregated in vast flocks; the males were often fighting and their fierce conflicts sometimes ended in death. They fed in compact groups, competing with each other for seeds, catkins and insects. Their habitat was in the dry uplands, gravelly or sandy soils, and open woods or coppice thickets of the interior of northern California. During a severe winter they would migrate in large flocks to warmer areas near the coastline.

The partridges would utter 'Quick-quick-quick' noises very slowly, 'with a gentle suspension of the voice between each syllable'. They made neat nests of grass and dry leaves in thickets, which were so carefully concealed that often only a dog could find them.

188   *Crested Bobwhite* (HCR)

The strange long crests of the males were usually held backwards almost reaching their backs, but when alarmed were thrown forward over their beaks. These birds were very common in the interior of California and during summer ranged northwards within a few miles of the Columbian valley.

This species is now called the Mountain Quail or Plumed Quail and lives in the mountains of Washington, Idaho, California and Nevada. The picture shows a pair (the female has a shorter crest), and several males are sparring in the background.

CALIFORNIA QUAIL (CALIFORNIAN PARTRIDGE)

CALLIPEPLA CALIFORNIA

Callipepla californica (Shaw)

PLATE 189

It was the beautiful live Californian Partridges brought to England and presented to the Zoological Society by Captain Beechey in 1830 that inspired Gould to find out more about the American par-

189   *California Quail* (HCR)

tridges and compile his monograph.

An account of the partridges in the wild was quoted from a description by Dr Gambel of Philadelphia. In California Gambel had seen them in immense flocks, sometimes as many as a thousand or more rising into the air. On the ground they were very watchful, but when alarmed would run at amazing speed to the safety of cover. Sometimes they suddenly flew on to the branches of trees, where their feathers which resembled the colours of bark formed a natural camouflage. They were very graceful, and their striking comma-

190   *Gambel's Quail* (HCR)

191   *Scaled Quail* (HCR)

shaped crests would either be thrown backwards when running or curved forwards when resting or searching for food in the brushes.

Now called the California Quail they range from Oregon to Baja California in western North America, and have been locally introduced in other parts of North America, New Zealand, Hawaii, central Chile and King Island.

of the Californian Range of mountains in 1841. In this arid country, where it was hard to believe any animals could survive, Gambel saw these partridges running about in flocks of fifteen to twenty. They fed on seeds and used the low spreading branches of desert bushes and cacti as cover. When flying their long crests were swept back by

the rush of air and they uttered a loud, sharp whistle.

The illustration of two males was drawn from specimens lent by M. Louis Coulon, Director of the Museum at Neufchâtel. Today these quail, with their bizarre head plumage, live in the arid plains of Nevada, Utah, Colorado, Arizona and Mexico.

GAMBEL'S QUAIL (PARTRIDGE)

CALLIPEPLA GAMBELII

Callipepla gambelii (Gambel)

PLATE 190

Gould wrote that he had previously thought the Californian Partridge to be the most beautiful of the American partridges but now believed that Gambel's Partridge was even finer. He himself had seen only two examples, one in the museum at Neufchâtel, Switzerland, and the other in France in the Jardin des Plantes, Paris.

Dr William Gambel of Philadelphia discovered the species on the eastern side

192   *Elegant Quail* (HCR)

J. Gould and H.C.Richter del et lith.

DENDRORTYX MACROURUS.

Walter & Cohn imp.

ODONTOPHORUS GUIANENSIS.

194 Marbled Wood Quail (HCR)

ELEGANT QUAIL (PARTRIDGE)

CALLIPEPLA ELEGANS

Callipepla douglasii (Vigors)

PLATE 192

Gould wrote that this species was 'conspicuous for the general elegance of its appearance, the beauty of its crest, and the delicate style of its markings'. The male had a buff crest, and grey, black, and rust colours on its body, whereas the female had a brown crest and feathers freckled with buff, brown and grey. Several specimens of both sexes from Mexico were in the Earl of Derby's collection and a fine male was in the national collection at the British Museum.

These partridges live in arid scrublands from western Chihuaha south to Jalisco, Mexico.

OPPOSITE:

193 Long-tailed Wood-partridge or Tree Quail (HCR)

SCALED QUAIL (SCALY PARTRIDGE)

CALLIPEPLA SQUAMATA

Callipepla squamata (Vigors)

PLATE 191

This species is less brightly coloured than other plumed partridges but is remarkable for the scale-like markings all over the front of its body. The illustration shows the birds from two angles, front and side, so that the crescent brown-edged patterning on the breast and belly can be seen clearly. The crest is short and silky, narrow at the base and then broadening out into a tip of white feathers.

Specimens of these birds were very rare, only one or two were at the Zoological Society, and the birds in the illustration came from the British Museum.

Now called the Scaled Quail, or nicknamed Cotton-top, these birds live among sparse undergrowth in arid areas of eastern Colorado and western Kansas south through Arizona, New Mexico and western Texas to central Mexico. They have been introduced elsewhere.

LONG-TAILED WOOD-PARTRIDGE OR TREE QUAIL (LARGE-TAILED PARTRIDGE)

DENDRORTYX MACROURUS

Dendrortyx macroura (Jardine and Selby)

PLATE 193

This species belongs to a group of birds that are larger and have longer brighter legs and feet than the other partridges of America.

Gould wrote that specimens of this bird were very rare and the only example he knew in England belonged to Sir William Jardine, who bought it at a sale of the contents of Bullock's London Museum. William Bullock, a London showman, after a six-month Mexican visit, displayed 200 birds, fish, minerals, ancient carvings and texts at his 'Ancient and Modern Mexico' exhibition of 1824 in the Egyptian Hall, Piccadilly. Another specimen from Paris was lent to Gould by the Prince of Massena, and this adult male was the model used for the illustration. Today it is found in the dense undergrowth of mountain forests in Mexico.

195   *Spotted Wood Quail* (HCR)

196   *Spot-winged Wood Quail* (HCR)

Marbled Wood Quail (Guiana Partridge)

Odontophorus guianensis

Odontophorus gujanensis (Gmelin)

PLATE 194

The illustration depicts a male and female of similar plumage, and a brood of seven chicks, one of which is tucked under its parent's wing. These partridges are now called the Marbled Wood Quail, and live in the tropical forests of the Neotropics from Costa Rica to Colombia, eastward to Venezuela and the Guianas, and south to Eastern Bolivia and central and north-eastern Brazil.

Gould was informed by Robert Schomburgk, botanical collector in Guiana, that unlike other quail which gather in coveys this species was usually seen as a pair or singly among the undergrowth.

Charles Waterton (later known as the eccentric squire of Walton Hall), in his *Wanderings in South America*, published in 1825, wrote that these forests birds had a loud early morning call which echoed through the woods and sounded like 'dura-quaura' often repeated. He thought that the young brood soon left their parents as more than two birds were seldom seen together.

Their calls could be imitated by hunters, and the birds were much prized for their delicate white flesh.

Spot-winged Wood Quail (Capueira Partridge)

Odontophorus dentatus

Odontophorus capueira (Spix)

PLATE 196

Gould wrote that this species, now called the Spot-winged Wood Quail, was often confused with the Guiana Partridge. Its habitat is in north-east Brazil, south to Paraguay and north-east Argentina.

An account of this bird by Prince Maximilian of Wied, a naturalist and traveller in Brazil, was extensively quoted. These birds lived in the thick woods, they ran about quickly and fed among the dry leaves on seeds, berries and insects. At

197 *Striped-face Wood Quail*

daybreak, the male birds uttered a rousing morning call like the farmyard cock of Europe; this cry (notated on a musical stave) of four notes quickly repeated reverberated at a great distance through the forest. In the evening the male birds perched on a branch near each other and frequently uttered the call of "uru".

The flesh of these quail, as of other species, was considered a delicacy.

Spotted Wood Quail (Guttated Partridge)

Odontophorus guttatus

Odontophorus guttatus (Gould)

PLATE 195

Several years previously Gould described this species in the *Proceedings of the Zoological Society*. Then he only knew of female birds and did not realize that the male had a beautiful tufted crest of orange feathers.

Gould believed that these quails could soon become domesticated in England, for they had laid eggs and reared young at the Earl of Derby's aviary at Knowsley. In captivity, they not only perched on trees but on any ledges or projections in the aviary. This species, now called the Spotted Wood Quail lives in tropical and mountain forests of southern Mexico to western Panama.

Striped-face Wood Quail (Ballivian's Partridge)

Odontophorus balliviani

Odontophorus balliviani Gould

PLATE 197

This species was discovered by Thomas Bridges, botanist and explorer in Bolivia, who is better known for sending to Kew Gardens the seeds of the giant Victoria Amazonian waterlily. Bridges asked that this partridge should be named after General Ballivian, President of the Bolivian Republic from 1842 to 1847, who had given him every encouragement to pursue his natural history researches, and 'whose love of science renders him worthy of such a compliment'.

This bird is now called the Stripe-faced Wood Quail because of the conspicuous long eyebrow markings on its face. Gould described the birds' breast and belly feathering of chestnut or coffee, minutely freckled in black with irregular patches of white, as being 'singularly rich and sparkling'. They inhabit the subtropical forests of Cochabamba and Cuzco in the Andes of Bolivia and southern Peru.

155

A Monograph of the Trochilidae or Family of Hummingbirds

Five volumes (1849–1861), 360 plates.

The *Monograph of Hummingbirds*, dedicated to Her Royal Highness the Princess Royal, spanned the mid-century years and was perhaps the most decorative of all Gould's series. The pictures delightfully illustrated the close relationship between bird and flower and the dependence of hummingbirds on plants for their food of nectar. The 'hummers' were small, varying from the size of a bee to that of a starling, and this was the only set of volumes in which all the birds could be depicted exactly life-size.

Gould's delight in these tiny glittering birds extended over many years. It had begun with his introduction to the unique collection of hummingbirds belonging to George Loddiges, botanist and flower illustrator, whose family owned famous exotic plant nurseries at Hackney. After Loddiges's death in 1846, Gould amassed his own collection and claimed in 1861 that it surpassed any other in the number of species and examples it contained. His 1,500 mounted hummingbirds were exhibited in especially designed cases at a pavilion in the Zoological Gardens, London, in 1851.

In the same year Gould displayed his 'new mode of representing the luminous and metallic colouring of the *Trochilidae*, or humming birds' at the Great Exhibition at Crystal Palace. The problem of capturing the iridescent colours of these tiny birds was immense. Gould supervised many costly experiments, and eventually a method was found of using a 'combination of transparent oil and varnish colours over pure gold leaf'. Similar attempts at metallic colouring were also made at that time in America by William Baily of Philadelphia, for an unpublished book on hummingbirds; the two trochilidists exchanged ideas, but Gould maintained that the method he used was entirely his own invention.

Gould himself saw only one species of hummingbird alive, when midway through the publication of his series he visited North America and watched a lone Ruby-throated Hummingbird in Philadelphia and then a large flock in Washington. Although he brought a live bird to England it survived for only two days, probably in a comatose state, at his home in London, and all the plates were based on stuffed specimens. The plants in the illustrations were drawn from dried flowers sent from South America, or grown in English hothouses, but many were carefully adapted from the plates by W.H. Fitch in *Curtis's Botanical Magazine*, a source which Gould gratefully acknowledged. Plants and birds were skilfully combined into intricate compositions verging on the balletic by Gould's accomplished artist, Richter.

As the expertise required for the production of the plates could only be found in a capital city, Gould felt that it was essential for him to remain in London to supervise personally the process of publication. He regretted that he had been unable to study more of the hummingbirds in their natural settings, but in his profession, he claimed, 'the traveller and historian are seldom united'.

198   *Saw-billed Hermit* (HCR)

VOLUME I

SAW-BILLED HERMIT (SAW-BILL)
GRYPUS NAEVIUS

Ramphodon naevius (Dumont)

PLATE 198

The original plate shows two males, a female, and a nest and eggs all of natural size. Gould received the nest from Rio de Janiero. It was of 'a lengthened, pointed form, composed of fine vegetable fibres and mosses, intermingled with which, especially on the lower part, are portions of dead leaves and pieces of lichen; and attached to the extremities of the leaves of apparently a species of Palm'.

The Sawbill is one of the group of hermit hummingbirds whose nests are made by the bird on the wing in a spectacular display of aerobatics. The male takes no part in nest-building or rearing the young, and the female flits to and fro collecting cobwebs, grasses and fibre threads from the surrounding vegetation. With her saliva or sticky nectar she glues the first strands on to a hanging leaf. Then using her bill as a sewing needle she pushes and pulls out strands to weave the intricate nest.

WHITE-TIPPED SICKLEBILL (SICKLE BILL)
EUTOXERES AQUILA

Eutoxeres aquila (Bourcier)

PLATE 200

'It is evident that its singularly-shaped bill is adapted for some special purpose, and we may readily infer that it has been expressly formed to enable the bird to obtain its food from the deep and remarkably-shaped flowers of the various Orchidaceous and other plants with curved tubular flowers so abundant in the country the bird inhabits, and for exploring which a bill of any other form would be useless.'

Gould knew that hummingbirds depended on plants to provide their diet of nectar, but probably did not know the extent to which many exotic plants relied on hummingbirds for their pollination and survival. Certain *heliconia* flowers have adapted to the exact curvature required to match the almost half-moon shaped beak of the sicklebill. As the sicklebills are heavier than most hummingbirds, they prefer to perch while feeding, and the flowers of the *heliconias* are arranged like branches of a tree to make this possible.

Gould himself did not visit South America and relied on travellers' descriptions to tell him which flowers the birds visited. This information was not always accurate, and today there is a much greater knowledge of flowers which are ornithophilous, that is, designed to be pollinated by hummingbirds. The White-tipped Sicklebill inhabits an area from Costa Rica south to Colombia, Ecuador and Peru.

199   *Pale-tailed Barbthroat* (HCR)

200   *White-tipped Sicklebill* (HCR)

PALE-TAILED BARBTHROAT (FAWN-TAILED BARBED-THROAT)

THRENETES CERVINICAUDA

Threnetes leucurus cervinicauda Gould

PLATE 199

'How constantly are we receiving novelties from the richly wooded districts bordering the River Napo, and how many fine birds appear to inhabit this luxuriant region! – a zone, as it were, intermediate between the elevated portions of the great Andean ranges and the flat lands of the eastern parts of South America.'

Gould was delighted that so many new hummingbird species were being discovered in the tropical forests of Ecuador and Peru, a region little known to Europeans. Here the birds, now known as Pale-tailed Barbthroats, are shown with the plant *Echites franciscea*, a creeper from Brazil growing in the hothouse at Kew Gardens, and featured in *Curtis's Botanical Magazine*, 1 November 1850.

SCALE-THROATED (EURYNOME) HERMIT

PHAETHORNIS EURYNOME

Phaethornis eurynome (Lesson)

PLATE 202

'All the nests that I have seen have been attached to the pendent leaves of palms and other trees growing in the neighbourhood of water or in humid situations, and the ingenuity with which these little birds attach their nests with cobwebs and other slight materials is truly wonderful: the beautiful nest represented is formed of the most delicate tendrils and roots of trees; it is a somewhat shallow and frail structure, lengthened to a point below. I believe that the eggs, which are white, are generally two in number.'

Hermit Hummingbirds have little room to sit in their cramped dangling nests, but the female appears to suffer no discomfiture by being forced to keep her head and tail stiffly erect. She incubates her two eggs for an average of eighteen days, and sits for about three hours at a time leaving the nest for short periods to bathe and feed.

This species is from south-east Brazil, east Paraguay and north-east Argentina.

201 *Reddish Hermit* (HCR)

202 *Scale-throated Hermit* (HCR)

REDDISH (LITTLE) HERMIT

PHAETHORNIS EREMITA

Phaethornis ruber (Linnaeus)

PLATE 203

'The nest, as will be seen, is ingeniously attached with spiders'-webs to the extrem-ity of a leaf of a Dicotyledonous plant, and is composed of various fine silky and cottony vegetable fibres mixed with spiders'-web and portions of a fungus(?) resembling wool; in form it is round, deep, cup-shaped, and tapers to a lengthened point at the bottom. The nest figured is in my own collection, and I also possess another containing two eggs, procured by Mr. Hawkswell at Buena Vista in June 1848.

'The eggs are two in number, of a pinky white, about seven-sixteenths of an inch in length by about five-sixteenths in breadth.'

The Little Hermit is a very small hummingbird and its eggs are some of the smallest in the world. The newly hatched young are blind and featherless without any downy plumage and look almost maggot-like. The nest is cup-shaped at the top, with a turned-in brim to prevent the nestlings from falling out in a swaying breeze. They are entirely helpless and rely on their mother to fly to and fro with food of nectar and insects.

REDDISH (PIGMY) HERMIT

PHAETHORNIS PYGMAEUS

Phaethornis ruber (Linnaeus)

PLATE 201

Gould described this little bird from southern Brazil as even smaller than the Little Hermit (see plate 203), but there are only minor differences in the illustrations and descriptions. They are almost certainly the same species.

'The figure of the beautiful nest represented on the accompanying Plate is copied from a drawing sent to me by Mr. Reeves. It will be seen that the interior of this delicate structure is formed of the softest materials – the wool-like fibres of some flowering plant, sparingly decorated on the outside with thistledown-like seeds.'

Hummingbirds' nests are masterpieces of constructive engineering. The tiny nests balanced precariously from the side of a leaf are corrected for any lopsidedness by small particles of soil woven into a long dangling extension as a counterweight. In an article for the Zoological Society of London Gould described how these hanging nests are carefully weighted on each side with earth or small stones until a perfect equilibrium is established.

203   *Reddish Hermit* (HCR)

VOLUME II

SOMBRE HUMMINGBIRD

APHANTOCHROA CIRRHOCHLORIS

Aphantochroa cirrochloris (Vieillot)

PLATE 204

'While the greater number of the Trochilidae are characterized by a splendid style of plumage, there are others, as will be seen on reference to the present Plate, in which these features are wanting; to most persons these sombre-coloured birds will be less pleasing than their more gaily attired congeners, but they are equally interesting in the eyes of the naturalist . . .

'I have received numerous examples from various parts of Brazil, Pernambuco, Bahia, and the neighbourhood of Rio de Janeiro, where Mr. Reeves states it is very common, and where it evinces a great predilection for the flowers of the Banana.'

Gould's artist, H.C. Richter, ingeniously displayed this dullish hummingbird against the rich purples and golds of a banana flower. Banana palms were one of the exciting attractions for visitors to the great Palm House at Kew Gardens, designed by Decimus Burton and opened in 1848.

CRIMSON TOPAZ

TOPAZA PELLA

Topaza pella (Linnaeus)

PLATE 205

'The countries of Cayenne, Trinidad, and Surinam, and the fluviatile regions of the Lower Amazon are the native habitats of this gorgeous species, which may be regarded not only as one of the gems of Ornithology, but as one of the most beautifully adorned species of the Trochilidae; I may also add it is one of the oldest known members of the family, being mentioned in the works of every writer on natural history, from the days of Linnaeus to the present time.'

Probably the first naturalist to describe the Crimson Topaz in the field was the traveller Charles Waterton (later the eccentric squire of Walton Hall, Wakefield, and founder of the first English nature reserve), who explored through Cayenne and Demerara (modern Guyana) in 1816.

In his *Wanderings through South America* Charles Waterton saw the Crimson Topaz in the forests among the red blossom: 'He is the largest of all the humming-birds, and is all red and changing gold green, except the head which is black. He has two long feathers in the tail, which cross each other, and these have gained him the name of Karabimiti, or Ara humming-bird from the Indians.'

204   *Sombre Hummingbird* (HCR)

205   *Crimson Topaz* (HCR)

206   *Fiery Topaz* (HCR)

FIERY TOPAZ

TOPAZA PYRA

Topaz pyra (Gould)

PLATE 206

Gould related that his naturalist friend, the late Mr George Loddiges, a hummingbird expert whose collection had been the inspiration for Gould's writings on the Trochilidae, had always thought that the Crimson Topaz was the finest of all the hummingbirds 'and will always remain so, for we cannot imagine a more beautiful species'. Unfortunately Loddiges died before the Fiery Topaz was discovered; Gould believed that if he had been alive he would have agreed that this new species surpassed even the Crimson Topaz in its magnificent colouring.

The Fiery Topaz lives in the river basin of the Rio Negro, a tributary of the Upper Amazon, Brazil, and neighbouring parts of Colombia, south Venezuela, Ecuador and

north-east Peru. Gould said that it differed from the Crimson Topaz by having a larger proportion of deep velvety black on the head, the whole of the body a rich fiery scarlet, and 'the three lateral feathers on each side purplish black instead of buff'. Some authorities consider it to be conspecific with the Fiery Topaz, *T. pella*, but they overlap in eastern Ecuador and are therefore left here as two specific species.

ECUADORIAN (CHIMBORAZIAN) HILLSTAR

OREOTROCHILUS CHIMBORAZO

Oreotrochilus chimborazo (Delattre and Bourcier)

PLATE 207

'This beautiful species of Hill-Star is an inhabitant of the celebrated volcanic mountain Chimborazo, where it is to be found at an elevation of from 12 to 16,000

feet [3,664–4,885 metres], or to the verge of perpetual snow; in these desolate regions it finds a home so congenial to its habits, that it is never known to descend to the warmer valleys below.'

The hillstars live high up on the slopes of the Andes below the ice-capped mountains in sometimes appalling conditions, where night-time temperatures regularly fall below freezing and the air is thin and low in oxygen. They survive in these sub-zero conditions by becoming torpid, with symptoms similar to hibernation – their body temperature lowers and their heartbeat is dramatically reduced. After the cold of the night the birds 'thaw' and come to life with the warmth of the morning sun.

These birds live on the nectar of alpine plants and insects. Gould shows two males and a female on the plant *Chuquiraga insignis*, while in the distance two immature males are sparring with each other. Mount Chimborazo can be seen faintly in the background.

162

207   *Ecuadorian Hillstar* (HCR)

EULAMPIS JUGULARIS.

J. Gould and H.C. Richter, del. et lith.

Hullmandel & Walton, Imp.

208 *Purple-throated Carib* (HCR)

White-sided Hillstar
Oreotrochilus leucopleurus

Oreotrochilus leucopleurus Gould

PLATE 209

'Hitherto this species has only been found in Chile, where it inhabits the sheltered valleys along the Andes . . . Mr. Bridges, from whom I have received numerous specimens, procured on the Andes of Aconcagua, states that the bird was not uncommon near the Ojos de Agua, on the road towards Mendoza, at an elevation of 10,000 feet [3,053 metres].'

Gould also depicts a 'beautiful nest, brought back direct from Chile . . . which appears to have been attached by means of cobwebs to the side of a rock or large stone; it is larger than is usually the case among the Trochilidae, and is a dense and warm structure composed of moss, fine vegetable substances and feathers.' Due to the cold and difficult weather conditions of the Andes the hillstar hummingbirds build sturdier nests and have longer nesting periods than other species. The female takes around two months to brood and raise her young.

Thomas Bridges (1807–1865) was an enterprising botanical collector who explored through the remote parts of South America. In 1846 he sent from Bolivia the first seeds of the *Victoria amazonica* water-lily to Kew Gardens, but the resulting plants died before flowering.

Green-breasted (Prevost's) Mango
Lampornis Prevosti

Anthracothorax prevostii (Lesson)

PLATE 210

'The figure of the male on the accompanying Plate was taken from a fine specimen in my own collection, received by me with many others of both sexes from Honduras, which country, together with the adjacent one of Guatemala, is the true habitat of the species.' Now called the Green-breasted Mango, it is distributed over an area from Mexico, to Honduras and Salvador.

Gould shows the birds with the plant *Lacepedea insignis*, Fragrant Lacepedea, a scented Mexican flowering shrub flowering at Kew Gardens, which featured in *Curtis's Botanical Magazine*, 1 August 1849.

Purple-throated (-breasted) Carib
Eulampis Jugularis

Eulampis jugularis (Linnaeus)

PLATE 208

'In the accompanying Plate, I have attempted to represent this bird as accurately as possible; but after all, I find, to my regret, that it conveys only a faint idea of its beauty.'

The Purple-breasted Carib, now known as the Purple-throated Carib, has beautiful glowing colours, with a purple-red gorget, black body and iridescent green wings. It

209   *White-sided Hillstar* (HCR)

210   *Green-breasted Mango* (HCR)

211   *Blue-fronted Lancebill* (HCR)

sharp, needle-like' bill was 'specially fitted for procuring its insect food from the smaller kind of tubular flowers, or from prickly spines of the Cacti'.

The Blue-fronted Lancebill holds the record for the deepest hummingbird's nest. This was a pendent structure attached by cobwebs to a rocky overhang near the bottom of a 250 foot (75 metre) shaft.

The species was named *Doryfera johannae* in memory of a daughter of George Loddiges, the orchid nurseryman and ornithologist whose collection of hummingbirds was greatly admired by Gould.

White-vented (Buffon's) Plumeleteer

Hypuroptila buffoni

Chalybura buffonii (Lesson)

PLATE 212

'The greater portion of these specimens (sent to Europe) have been received from two sources, namely, Bogota and the Caraccas. The bird is strictly a hill species and Mr. Mark (British Consul at Bogota) informs me that Bogota specimens are generally collected about "La Mesa" or the

can be found in the forests, clearings and banana plantations of the Lesser Antilles islands.

Gould remarked that despite its beauty it was not a rare bird, and that 'for a few shillings each, the collector may obtain from any of the Parisian dealers as many of the finest examples as he could wish'. Unfortunately the disappearance of tropical rain-forest habitat threatens the numbers of these birds even more than the greedy skin collectors of the past.

The birds are shown hovering over the *Nymphaea amazonum*, Amazon water lily, and the colouring of the caribs is echoed in the purple undersides of the green lily-leaves.

Blue-fronted Lancebill

Dorifera Johannae

Doryfera johannae (Bourcier)

PLATE 211

Gould described the Blue-fronted Lancebill as one of the rarest hummingbirds, belonging to the forests of the eastern Andes in Colombia, Ecuador and north-east Peru. It is a small bird measuring about 3½ inches (9 centimetres) excluding the bill. Gould surmised that the Lancebill's 'straight,

212   *White-vented Plumeleteer* (HCR)

table mountains, and near the village of San Antonio, both localities being about six or seven thousand feet [1,800–2,000 metres] above the sea-level, and about a day's ride from Bogota.'

It is also found on the hills and in the woods of Panama, Venezuela, south-west Ecuador, north-west Peru and the eastern Andes of Colombia.

The two males and a female are depicted with differing plumage. The cock has striking iridescent underparts 'of a lively emerald-green, each feather finely fringed with greyish white, giving the whole a scale-like appearance', whereas the hen is duller with underparts of 'light grey with a few specks of green on the flanks'.

The species, now called the White-veined Plumeleteer, was originally named in 1831 in honour of the Comte de Buffon (1708–1788), the renowned French philosopher-naturalist whose long series of illustrated books, the *Histoire naturelle*, first appeared in 1749.

Green-crowned Brilliant

Heliodoxa jacula

Heliodoxa jacula Gould

PLATE 213

'In vain have I laboured to represent in the accompanying illustration the gorgeous metallic lustre pervading nearly the whole of the plumage of this wonderful bird, which, when flying, must present the appearance of a moving mass of brilliant light, almost too dazzling for the eye to dwell upon; so resplendent indeed, is it, that no art can depict or description convey its true portraiture.'

Gould describes the bird as a flying jewel. 'The entire crown and all the under surface are alike luminous, but the green colouring of those parts is relieved by a throat mark of equally luminous blue; while the dull green, tinged with rust-red, of the remainder of the plumage serves as a contrast to show off those parts which are metallic.'

The birds are depicted against the pinks and mauves of a beautiful orchid, *Cattleya maxima*, which Gould acknowledged to be 'partly taken from Curtis's "Botanical Magazine", a work replete with interest, both for the accuracy of the drawings and the scientific character of the letterpress'.

Streamertail
(Black-capped Humming Bird)

Trochilus polytmus

Trochilus polytmus Linnaeus

PLATE 214

The male Black-capped Hummingbird, known as the Streamertail, has a spectacular long, deeply forked tail which is important in courtship display, and produces a whirring sound when accelerated in flight. In Jamaica, where it is widespread, it is commonly called the 'doctor bird' sup-

posedly because its black crown bears a fanciful resemblance to an old-fashioned doctor's black top hat.

For a detailed account of the birds Gould recommended P.H. Gosse's *Birds of Jamaica* (published in 1847), which provided 'a rich store of observations' and 'various attempts made by that gentleman at domesticating this lovely species'. Philip Gosse (1810–1888) travelled to Jamaica as a collector for the British Museum; he later became well known for his exquisitely illustrated books on marine biology and his anti-Darwinian theories.

213   Green-crowned Brilliant (HCR)

Fork-tailed (Refulgent) Woodnymph

Thalurania Refulgens

Thalurania furcata refulgens Gould

PLATE 215

Gould gave little information about this woodnymph except its extreme beauty and strongly contrasted markings of velvety black head, metallic green throat, purplish-blue breast and shoulders, purplish brown wings and black tail.

To emphasize its attractive colouring Gould had it placed against the pinks of an exotic dipladenia. 'It will be seen that I have united with this bird one of the most delicate and beautiful flowering plants which America has yet given us; the drawing was made by Mr. Richter from a freshly expanded blossom which flowered in the stove at Berry Hill, at Taplow in Buckinghamshire; and it gives me great pleasure to offer thus publicly my thanks to Mr. Noble, for his kindness in directing this beautiful specimen of the *Dipladenia splendens* to be placed at my disposal for the purpose of figuring, thereby adding another to the many acts of liberality proffered by this gentleman for the furtherance of art and science.' Mr John Noble, Gould's friend and subscriber, lived at Taplow, near Maidenhead on the Thames, a favourite spot where Gould went fishing and bird-watching.

215 *Fork-tailed Woodnymph* (HCR)

214 *Streamertail* (HCR)

White-necked Jacobin (Jacobin)

Florisuga Mellivora

Florisuga mellivora (Linnaeus)

PLATE 216

The White-necked Jacobin is a widespread and common tropical species, seen from southern Mexico to Peru and Brazil, also in Trinidad and Tobago. It was well known to early explorers in South America and first described in 1758.

In courtship the male White-necked Jacobin flaunts the white underparts of his plumage, spreading out the underside of the tail in front of the female so that it appears like a beautiful snow-white flower edged with blue.

The two males and female are shown with a spray of red flowers, described by Gould as the *Erythrina umbrosa* of Humboldt and Bonpland. Experiments have shown that hummingbirds are attracted by strong colours and prefer food from feeders coloured red and orange. Many rain-forest plants are brightly coloured to attract birds rather than perfumed to encourage insects as pollinators, perhaps because birds are longer-lived and can cope better with wet weather conditions.

FLORISUGA MELLIVORA.

216   White-necked Jacobin (HCR)

VOLUME III

TUFTED COQUETTE

LOPHORNIS ORNATUS

Lophornis ornata (Boddaert)

PLATE 221

The tiny Tufted Coquettes are about 2¾ inches (7.5 centimetres) in length, and the males have long spangled neck-plumes, which they show off in courtship display. These plumes are light chestnut-red and each has a spangle of luminous green at the tip. Gould thought that for 'grace and beauty' the dainty coquettes were 'second to none in the great family of the Trochilidae'.

In Gould's time the Tufted Coquettes could be found extensively over eastern South America, but they are now found in lowland areas of north-east Venezuela, Trinidad, the Guianas and extreme north Brazil. The plate shows two males and a female with an orchid copied from a drawing of a Brazilian species sent by Mr Reeves of Rio de Janeiro.

DOT-EARED (GOULD'S) COQUETTE

LOPHORNIS GOULDI

Lophornis gouldii (Lesson)

PLATE 217

Gould remarked that he seldom used 'complimentary' names for newly discovered species, and preferred descriptive names, so he did not wholeheartedly agree with the French naturalist R.-P. Lesson attaching the Gould name to such a rare and beautiful hummingbird. Gould knew of only a few specimens of this scarce coquette and these had been found in the remote forests of the Amazon. They differed from the Tufted Coquette by having pure white instead of brown neck-plumes with broader and rounder spangles.

Gould's Coquette is now called the Dot-eared Coquette but retains the same scien-

OPPOSITE:

Top Left: *217 Dot-eared Coquette* (HCR)

Top Right: *218 Frilled Coquette* (HCR)

Bottom Left: *219 Spangled Coquette* (HCR)

Bottom Right: *220 Ruby-throated Hummingbird* (HCR)

tific name. Its habitat is the lower Amazon valley in central Brazil. Gould's name is also commemorated by the dazzling Gould's jewel-front *Polyplancta aurescens*.

FRILLED COQUETTE

LOPHORNIS MAGNIFICUS

Lophornis magnificus (Vieillot)

PLATE 218

The Frilled Coquette is a tiny bird, about 2½ inches (7 centimetres) long. The males are very showy with their striking chestnut-brown crest, iridescent green throat, and bright white bib feathers which sparkle with green. In their courtship display they extend their bright crests and bibs, gyrate, swoop, dive, circle and make buzzing sounds in front of the females. They inhabit tropical forests in central and south-eastern Brazil, and despite their diminutive size are very aggressive in protecting their territory.

Gould described the nest as 'a small round cup-shaped structure, composed of a rufous-coloured fungus-like substance, coated externally with cobwebs and fine vegetable fibres, and decorated with small pieces of lichen'.

SPANGLED COQUETTE

LOPHORNIS REGINAE

Lophornis stictolopha Salvin and Elliot

PLATE 219

'As I had frequently been informed of the existence of a species of *Lophornis* with a crest, which, when outspread, resembled the tail of a Peacock, it was with no ordinary sensations of pleasure I first beheld the lovely little bird here depicted; specimens of which arrived in Europe for the first time in the year 1847.'

Gould further described each feather of the rusty-red crest as being 'surmounted by a ball-like, dark bronzy-green tip, which must render the bird a most conspicuous and pleasing object when the feathers are fully displayed'. This extraordinary plumage now seems more reminiscent of Rastafarian dreadlocks! The Spangled Coquette can be seen in scattered localities in western Venezuela, eastern Colombia and eastern Ecuador.

WIRE-CRESTED (POPELAIRE'S) THORNTAIL

GOULDIA POPELAIRI

Popelairia popelairii (DuBus)

PLATE 222

'Were it possible to visit the planets, in search of the hidden secrets of nature, one could scarcely expect to find a greater number of remarkable novelties, in the way of birds, than have been revealed by the more recent explorations among the great Andean ranges. . . . ' Gould marvelled at the elegance of this thorntail, the male of which sported a green crest with two very long black plumes and an unusual jagged-shaped steel-blue and white tail. Now called Wire-crested Thorntail, it is found in eastern Colombia, eastern Ecuador and north-eastern Peru. The species was first named after Baron Popelaire de Terloo, who discovered it in Peru and gave the first specimen in Europe to the Brussels Museum.

The three cocks and a hen are shown with the Andean blossom, *Loasa picta*, Painted-flower Loasa, copied from *Curtis's Botanical Magazine*, 1 February 1849, which Gould acknowledged as 'a work of great merit and usefulness, whether we regard the scientific descriptions by Sir William J. Hooker and Mr. Smith or the artistic figures by Mr. Fitch'.

RUBY-THROATED HUMMINGBIRD

TROCHILUS COLUBRIS

Archilochus colubris (Linnaeus)

PLATE 220

The Ruby-throated Hummingbird is the only species of hummingbird to be found in the eastern states of North America and southern Canada. Although a tiny bird, 3½ inches (9 centimetres) long, it performs a most remarkable feat of endurance by migrating up to 2,000 miles (3,200 kilometres) from eastern U.S.A. to wintering grounds in Mexico, Central America and as far south as Panama. Part of its journey is a non-stop hop of some 622 miles (1,000 kilometres) across the Gulf of Mexico.

'It was on the 21st of May, 1857,' Gould wrote 'that my earnest day-thoughts and not unfrequent night-dreams of thirty years

221 Tufted Coquette (HCR)

were rewarded by the sight of a living Humming-bird.' To Gould the Ruby-throated Hummingbird was of special interest as it was the only species he saw alive, first as a single bird in Bartram's Gardens, Philadelphia, and afterwards in a flock in the Capitol Gardens, Washington. For a short time Gould kept one in captivity, feeding it from a bottle with sugar and water, and placing it in a gauze bag suspended from his coat button to travel. A pair travelled with Gould across the Atlantic but died soon after the journey, one in the English Channel and the other after two days in London at Gould's home in Broad Street.

VERVAIN (LITTLE) HUMMINGBIRD

MELLISUGA MINIMA

Mellisuga minima (Linnaeus)

PLATE 223

A minute hummingbird, only about 2½ inches (6 centimetres) long, this bird inhabits Jamaica, Hispaniola and adjacent islands. It is now called the Vervain Hummingbird and is named after one of its favourite food plants. Its nest of lichen, silk and cotton is one of the smallest bird's nests in the world, about the size of half a walnut shell. The eggs, the size of small peas, are around ⅜ of an inch (10 mil-

limetres) long and weigh just over 1/100 ounce (0.365 gram). The Vervain Hummingbird is a contestant with the Bee Hummingbird for the title of the world's smallest bird.

ANNA'S HUMMINGBIRD (ANNA'S CAYLPTE)

CALYPTE ANNAE

*Calypte anna** (Lesson)

PLATE 224

Gould was bemused by the idea that it might not be merely coincidence that areas where precious metals were found also produced hummingbirds whose plumage had rich metallic brilliancy. He was referring to the Costa's and Anna's Hummingbirds of California, which have 'not only the throat, but the entire head as glitteringly resplendent as if they had been dipped in molten metal'.

Anna's Hummingbird remains in California and adjacent areas throughout the year. In winter and early spring during the main rainy season it breeds in gardens and low hills and in the summer moves high into the mountains away from the heat and drought of the lower country.

This hummingbird was named after

222 Wire-crested Thorntail (HCR)

Anna, Duchess of Rivoli. Gould shows it on the plant *Ceanothus floribundus*, Copious-flowering Caenothus, a hardy, mazarine-blue flower from California.
*Some authorities keep the name *Calypte annae*

223 Vervain Hummingbird (HCR)

BEE HUMMINGBIRD (HELENA'S CALYPTE)

CALYPTE HELENAE

*Mellisuga helenae** (Lembeye)

PLATE 225

'I have always considered this diminutive but truly beautiful Humming-bird to be one of the gems of my collection, which contains an example of each sex, both which bear the appearance of being fully adult.'

Today this hummingbird, aptly called the Bee Hummingbird is reputed to be the smallest bird in the world, the male being less than a mere 2¼ inches (5.7 centimetres) long and weighing just ½0 ounce (1.6 grams). Females are slightly larger. There is, however, so little difference between the tiny species that even a sip of water can make one bird seem heavier than the other. It is thought that the hearts and bones of these birds have reached the limits of miniaturization and that any smaller bird could not find the energy needed to feed.

The Bee Hummingbird's habitat is con-

fined to isolated patches of woodland and scrub in Cuba and the Isle of Pines. It was named after Princess Hélène d'Orleans (1814–58) of Mecklenburg, East Germany, who married the Duke of Orleans in 1837.
*Some authorities keep the name *Calypte helenae*

RUFOUS HUMMINGBIRD (FLAME-BEARER)

SELASPHORUS RUFUS

Selasphorus rufus (Gmelin)

PLATE 226

The Rufous Hummingbird measures only 3¾ inches (9.5 centimetres) long and weighs just over 1/10 ounce (only 4 grams) yet breeds as far north as the southern Alaskan coast, and migrates south through Mexico to Panama, a distance of some 2,000 miles (3,200 kilometres). It nests in northern pine and birch forests, where food can be obtained from insects and flowering plants, stops in autumn at woodlands near the Californian coast, recuperates and winters in Central America. Thus it makes a similar incredible journey of migration down the western coast of America to that achieved by the Ruby-throated Hummingbird along the east coast.

The explorer Captain Cook reported many of these birds at Nootka Sound, Canada, and further travellers saw them at the mouth of the Columbia River. From

224 Anna's Hummingbird (HCR)

this area in April 1834 Thomas Nuttall sent a description quoted in Audubon's *Ornithological Biography* of the male looking 'like a breathing gem, or magic carbuncle of glowing fire, stretching out its gorgeous ruff, as if to emulate the sun itself in splendour'.

225 Bee Hummingbird (HCR)

FLORESI'S FLAMEBEARER

SELASPHORUS FLORESII

Selasphorus sasin × Calypte anna

PLATE 227

This bird was named after Signor Damiano Floresi d'Areais, a hummingbird enthusiast who lived in Mexico, and died prematurely of fever in Panama. In 1845 he sent a fine specimen with brilliant colouring to George Loddiges. Gould commented that its crown and gorget of bright flame were 'difficult, if not impossible to represent . . . by any artistic means at our command'.

The two Flamebearers are shown with the plant *Echinocactus visnaga*, Visnaga or Monster Cactus. One of the main attractions at Kew Gardens in 1846 was a huge Visnaga cactus weighing over a ton which had been transported from Mexico. Unfortunately this plant rotted and did not long survive, but a smaller flowering one, weighing 713 pounds (329 kilograms), flourished and was illustrated in *Curtis's*

Botanical Magazine in January 1851.

The birds illustrated in Gould's monograph are now considered to be hybrids between Allen's Hummingbird, *Selasphorus sasin*, and Anna's Hummingbird *Calypte annae*.

CALLIOPE HUMMINGBIRD (MEXICAN SATELLITE)

CALOTHORAX CALLIOPE

Stellula calliope (Gould)

PLATE 231

Now called the Calliope Hummingbird, this tiny creature is the smallest bird that inhabits North America and measures only 3¼ inches (8 centimetres) in length. It travels along the western coast in a long migratory journey similar to that of the Rufous Hummingbird, on a route as far as Mexico. It too breeds in the pine forests and mountain woodlands of the northwestern American states.

The male Calliope is depicted with its pinky-scarlet and white bib feathers distended in courtship display. Although the bird is named after the sweet-voiced Greek Muse Kalliope, it does not sing, but utters occasional 'bzzt' sounds during U-shaped swoops in an elaborate display dance.

226 Rufous Hummingbird (HCR)

Marvellous Spatuletail (Humming-Bird)

Loddigesia mirabilis

Loddigesia mirabilis (Bourcier)

PLATE 228

This amazing species is one of the rarest and most unusual of all hummingbirds. Its tail has an extraordinary shape, for it has only four instead of the normal ten tail-feathers. In flight the two outer wire-like feathers cross each other twice, at the base and in the middle. At the tips of these feathers are purplish-black 'spatules' which when brought together can make a loud clapping sound.

'I scarcely know how to commence my account of a Humming-Bird which has for so many years been an object of the highest interest, not only to myself, but to every one who has paid attention to the *Trochilidae*.' Gould based his knowledge on a lone example sent to George Loddiges by Andrew Mathews, a botanical collector based at Lima, Peru, who died at Chachapoyas in 1841. Throughout his life Gould repeatedly offered a large sum to travellers to bring back a specimen for his own collection but never succeeded in obtaining a single example. In 1880 a Polish collector, Jean Stolzmann of Warsaw, visited Chachapoyas and succeeded in rediscovering the species.

Now called the Marvellous Spatuletail it inhabits the montane scrub and forest edges on the east side of the Utcubamba valley 7,000 feet (2,133 metres) up in the Andes in a wild part of north Peru. Little is known, even today, of its life history, but recently such habitats in the southern Amazonas have come under constant threat of destruction.

Booted (White-Booted) Racket-Tail

Spathura Underwoodi

Ocreatus underwoodii (Lesson)

PLATE 229

The male Booted Racket-tails are remarkable for their unusual tails which have two very long outer feathers with large 'spatules' at the ends. They also have prominent tufts of white feathers on their legs. In flight they carry their tails horizontally, and their fast wing-beats of as many as seventy times a second make a loud humming sound.

Gould described the plumage of the two sexes as widely different, for the female has duller colours and 'only a rudiment of the white boots so conspicuous in the male'.

These birds inhabit subtropical regions of Venezuela and Colombia south through Ecuador and Peru to Bolivia. They are depicted with the passionflower, *Passiflora*

227 Floresi's Flame bearer (HCR)

228 Marvellous Spatuletail (HCR)

ligularis, a plant which has adapted to pollination by hummingbirds. When the birds probe deep inside the flower to the base of the petals for nectar, the tops of their heads are dusted with the protruding pollen grains.

229   *Booted Racket-tail* (HCR)

GREEN-TAILED TRAINBEARER (NOUNA-KOALI)

LESBIA NUNA

Lesbia nuna (Lesson)

PLATE 230

Now known as the Green-tailed Trainbearer this species has a trailing forked tail about 3½ inches (9 centimetres) long. It has a short straight bill, which it uses to snap up insects during its rapid flight.

The French naturalist R.-P. Lesson, charmed by its elegance, named it in 1832 after the American heroine Nouna-Koali, from Ferdinand Denis's historical romance *Ismael Ben Zaizar, or the Discovery of the New World*. Its other name Lesbia comes from *lesbias*, a precious brilliant-coloured stone found on the island of Lesbos.

Green-tailed trainbearers are found in the temperate zones of the Andes in Colombia, west Venezuela, Ecuador, Peru and Bolivia.

RED-TAILED (THE SAPPHO) COMET

COMETES SPARGANURUS

Sappho sparganura (Shaw)

PLATE 232

'We are continually receiving fresh evidence that the richest botanical and zoological districts of South America are those to the eastward of the Peruvian and Bolivian Andes; the great primaeval forests of which are as yet a *terra incognita* and their zoological products equally unknown. It is only the outskirts of this fine country that have yet been partially investigated.'

Gould had heard reports from many parts of Bolivia of this gorgeous but belligerent bird with a long glittering tail which 'appears and disappears like a flash of coloured light'.

Today it is found in the Andes of southern Bolivia and western Argentina adjacent to Chile and possibly southern Peru.

The plant depicted is the *Cantua buxifolia*, a blossom of yellow and scarlet tubular flowers from the Peruvian Andes, which is much used by the native Indians for decoration at festivities.

230   *Green-tailed Trainbearer* (HCR)

231   *Calliope Hummingbird* (HCR)

RED-TAILED (THE PHAON) COMET

COMETES PHAON

Sappho sparganura (Shaw)

PLATE 233

'In classic love Phaon is said to have been tenderly loved by Sappho, and here certainly is an object so beautiful as to afford a sufficient excuse for the most frenzied passion; but so tender a feeling would never seem to enter into the breasts of Hummingbirds, their general conduct appearing to be actuated by the Furies rather than the Loves, engaged as they are in one continuous strife with one another.' This rather ponderous passage, with its comment on the inappropriateness of the lovers Phaon and Sappho for such belligerent birds, reveals that Gould could boast of some classical knowledge, but it is thought that as a gardener's son his schooling in Latin and Greek literature was probably very rudimentary.

The Phaon and the Sappho Comets are now considered to be the same species, the Red-tailed Comet. They are shown with a species of *Bilbergia* copied from a drawing sent by Mr Reeves of Argentina.

175

232   Red-tailed Comet (HCR)

Great (Temminck's) Sapphire-wing

Pterophanes Temmincki

Pterophanes cyanopterus (Fraser)

PLATE 236

This species is one of the largest humming-birds, measuring 6½ inches (16.5 centimetres) long, and has brilliant shining deep-blue wings. It lives in mountainous areas of Colombia, Peru and Bolivia. Gould remarked that it was appropriately named after the eminent Dutch zoologist Professor Coenraad Jacob Temminck (1778–1858), 'the Father of living ornithologists', who was Director at the Natural History Museum, Leyden, Holland.

In the Philadelphia Academy of Natural Sciences is a preparatory watercolour of Temminck's Sapphire-wing inscribed 'Original rough design/J Gould/May 9, 1848/ given at the request of Mr. Wilson'. Gould donated this drawing during his visit in 1857 probably to show that he himself made the preliminary sketches for the finished plates in his books.

The adult male and female are shown below a young bird on the plant *Tasconia mollisima*, Downy-leaved Tasconia. Gould gave a detailed acknowledgment for the source for his picture to *Curtis's Botanical Magazine*, vol. 1. Third Series, Tab. 4187.

Shining Sunbeam

Aglaeactis Cupreipennis

Aglaeactis cupripennis (Bourcier)

PLATE 236

Gould described the Shining Sunbeam as one of his favourite hummingbirds because of the rich hues of its glittering back. From the front the bird seemed blackish-brown but viewed from behind it had an amazing variety of colours changing from luminous purplish-crimson to copper and grass-green on the rump. It is of average size, 4½ inches (12 centimetres), and is one of the commoner South American hummingbirds living in temperate areas of the Andes,

233   Red-tailed Comet (HCR)

Colombia, Ecuador and Peru.

The Sunbeams are displayed against the magnificent flower of the cactus *Cereus macdonaldiae*. Gould did not mean to suggest that the sunbeams fed from this plant but thought it was one they might occasionally have visited. This Great Night-flowering Cactus came from Honduras and was a 'floral spectacle' at Kew Gardens, but only a fortunate few saw it in full glory as its blossoms expanded at night.

234   Black-hooded Sunbeam (HCR)

Black-hooded (Pamela's) Sunbeam

Aglaeactis Pamela

Aglaeactis pamela (d'Orbigny)

PLATE 234

Now called the Black-hooded Sunbeam, this species is found in the temperate regions of the Bolivian Andes. Gould received specimens from the plant collector Thomas Bridges, who travelled in Bolivia during 1844–1845 and found the sunbeam feeding among the lily *Alstroemeria* 'at Unduave, and in the Yungas of Cochabamba; far up in the mountains, near the limit of vegetation, at an altitude of 10,000 feet [3,053 metres]'.

Like the Shining Sunbeam this bird is best seen from behind, as the iridescent parts of its plumage appear on its back. Gould imagined that when it glistened in the sunlight it must appear 'a truly gorgeous object' for its entire back was covered with 'glittering metallic-green feathers, as if encased in a coat of mail'.

The showy male and the duller female are displayed with the plant *Diplandenia acuminata*, which appeared in *Curtis's Botanical Magazine* in January 1855.

235   *Great Sapphire-wing* (HCR)

236   *Shining Sunbeam* (HCR)

237 Bearded Helmet-crest (HCR)

BEARDED (GUERIN'S) HELMET-CREST
OXYPOGON GUERINII

Oxypogon guerinii (Boissoneau)

PLATE 237

'Although it is not adorned, like many of the Humming Birds, with bright metallic colours, the beautiful lengthened crest and throat feathers render it a showy and conspicuous species.' This species is now called the Bearded Helmet-crest because of its 'beard', a distinctive tuft of long green and white throat feathers.

The helmet-crests live at high altitudes in the Andes of Colombia and Venezuela. Because of the low oxygen levels in the mountains they conserve their energy by perching and feeding from low-growing flowers rather than hovering in the air.

The plate shows four cocks and a young hen at the top left-hand corner. In the foreground two cocks are shown squabbling 'in one of those conflicts which so frequently occur with all the species of this family'.

BLUE-MANTLED (SOUTHERN) THORNBILL
RAMPHOMICRON VULCANI

Chalcostigma stanleyi vulcani (Gould)

PLATE 238

Gould describes these thornbills as mountain species which probably inhabit 'the shrubby sides of the interior of some extinct volcano'. In the background is depicted the smouldering crater of the volcano Pinchincha, near Quito, Ecuador.

These birds have short bills, less than half an inch in length (1.3 centimetres), which are suitable for searching for insects on rocks and low-lying plants. They perch rather than hover and have larger, more developed feet than most hummingbirds. Like most mountain species they are larger than average, 4¾ inches (11 centimetres) in length, and their colours are less flamboyant. Now called the Blue-mantled Thornbill, this bird is found in Ecuador, south-eastern Peru and Bolivia.

238 Blue-mantled Thornbill (HCR)

VOLUME IV

RUBY-TOPAZ HUMMINGBIRD (RUBY AND TOPAZ)

CHRYSOLAMPIS MOSQUITUS

Chrysolampis mosquitus (Linnaeus)

PLATE 242

'If any one species of this extensive family of birds be better known than another, it is undoubtedly the Ruby and Topaz Humming Bird here represented, for it is not only one of those earliest discovered, but its beauty is of such a character as at once to fix the attention of every observer.'

The Ruby and Topaz was first described in 1758. As it was a common species and found over a widespread area, large numbers were trapped to be sent to Europe for mounting under glass shades as drawing-room ornaments. The flashing colours of their ruby crowns and topaz gorgets made them particularly sought after for elaborate taxidermic displays.

Today the tiny 3½ inch (9 centimetre) Ruby-topaz Hummingbird is widely distributed through northern and eastern South America. The scaly plumage on their heads and gorgets reflects the light rays of the sun and can change colour from ruby red to dazzling golden-yellow. When viewed from the side these bright colours do not always show and at certain angles the Ruby-topaz can appear very dull.

In Richter's illustration the male and female are depicted with a nest 'composed of cottony materials, and decorated with leaves and small patches of lichen'.

BLACK-EARED (BRAZILIAN) FAIRY

HELIOTHRIX AURICULATUS

Heliothryx aurita (Gmelin)

PLATE 239

Gould considered that the 'trivial name of Fairy' was very appropriate for this group of hummingbirds, 'since the elegance of their form and the peculiar chasteness of their colouring readily recall to memory the ideas of grace and beauty connected with those imaginary beings'. Fairies with their wraithlike bodies and tiny gauzy wings abounded in the works of such mid-Victorian writers and artists as Christina Rossetti, William Allingham and Richard 'Dicky' Doyle.

The Brazilian Fairy, now called the Black-eared Fairy, has a crown and upper surface of glossy golden-green, and a black

239 *Black-eared Fairy* (HCR)

240 *Green Violet-ear* (HCR)

241   Giant Hummingbird (HCR)

erected in display or when the birds are angry or excited.

Unusually for hummingbirds, the sexes are similar, and the male Sparkling Violet-ear has been seen sharing with the incubation of the eggs.

Now called the Green Violet-ear, this species lives in the highlands of middle America from Mexico through eastern South America to north-west Argentina. As they are not rare, observations have been made of their habits in captivity. It has been recorded that the average speed of their courtship flights is fifty-five miles an hour, and that two birds chasing one another have achieved as much as ninety miles an hour.

The Sparkling Violet-ear was the first live hummingbird to be kept in a European zoo and arrived at Regent's Park in London in November 1905. Unfortunately, its diet was not properly understood and it died after fourteen days.

GIANT HUMMINGBIRD
PATAGONA GIGAS
Patagona gigas (Vieillot)

PLATE 241

'The figures of the accompanying Plate give a faithful representation, the size of life, of this the largest of the Humming

242   Ruby-Topaz Hummingbird (HCR)

ear-patch terminating in a small tuft of violet-blue feathers.

The male and female are depicted with the orange flowers of a bulbous plant sent to Gould by Mr Reeves of Rio de Janeiro, which were portrayed as 'a pleasing contrast' in colour rather than as a plant to which the birds were particularly attracted.

GREEN (MEXICAN) VIOLET-EAR
PETASOPHORA THALASSINA
Colibri thalassinus (Swainson)

PLATE 240

The violet-ears are particularly attractive medium-sized hummingbirds with characteristic purplish-blue ear tufts which can be

243 *Sword-billed Hummingbird* (HCR)

244 *Empress Brilliant* (HCR)

birds, which has been truly designated as the giant of its family, for by no other species is it approached in size.' The Giant Hummingbird, the largest hummingbird of all, is about the size of a starling, 8¾ inches (22 centimetres). Its weight, however, is only half a starling's, and at 0.7 ounces (20 grams) is more like that of a well-fed Great Tit.

This large hummingbird is found high up in the southern Andes from Ecuador to Chile, at bleak altitudes up to 14,000 feet (4,250 metres). The Giant has a lower wing-beat than other hummingbirds, flapping its wings at a relatively gentle rate of 10 beats per second compared with the average hummingbird rate of 24. In flight it appears to swoop and glide, with wing-beats occurring in bursts. Despite its large size and slow wing-beat the Giant is still capable of hovering, flying backwards, and manœuvring in the air.

The Giant lacks the brilliant plumage of other hummingbirds and is dull brown with

a rusty-red throat and chest. It feeds from plants such as the tall puyas and agaves of the Andes.

SWORD-BILLED HUMMINGBIRD (SWORD-BILL)

DOCIMASTES ENSIFERUS

Ensifera ensifera (Boissoneau)

PLATE 243

'Mr. Hartweg, the celebrated botanical traveller, informs me that he has seen this bird in a state of nature, and that he frequently saw it engaged in procuring its insect food from the lengthened corollas of the *Brugmansia*, for which exploring its lengthened bill is so admirably fitted; affording another instance of the wonderful adaption of structure to a given purpose so frequently observable in every department of Nature's works.' Theodore Hartweg (1812–1871) was sent by the Horticultural

Society, London, in 1836 to collect plants, particularly orchids, in Mexico, Guatemala and Colombia.

The Sword-billed Hummingbird has the longest bill relative to body size of any bird. The bill measures up to just over 4 inches (10.5 centimetres) and is longer than the rest of its head and body. With its long bill and tongue the Sword-billed can reach nectar at the base of the elongated corolla tubes (6 to 8 inches or 15 to 20 centimetres long) of especially adapted species of datura and passion flower. Its bill does not appear to be an encumbrance in other activities for it can build nests and feed its young with great dexterity.

The habitat of the Sword-billed ranges over a wide area of the Andes from Venezuela, to Colombia, Ecuador, Peru and Bolivia. The two adults and a young male are shown on the Scarlet Trumpet Flower, *Brugmansia sanguinea*.

EMPRESS BRILLIANT (HUMMING BIRD)

EUGENIA IMPERATRIX

Heliodoxa imperatrix (Gould)

PLATE 244

'The *Eugenia Imperatrix* is remarkable for its large size, deeply forked tail, and the harmonious hues of its plumage, which, although less glittering and metallic than in many other species, is nevertheless strikingly beautiful. The name of *Victoria regia* has been given to one of the finest flowers of South America, I have dedicated this new Hummingbird to the Empress of the French, as a just tribute to one, whose many virtues add lustre to the lofty position in which she is placed.'

Gould previously wrote that he disapproved of 'complimentary' names, but on this occasion it is obvious that he was not always true to his word. The scientific name *Eugenia*, after Eugenie, wife of Napo-leon III, has nevertheless survived, and the species is today called the Empress Brilliant, *Eugenia imperatrix*. Recent authorities have, however, included *Eugenia* in the genus *Heliodoxa*. This showy bird lives in temperate forest areas of Colombia and Ecuador. The two males and a female are shown with a species of the plant *Datura*.

LONGUEMARE'S SUNANGEL (SUN ANGEL)

HELIANGELUS CLARISSAE

Heliangelus amethysticollis clarisse (Longuemare)

PLATE 245

'Ordinarily the skins of birds are collected for scientific cabinets, or for the decoration of the drawing-room or other apartments; but the great beauty and metallic hues of the Humming Bird have attracted the notice of the plumassier and artificial florist, and their feathers are now extensively used for the decoration of head-dresses, etc. I have known as many as two thousand examples of a single species sold at one time in Paris for such purposes alone, and the beautiful bird on the accompanying Plate, although not known or described until 1841, is now transmitted, particularly to France, in such abundance, that . . . I believe not a few fall into the mutilating hands of the plumassiers.'

This contemporary account conveys some idea of the enormous fashion market in hummingbird skins used for costume jewellery and millinery in the Victorian era. It was not until 1889 that a group of ladies at Didsbury, Manchester, met to protest against this outrageous plumage trade and set in motion the beginnings of the Society for the Protection of Birds.

This subspecies of the Amethyst-throated Sunangel is found in temperate

245 *Longuemare's Sunangel* (HCR)

246 *Ameythst-throated Sunangel* (HCR)

regions of the Andes in Colombia and Venezuela. It was named *clarissae* in honour of Madame Parzudaki, wife of a naturalist in Paris.

247 *Green-backed Firecrown* (HCR)

Amethyst-throated (Amethystine) Sunangel

Heliangelus amethysticollis

Heliangelus amethysticollis (d'Orbigny and Lafresnaye)

PLATE 246

Gould described this rare species, found in the temperate areas of Peru and Bolivia, as similar in shape to the Sun Angel but dissimilar in colouring.

Its differences were a buff-colour gorget merging into the bronzy-green of its flanks and a glittering green spot on its forehead which extended towards the crown.

Now both are considered to be subspecies of the same species, the Amethyst-throated Sunangel. Its name 'amethystine', derived from the purple-violet colour of the semi-precious stone, described the luminous violet-reds and blues of its throat.

Collared Inca

Bourcieria torquata

Coeligena torquata (Boissoneau)

PLATE 249

The Collared Inca, like the Sword-billed has a long straight bill suitable for obtaining nectar from flowers with elongated tube-like corollas. Such flowers, among them the daturas, have narrow openings and no platform on which insects can land. The Inca Hummingbirds are strong fliers and are able to feed while hovering in the air. They are remarkably efficient at approaching the openings of flowers with great accuracy.

The colours of the Collared Inca, unusually for hummingbirds, are predominately black and white, 'the white breast of the fully adult birds offering a striking contrast to the jet-black of the surrounding plumage'. The male differs from the female in having a triangular mark of blue on its crown. These birds are widely distributed from Colombia, Venezuela, through Peru, Ecuador and northern Bolivia.

Green-backed (Chilean) Firecrown

Eustephanus galeritus

Sephanoides sephanoides (Lesson)

PLATE 247

'If our celebrated Captain Cook added to his renown as a circumnavigator by discovering that the Rufous Flame-bearer *Selasphorus rufus* is an inhabitant of the high north-western regions of America, scarcely less interesting was the discovery made by Captain King, that the present fine species is a denizen of Terra del Fuego, the extreme southern limits of that great continent, where it was observed by him flitting about among flowering shrubs in the midst of a snowstorm.'

The Chilean Fire-Crown, now called the Green-backed Firecrown, travels many hundreds of miles to the far south of South America, and during summer breeds amongst the wild fuschias in the dense dark woods of southern Chile, Argentina, and Tierra del Fuego. Occasionally it has been seen as a vagrant in the Falkland Islands. It flies northwards to return to drier arid areas for the winter.

Rear Admiral P.P. King (1793–1856) was in command of HMS *Adventure* during a government coastal survey of South America from 1826 to 1830. Charles Darwin also saw these birds and described them in his *Zoology of the Voyage of H.M.S. Beagle* published 1838–1841.

*Sephaniodes and not *sephanoides* is correct according to Sibley and Monroe 1990, misspelt in Peters (see Schavenesee 1966 p. 183 and Morony *et al.* 1975 p. 161).

248 *Juan Fernandez Firecrown* (HCR)

Juan Fernandez Firecrown (Stokes' Humming Bird)

Eustephanus stokesi

Sephanoides fernandensis (King)

PLATE 248

'Nothing has yet been recorded respecting this or the other Humming Birds inhabiting the island of Juan Fernandez, the extent of which is considerably less than the Isle of Wight, but in which we are told there are many lofty mountains, interspersed with pleasant valleys, clothed with an abundant vegetation. It is in these valleys, and among the shrubby trees close to the sea-shore, that this bird finds a congenial habitat.'

The Juan Fernandez Islands, Mas a Tier-

249 Collared Inca (HCR)

250   *Coppery-bellied Puffleg* (HCR)

251 *Azure-crowned Hummingbird* (HCR)

252 *Blue-capped Puffleg* (HCR)

ra (believed to be the setting of Defoe's *Robinson Crusoe*) and Mas Afuera, off the coast of Chile are the home of this rare species, now called the Juan Fernandez Firecrown. It is thought that there is a population of less than 500 remaining on the islands and conservation measures are needed to prevent a further decline.

The birds depicted with the fern *Dicksonia berteroana* are females.

COPPERY-BELLIED PUFFLEG

ERIOCNEMIS CUPREIVENTRIS

Eriocnemis cupreoventris (Fraser)

PLATE 250

'The great beauty of the *Eriocnemis cupreiventris*, and the large size of the white tufts clothing its legs, render it a very conspicuous object. It is much sought after by collectors; and, judging from the great number of specimens sent to Europe from Santa Fé de Bogota, it would seem to be one of the most abundant of the Humming Birds inhabiting that country.'

The pufflegs have long, fluffy feathers forming powder-puffs around their feet and are still fairly widespread in north-west Colombia and western Venezuela. Because of overcollecting and the destruction of much of their habitat some of the rarer species of pufflegs have been placed on the international Council for Bird Protection world checklist of threatened birds.

GLOWING PUFFLEG

ERIOCNEMIS VESTITUS

Eriocnemis vestitus (Lesson)

PLATE 253

Gould's visitors always exclaimed with admiration at their first sight of this specimen with its 'striking beauty and the glow-

253 *Glowing Puffleg* (HCR)

254   *White-tailed Emerald* (HCR)

worm like splendour of its upper tail-coverts'. Its brilliancy was most apparent at certain hours of the day, especially in the evening after sunset, when its glowing colours contrasted with the dark hues of its tail-feathers.

The Glowing Puffleg has been a popular bird in captivity. Gould believed that it was easily procured in the wild because 'its large snow-white boots must render the bird a very conspicuous object'.

He felt that it was impossible to capture the resplendent colours of this bird on paper and exclaimed, 'Would that it were possible for me even faintly to depict it! but no, even the most finished drawing can be but a phantom of the original.'

BLUE-CAPPED (D'ORBIGNY'S) PUFFLEG

ERIOCNEMIS D'ORBIGNYI

Eriocnemis glaucopoides
(d'Orbigny and Lafresnaye)

PLATE 252

'A single specimen (apparently an adult male) of this bird graces the collection in the Museum of the Jardin des Plantes, at Paris. This individual was, I believe, brought to Europe by M. D'Orbigny, procured either in Peru or Bolivia.'

Professor Alcide D'Orbigny (1803–1857), a French zoologist, travelled in South America from 1826 to 1833 and was Professor at the Museum of Natural History, Paris.

The birds are shown with the flower *Howardia caracasensis*, a drooping plant native to the province of Caracas in Venezuela, which featured in *Curtis's Botanical Magazine* in April 1859.

AZURE-CROWNED HUMMINGBIRD (BLUE-NECKED AZURE-CROWN)

CYANOMYIA CYANOCOLLIS

Amazilia cyanocephala (Lesson)

PLATE 251

The Azure-crowns were described by Gould as having 'glittering hues predominating on the sides and nape of the neck – parts not generally adorned with any fine colouring'. Their iridescence was so splendid that Gould believed it was beyond his artistic power to portray it.

Gould's artists attempted to depict the hummingbird's metallic sheen by a special method of painting with colours and transparent varnishes on top of small areas of gold leaf. Gold had previously been used in bird illustration but the Gould receipe was the most successful of all in capturing the iridescence of these tiny birds' plumage.

Gould described the habitat of this hummingbird as extending from the temperate regions over a wide area from Mexico to Peru, but if the birds illustrated are in fact Azure-crowned Hummingbirds then they are distributed from Mexico to Nicaragua. There is some confusion, however, and possibly the species illustrated is the Andean Emerald *Amazilia franciae* of Colombia to northern Peru.

WHITE-TAILED EMERALD

THAUMATIAS CHIONURUS

Elvira chionura (Gould)

PLATE 254

The Emeralds are characterized by their bright green upper surfaces, and white undersides. In the forests the green and white may be a camouflage against predators, as the emeralds are difficult to see from above or below. Gould described the White-tailed Emerald as different from most other hummingbirds in having a flashing white tail. It was found in Pana-

255 *Blue-throated Goldentail* (HCR)

ma, 'near David, in the province of Veragua, at an altitude of from two to three thousand feet'.

The two males and a female are shown with the plant *Sobralia macrantha*, a deep purplish-rose orchid collected from Guatemala which featured in a double page of *Curtis's Botanical Magazine*, June 1849. This species is now found in south-western Costa Rica.

VOLUME V

BLUE-THROATED (ELICIA'S) GOLDENTAIL

CHRYSURONIA ELICIAE

Hylocharis eliciae (Bourcier and Mulsant)

PLATE 255

'Of this charming bird little or nothing is known further than that it is a native of Central America . . . Although the *Chrysuronia elicia* is not distinguished by any great brilliancy of colouring, its blue throat and rich bronzy tail harmonise so well, as to render it as I have termed it above, a very charming little bird.' The species was named by Jules Bourcier (1797–1873), French Consul General and naturalist in Ecuador from 1849 to 1850, in honour of Madame Elicia Alain.

The birds are shown with fernery and the plant *Stanopea ecornuta*, Hornless Stanopea, which featured in *Curtis's Botanical Magazine*, November 1855. Now called the Blue-throated Goldentail, this species is found from southern Mexico to west Panama and extreme north-west Colombia.

SAPPHIRE-SPANGLED EMERALD (BLUE-BREASTED SAPPHIRE)

HYLOCHARIS LACTEA

Amazilia lactea (Lesson)

PLATE 256

Now called the Sapphire-spangled Emerald this bird is found in Peru, Bolivia and Brazil. It has a green upper surface and throat of a rich shining violet-blue. One bird is shown drinking; it dips its tube-like tongue, normally as long as the bill, in the water and sucks up the liquid. In the wild hummingbirds spend much of their time by pools and waterfalls where they delight in bathing and preening. The plant depicted is the *Nymphea amazonum*, the Amazon Waterlily.

FORK- (LONG-) TAILED EMERALD

CHLOROSTILBON AURICEPS

Chlorostilbon canivetii (Lesson)

PLATE 257

Gould described this bird as having 'the forehead and crown of the head a glittering metallic golden hue, upper surface and wing-coverts golden-green; throat, and the whole of the under surface lustrous metallic green'. Gould's artists indeed had a challenge in attempting to capture the golden-green sheens of this glittering creature!

Now called the Fork-tailed Emerald, it lives in Mexico and Guatemala, south to Nicaragua and Costa Rica.

SHORT-TAILED (POORTMAN'S) EMERALD

CHLOROSTILBON POORTMANI

Chlorostilbon poortmani (Bourcier)

PLATE 258

Gould placed this small insignificant bird with the extra large *Victoria regia* water-lily. He did not know if the birds fed from the flower but the juxtaposition was made because 'the Humming-Birds examine individually most of the plants in the regions they frequent, whether in woods or savannahs, and the chances are, therefore, that the *Victoria regia* is not unvisited by this bird during its peregrinations.'

The flowering of the giant water lily caused great excitement in 1849 when a race took place as to whether the Kew Gardens' or the Duke of Devonshire's plant at Chatsworth would bloom first. The Duke's plant cultivated by Sir Joseph Paxton won, but in the following years Kew's annual tropical lily, named *Victoria amazonica* after the Queen, became one of the most famous sights of the Gardens.

Now called the Short-tailed Emerald, this bird lives in Colombia and north-west Venezuela.

SWALLOW-TAILED HUMMINGBIRD (WESTERN SWALLOW-TAIL)

EUPETOMENA HIRUNDO

Eupetomena macroura hirundo Gould

PLATE 259

This large hummingbird, 6½ inches (16.5 centimetres) in length, came from 'Huiro, in the Valley of Santa Ana, Peru, at an

CHLOROSTILBON AURICEPS, *Gould*

256 *Sapphire-spangled Emerald* (HCR)

257 *Fork-tailed Emerald* (HCR)

258   *Short-tailed Emerald* (HCR)

elevation of 4 800 feet [1.465 metres]'. It was described as having the habits of a swallow and was seen 'flying over the open plains in search of insects'. H.C. Richter illustrated a Swallow-tail in Plate 1 of the second volume of Gould's masterwork *The Monograph of the Trochilidae* (1849–1861), but some twenty years later in the Supplement this further species was illustrated by William Hart. Now known as the Swallow-tailed Hummingbird, this bird lives in savannah and scrub east of the Andes from the Guianas through Amazonian Brazil to southern Peru and northern Bolivia.

SUPPLEMENT

ELLIOT'S TOPAZ

LAMPORNIS CALOSOMA

Anthracothorax nigricollis × *Chrysolampis mosquitus*

PLATE 260

Gould was puzzled as to whether this hummingbird belonged to the genus Topaz *Chrysolampis* or Mango *Lampornis*. The specimen, which possibly came from the West Indies, was a unique male belonging to Mr Elliot – perhaps the American zoologist Dr D.G. Elliot (1835–1915). William Hart, Gould's artist, depicted the front and back view of the bird in order to show its brilliant emerald-green throat and tail of outspread coppery-brown and purple feathers.

This bird is now considered to be a hybrid between the Black-throated Mango, *Anthracothorax nigricollis*, and the Ruby-Topaz Hummingbird, *Chrysolampis mosquitus*.

BEARDED MOUNTAINEER

OREONYMPHA NOBILIS

Oreonympha nobilis Gould

PLATE 261

Gould was very impressed by this large hummingbird, of which the male was 6 inches (15.2 centimetres) in length and had unusual feathering of a blue crown and red beard. It came from the mountains of Peru, at a height of 11,500 feet (3,500 metres) above sea level.

The plate shows two males and a female with the orange flower *Chuquiraga insignis*. Earlier in the series, on Plate 68 of Volume II, the Chimborazian Hill-star was shown feeding from this shrub on the slopes of a volcano. The picture of the plant had been made from an unpressed specimen, a sprig sent home by Professor Jameson of Quito University, which 'was hung up in the shade and not put under pressure'.

BARTLETT'S EMERALD

AGYRTRIA BARTLETTI

Amazilia lactea bartletti (Gould)

PLATE 262

The Supplement to *A Monograph of the Trochilidae, or Family of Hummingbirds*, was completed after Gould's death by his colleague Dr Richard Bowdler Sharpe, who contributed the text for this species. He reported that it was discovered by Edward Bartlett on the Lower Ucayali River in Eastern Peru. Edward Bartlett (1836–1908), son of Abraham Bartlett, superintendeur of the London 200, travelled by steamer along the Amazons to the Ucayali River, in 1865.

Now considered to be a subspecies of the Sapphire-spangled Emerald this bird is found in east and south-east Peru to north Bolivia.

OPPOSITE:

TOP LEFT: *259 Swallow-tailed Hummingbird* (WH)

TOP RIGHT: *260 Elliot's Topaz* (WH)

BOTTOM LEFT: *261 Bearded Mountaineer* (WH)

BOTTOM RIGHT: *262 Bartlett's Emerald* (WH)

The Birds of Asia

Seven volumes (1849–1883), 530 plates.

The Birds of Asia is perhaps the least known and was certainly the most protracted in production of all Gould's sets of volumes. He started to publish the series in 1849 when he had finished *The Birds of Australia*, was embarking on *The Mammals of Australia* and *The Monograph of the Humming-Birds*, and had *The Partridges of America* already in hand. As so much work was in progress Gould issued the prints only once or twice yearly and it eventually took thirty-four years for the thirty-five parts, each with about seventeen plates, to be published. Not only Gould but some of his original subscribers died before the set was completed. The last three parts appeared posthumously and were prepared by his protégé Richard Bowdler-Sharpe with William Hart's illustrations.

The Asian birds came from an extensive area, including Russia, India, Malaysia, China and Japan, with a vast range of habitat, which Gould described: 'the grandest mountain-ranges alternate with steppes, sandy deserts, inland seas, and interminable forests of gigantic growth.' The highlights of the series are Wolf's and Richter's gorgeously coloured pheasants, Wolf's impressive birds of prey and Richter's dramatic magpies. A transition of styles can be seen from H.C. Richter's birds set against carefully drawn flowers and foliage to the later plates with Hart's elaborate landscape backgrounds. Although the series was so long in preparation, Gould never lost interest in extending his knowledge of Asian birds, and was delighted when he was shown the latest discoveries of new species.

Sharpe wrote in the introduction, dated 1883, that Gould's first volume *A Century of Birds from the Himalayas*, published fifty years previously, had heralded the beginning of a golden age in knowledge of the birds of Asia. The writings of B.H. Hodgson, British resident in Nepal, and the *Catalogue of Birds in the Museum of the Hon. East India Company* by Dr T. Horsfield and F. Moore, were followed by standard works by E. Blyth and Dr T.C. Jerdon on the birds of India. Towards the end of the century A.O. Hume edited an interesting journal of important papers on Indian birds under the curious title *Stray Feathers*. Consul R. Swinhoe had added knowledge about the birds of China, and fine illustrations of Japanese birds had appeared in *Fauna Japonica* by P. Siebold, C.J. Temminck and H. Schlegel.

As a tribute to its long and valuable service to scientific knowledge, Gould dedicated *The Birds of Asia* to the Honourable East India Company.

263   Red-napped or Barbary Falcon (JW)

VOLUME I

INDIAN BLACK OR KING (BLACK) VULTURE

OTOGYPS CALVUS

Sarcogyps calvus (Scopoli)

PLATE 264

'The *Otogyps calvus* is a truly Indian species, for it inhabits every part of that great peninsula; but it is not so gregarious, not found in such great numbers, as other members of the genus.'

This vulture is noticeably less sociable both when feeding at carcasses and when breeding than other vultures, and usually not more than four or five are seen together. They stand round the edge of a mixed feeding group waiting for a clear moment to snatch at a piece of carrion. They are greedy eaters, and Gould quoted an account of a vulture shot while drinking at a stream, which disgorged 'the entire leg of a cat'.

The Black Vulture could be seen flying over the hills 'in circles, with the wings extended, apparently without motion, and with their tips outwards, the legs being stretched out beneath the tail'.

This species is thinly distributed throughout the Indian subcontinent except

for Sri Lanka, south-east Asia and south Yunnan, and is distinctive for its black plumage, red bare-skinned face and white ruff at the base of the neck. Joseph Wolf's drawing of a fine, fully grown male was made from a living bird.

RED-NAPPED OR BARBARY FALCON

FALCO BABYLONICUS

Falco peregrinus babylonicus (Sclater)

PLATE 263

This falcon, now called the Barbary Falcon and also known as the Shaheen, is so similar in habits and size to the Peregrine Falcon that it is usually regarded as a subspecies of the Peregrine. Some authors, however, consider it to be a separate species, *Falco pelegrinoides*. Wolf's illustration depicts the Asian form which lives in the north-west Himalayas and Afghanistan east to Mongolia.

British soldiers defending the Khyber Pass during the mid-nineteenth century watched these falcons breeding among the rocks in the mountains. Gould quoted an account by Major E. Delmé Radcliffe, who remarked that they were valued for their hunting ability and that certain breeding pairs were known to native chiefs who obtained young hawks for training every year. As they were docile and good-

tempered they were 'very easily broken in the hood'.

Major Radcliffe often watched the young falcons soaring and swooping at the hill-crows and ravens. Suddenly the noise of the crows' croakings and cawings would cease and there would be silence while they made for cover in the pine trees. The falcons appeared to enjoy terrorizing the crows, but their real prey was Green Pigeons and Chukar Partridges.

SAKER FALCON

FALCO SACER

Falco cherrug Gray

PLATE 267

This falcon is found in steppe country and open plains throughout western and central Asia and northern India. Its western range extends as far as parts of south-eastern Europe, although in this area it is a rare bird. It resembles the Lanner or Jugger Falcon but is somewhat larger.

As a hunting bird, the Saker Falcon was trained by Indians and Arabs to catch hares, bustards and even larger prey such as gazelles. However, its reputation for courage was not considered among falconers to be as high as that of the Peregrine or the Gyrfalcon.

The name 'Saker' was of Arab origin, and had been used for many centuries as a general word for falcons. When the Arab word was adopted by the Europeans it had sometimes become confused with the Latin 'sacer' meaning 'sacred'. This error had even led to the bird being wrongly associated with the sacred falcon of Egyptian mythology.

LANNER FALCON

FALCO LANARIUS

Falco biarmicus Temminck

PLATE 265

This falcon is an African species and is also found in south-eastern Europe through to Asia Minor. There were instances of it reaching Spain and Greece, and on one occasion it was shot in England. The Lanner resembles the Saker Falcon, and it inhabits plains or deserts, preying upon small mammals and birds. It was also trained as a hunting bird by falconers but considered less powerful and courageous than the Peregrine.

'Of all the Falcons I have had opportunities of being acquainted with in a living state, this is at once the most beautiful and the most docile', wrote Gould. He added that Wolf's illustration was drawn 'with great care from a living example perched on my arm, which appeared to be as inquisitive and as interested in the delineation of his figure as the draughtsman himself'. 'This fine bird', Gould remarked, 'is now (in March 1868) living in the aviary at the Zoological Society of London in the Regent's Park.'

266 Laggar (JW)

LAGGAR (LAGGER FALCON)

FALCO JUGGER

Falco jugger Gray

PLATE 266

The Laggar Falcon is the commonest of the large falcons in India. It inhabits open country, plains and foothills throughout Afghanistan, the Indian subcontinent, except Sri Lanka, and central Burma.

Gould wrote that the birds portrayed had been lent to him by Andrew Murray of Edinburgh, whose brother Dr John Murray had formed a fine collection of birds when a civil surgeon at Agra. At this time, in the mid-nineteenth century, much of the information about Indian species came from

British professional and military men who observed, shot and collected birds in their spare time.

These falcons were trained for falconry and sport, but although powerful fliers, were considered to be heavier and slower than other Indian falcons.

Wolf originally illustrated a male and female of life size.

SULAWESI OR CELEBES SERPENT-EAGLE (RUFOUS-BREASTED SPILORNIS)

SPILORNIS RUFIPECTUS

Spilornis rufipectus Sclater

PLATE 268

This striking bird of prey, now called a Serpent-eagle, is found in Celebes (now Sulawesi) and the Sula Islands. It feeds upon rodents, lizards and other reptiles, chiefly snakes. A very dark-coloured bird, it shows white bars on its under-wings in flight. It has a black throat, a rich rufous-brown breast, and its belly and under-tail coverts are chocolate-brown barred and spotted with white.

Joseph Wolf's illustration of this eagle was drawn from a specimen collected by Alfred Russel Wallace during his famous travels in Indonesia (1854–1862) later described in *The Malay Archipelago*. The bird was obtained on the island of Celebes, in the vicinity of its capital town Macassar.

Gould was intrigued by these rare birds, 'whose habits and mode of life appear to be very peculiar; it would seem, also, that their structure is especially adapted for living upon snakes and lizards'. He was very grateful for the loan of Wolf's drawing from J.H. Gurney, an expert on raptorial birds, so that it might be copied and lithographed by H.C. Richter.

BLACK OR PARIAH (GOVINDA) KITE

MILVUS GOVINDA

Milvus migrans govinda Sykes

PLATE 269

These kites, now considered to be a race of the Black Kite, could be seen throughout India, and were especially numerous in areas where man was present.

From information supplied by Dr T.C. Jerdon, author of a catalogue and books on

FALCO SACER.

J.Wolf & H.C.Richter del. et lith.

Walter Imp.

267 *Saker Falcon* (JW)

SPILORNIS RUFIPECTUS, *Gould*

J. Wolf and H.C.Richter del et lith.   Hullmandel & Walton, Imp.

268 *Sulawesi or Celebes Serpent-eagle* (JW)

Indian birds, Gould recounted their success as bold and fearless scavengers. The kites were constantly seen soaring round villages and camps, always on the look-out for refuse of every kind. An account by Colonel Sykes, another expert on Indian birds, described how they circled the air, watching for an opportunity to dart upon a chicken or upon animal scraps thrown out from the cook-room. Occasionally they would even have the audacity to swoop down on a dish of meat which was being carried from the cook-room to the house.

Wolf's illustration depicts an adult and a young bird with some white plumage on its head and neck.

areas of south Asia from north-east India to Borneo and Java. Their short wings and tails enable them to hunt through dense young trees. As they are strictly nocturnal and seldom seen, little has been discovered of their habits.

Gould quoted reports of the native Indians' belief that these owls lived near the haunts of tigers, with whom they were on good terms. The owls' familiarity with these creatures supposedly meant that they had no fear of alighting and riding on the tigers' backs.

Eastern Grass Owl (Grass Owl)
Strix candida
Tyto longimembris (Jerdon)

PLATE 271

This owl resembles the European Barn Owl, but differs from all other owls in its much longer, sparsely feathered legs. Gould wrote that its long legs 'were admirably adapted for standing upon the grassy plains in the midst of which it principally dwells, and for rising therefore with much greater ease than the shorter legged members of its genus, which generally frequent trees, rocks, towers and other buildings'.

269 Black or Pariah Kite (JW)

Oriental Bay Owl (Bay Owl)
Phodilus badius
Phodilus badius (Horsfield)

PLATE 270

Richter's illustration of a male and female was based on a drawing lent to Gould, 'taken from life of the face, ears, and discs of this highly curious owl'. Gould added, 'the rich chestnut tint of their upper surface relieved with spangles of black and white, renders them very pretty objects.' As their plumage seemed soft and yielding, he thought that their flight was probably noiseless.

These rare owls live in deeply forested

270 Oriental Bay Owl (HCR)

201

These owls roost during daylight hours in hollows or tunnels among tussocks of long grass and sedges. They do not build a nest, but lay their eggs in a bed made of trampled vegetation; this site is often linked to runs formed under the grass. Their young are tawny coloured, unlike the European Barn Owl chicks which are snowy white. They live in India, south-east Asia, and related forms live in eastern Australia and New Guinea. They feed on small rodents, birds, reptiles and insects.

ASIAN PALM-SWIFT (PALM-ROOF SWIFT)

CYPSELUS INFUMATUS

Cypsiurus balasiensis (Gray)

PLATE 272

These swifts, living in India, Burma, and Malayasia, nest on the roofs of huts thatched with palm leaves. Richter's detailed

271 Eastern Grass Owl (HCR)

illustration was copied from a drawing lent to Gould by Major Godwin-Austen, which showed 'the bungalows, or native-dwellings, under which this bird builds'. Gould remarked that 'such sketches are in the highest degree useful to the ornithologist, and it is to be regretted that similar [studies of] breeding-habits of birds are not more frequently made'.

Today, photographers and film-makers can capture amazing aspects of birds' daily life in wild-life films and documentaries. In Gould's time outdoor photography was in its infancy, and few pictorial records were made of birds' nesting habits in the field. Almost all illustrations in ornithological books were based on specimens or captive birds in zoos and private collections.

These swifts are of a deep sepia-brown colour with slight green iridescence. They darted through the air, swooping for insects in a manner resembling the Common Swifts of Europe.

Some authors consider the African and Asian Palm-swifts are all one species *Cyp-*

272 Asian Palm-swift (HCR)

273 Wire-tailed Swallow (HCR)

siurus parvus and include a number of subspecies. More recently the Asian Palm-swift has been separated as the species *C. balasiensis*.

274   *Dusky Broadbill* (HCR)

WIRE-TAILED SWALLOW

HIRUNDO FILIFERA

Hirundo smithii filifera Stephens

PLATE 273

'Elegant in contour as our members of the *Hirundinidae* [Family of Swallows] are generally, I question if any Swallow yet discovered can excel the *Hirundo filifera* in this respect, neither is there one among them whose aerial movements are more graceful.'

Gould commented that the swallows' characteristically long forked tail-feathers and elegantly proportioned wings were especially structured to ensure 'sustained flight and a variety of aerial evolutions'. In some swallows the tail-feathers were 'more or less broad, while in others they diminish to the thread-like form seen in the present bird'. The male swallow usually had longer tail-feathers than the female.

These swallows frequent watery areas, fields, gardens and open plains, but their thread-like tail-feathers are not very noticeable in flight and can only be seen from a few yards' distance.

The Asian form of Wire-tailed Swallows *H. smithii filifera* are found in south Asia, east to India, Burma, Thailand, Laos and Vietnam.

INDIAN ROLLER

CORACIAS INDICA

Coracias benghalensis (Linnaeus)

PLATE 275

This species of roller is found from Iraq, Iran, north-west Arabia east to India and south-east Asia. It is sometimes erroneously called a 'blue jay' and during flight displays brilliant turquoise and blue patterns on its wings.

Gould wrote that the roller was frequently seen perching in some prominent position, 'such as the top of a pole, the bare branch of a tree, or on some low bush in groves and gardens in the immediate vicinity of villages'. Often some moving object caught its eye, 'a grasshopper on the ground, or an insect in the air,' and it would fly off to capture its prey and return to eat it on the site it had just left. Its food

275   *Indian Roller* (HCR)

consisted of insects, caterpillars, and occasionally mice, small lizards and other creeping reptiles.

Gould thought that this bird must be very plentiful in India because of the enormous export trade in its feathers. 'I may mention that between three or four hundred flat skins were shown to me on the 10th March, 1869, by a plumassier of Oxford Street, which, he said, had just come from India, adding that these were a continuation of former sendings, and that hundreds more would probably follow.' Gould stressed that 'it must be a source of regret to all right-minded persons . . . to learn that the annihilation of this beautiful bird is almost certain, unless a law be promulgated in India similar to that which we hope is about to be passed for the protection of some of our own birds.'

DUSKY BROADBILL (GREAT EURYLANE)

CORYDON SUMATRANUS

Corydon sumatranus (Raffles)

PLATE 274

This sturdy bird, now called the Dusky Broadbill, lives in the high canopies of the forests of south-east Asia from southern Burma, Thailand, Indochina, Sumatra and Borneo.

The Dusky Broadbill is one of the largest members of its species, about 11 inches (25 centimetres) long, and has an extremely wide and rounded pink bill which looks almost grotesque. During its heavy and slow-moving flight it uses its hooded, almost hawk-like bill to catch large insects in the air. It can also leap upwards from a perch and snatch insects from the forest foliage.

These broadbills are gregarious and mix in noisy groups of up to ten strong. Members of a flock co-operate in the construction of large, pouch-shaped nests of fibrous material, which are slung from branches or creepers.

Unlike other broadbills which are brightly coloured, this species is predominantly sooty black. In the illustration its dark plumage was relieved by some lighter markings, described by Gould as 'a large blood-coloured patch on the back and dingy brownish-white patch on the throat'.

EURASIAN (INDIAN) HOOPOE

UPUPA NIGRIPENNIS

Upupa epops Linnaeus

PLATE 276

Gould believed that the hoopoe of southern India differed from the Common Hoopoe of Europe by the absence of a white bar on its crest. Today there is considered to be only one species which ranges through Europe, Africa, Madagascar, India, Malaysia, and central Asia as far east as Japan. It is an occasional spring visitor to England.

Gould quoted an account of hoopoes which were seen near the houses of the English residents at Jaffna, from Captain Vincent Legge's *Birds of Ceylon*. 'In its nature it is a tame bird. When flushed it will take refuge in a neighbouring tree, where it will sit quietly, giving out a soft

276   *Eurasian Hoopoe* (WH)

204

melodious call, "hoo-poo, hoo-poo", accompanied by a movement of its handsome crest, and an oscillation to and fro of its head at each note . . . It feeds entirely on the ground, strutting about with an easy gait, and scratching vigorously for insects in the dry soil.' The hoopoes bred in the holes of trees, and even in the mud walls which surrounded Jaffna fort, but were notorious for their foul, smelly nests.

This illustration has the detailed landscape background of the plates made in the last years of Gould's publications.

VOLUME II

ASIAN PARADISE-FLYCATCHER (PARADISE FLYCATCHER)

MUSCIPETA PARADISI

Terpsiphone paradisi (Linnaeus)

PLATE 277

The Paradise Flycatcher is widely distributed in woodland clearings, shady gardens and shrubberies, especially near water. This species is found throughout south Asia from Afghanistan through to southeast Siberia and south India and east to Sumatra and Java. The flycatchers perch on branches and are very graceful as they swoop to catch insects in the air.

For many years ornithologists were puzzled by the different colourings of the Paradise Flycatcher's plumage, and it was thought that there were two, or even three different species. Gould carefully examined many examples and came to the conclusion that the white birds were invariably males, that the chestnut-brown birds with long tails were female, and the short-tailed birds were the young of both sexes.

He was, however, not entirely correct. We now know that females and immature birds have similar plumages with blackish heads, rufous upper parts and short tails, while older males are either of similar colours as females but with conspicuous long ribbon-like rufous central tail-feathers, or are mainly white with black head and long white tail-feathers. Confusingly, males often lack the long tail feathers, and even now male plumages are not fully understood. The illustration shows in the foreground two adult males in different colour phases, and in the back-

ground what must be another male, and what is probably a female.

MRS GOULD'S OR GOULD'S SUNBIRD

NECTARINIA GOULDIAE

Aethopyga gouldiae (Vigors)

PLATE 278

This sunbird was first illustrated by Elizabeth Gould in *A Century of Birds from the Himalayas* (see also plate 7). It was dedicated to her by Nicholas Vigors, the first secretary of the Zoological Society of London. Richter's illustration of two males and a female with the exotic plant *Nepenthes ampullaria* seems much more life-like than the stiff, quaint little birds drawn by Elizabeth Gould.

Gould wrote that nearly forty years had passed since Vigors's description but so few specimens had been obtained and so little was known that 'its history is still almost a blank'. It was much sought after by collectors in the Himalayas.

MUSCIPETA PARADISI.

277 *Asian Paradise-flycatcher* (HCR)

These sunbirds feed on nectar from flowers, small insects and spiders. They are found in Assam, south-east Tibet, the Himalayas, the Burma-Vietnam area and southern China. The back of the male is deep reddish-brown, except for the rump which is brimstone yellow. Its breast is yellow with streaks of orange. The crown of its head, throat, tail-feathers and a patch on either side of its breast are glossy steel-blue with purple reflections. The female is a much duller olive-green, apart from a yellow band across the rump.

278   *Mrs Gould's Sunbird* (HCR)

Beautiful Nuthatch

Sitta formosa

Sitta formosa Blyth

PLATE 280

Gould wrote of the Beautiful Nuthatch, 'Great as have been the discoveries in our Indian possessions during the last twenty years in every department of science, few can have exceeded in interest the Beautiful Nuthatch figured in the accompanying Plate; I (and doubtless other ornithologists) was quite unprepared to find a species pertaining to this little group of creeping birds, so gorgeously attired.'

The wings and back of these nuthatches are black with stripes of variegated shades of ultramarine blue.

The nuthatches live in woods and search for insects by walking up, down and around

279   *Sultan Tit* (HCR)

tree trunks. They also eat seeds or nuts and store them by wedging them into holes and crevices. Their nest is made in the hollow of a tree and walled up with mud, so that there is only just enough space for the bird to enter.

These birds live in the east Himalayas, northern Burma, northern Laos and northern Vietnam.

Sultan Tit

Melanochlora sultanea

Melanochlora sultanea (Hodgson)

PLATE 279

This tit is described as a sultan because of its colourful, exotic plumage, which is glossy blue-black, offset by a bright golden-yellow crest, chest and under-parts. The sexes are alike, except that the female,

shown at the top of the picture, has a greenish-olive throat, while the male's is steel-blue.

The Sultan Tit is the largest member of its family, and is an enormous size for a tit. It is about 8¾ inches (22 centimetres) long and weighs more than 1 ounce (30 grams). Most tits are very small and measure less than 6 inches (15 centimetres) in length.

The Sultan Tits are rarely seen but often heard. They live in hill forests and feed on arboreal insects. They are found from north-east India and south China south through south-east Asia.

Volume IV

Tailorbird

Orthotomus longicaudus

Orthotomus sutorius (Pennant)

PLATE 281

The Tailorbird is one of the most ingenious of all nest-builders, and is found in scrub-jungle, grassland, low herbage and field edges throughout India, Burma and southern China and south through south-east Asia to Java.

This tiny bird uses spiders' silk or plant fibres to create a cup by sewing together the edges of one or more living leaves. Holding a length of thread in its pointed beak, it pierces a hole in the leaf, and pushes the thread through, tying a knot at the end on the outside. It then does the same on the other side so that the two leaf surfaces are secured together. Each stitch is made separately, and the threaded leaves form a receptacle, which is lined with fine grasses, down and animal hairs to complete the nest.

Richter's illustration of the nest was copied from a drawing made in China, and the birds were drawn from Chinese specimens. Gould quoted from the revised *Catalogue of the Birds of China*, which gave an account by R. Swinhoe of the Tailorbird's nest. 'The prettiest construction of the kind I have seen was a nest flanked in by three orange-leaves, and places at the extremity of a bough of an orange-tree.'

This species has a long tail, which is often cocked stiffly over its back. Gould observed: 'The two central feathers of the male gradually lengthen until May, when they are about an inch and a half [4 centimetres] longer than the others which are all somewhat graduated . . . these lengthened feathers soon become worn, and usually drop after the first nesting, to be replaced by others only slightly longer than the rest.'

281   Tailorbird (HCR)

282   Red-billed Blue Magpie (HCR)

283 *Formosan or Taiwan Blue Magpie* (HCR)

VOLUME V

FORMOSAN OR TAIWAN BLUE MAGPIE (FORMOSAN BLUE PIE)

UROCISSA CAERULEA

Urocissa caerulea Gould

PLATE 283

'It will be seen by the number of species of Blue Pies figured in the present work, that this genus of birds forms a very conspicuous feature in Asian ornithology.' Gould considered that this particular species from Formosa now called Taiwan or Formosan Blue Magpie was exceptional among other members of its genus for its remarkable blue colouring.

He quoted from an account of this bird by Consul R. Swinhoe, who studied birds in China: 'The Mountain Nymph is by no means uncommon in the large camphor-forests of the mountain-range. It is there to be met with in small parties of six or more, flying from tree to tree, brandishing their handsome tail appendages, and displaying brightly contrasted black, azure, and white plumage, and their red bill and legs, among the deep tinted foliage of the woods . . . They feed on wild figs, mountain berries, and insects.'

RED-BILLED BLUE MAGPIE (NEPAULESE BLUE PIE)

UROCISSA OCCIPITALIS

Urocissa erythrorhyncha (Boddaert)

PLATE 282

Elizabeth Gould first illustrated this blue magpie in *A Century of Birds of the Himalayas* (see also plate 4). Richter's picture of some thirty years later is a much more elegant portrayal of this handsome bird with its very long tail.

This species, now called the Red-billed Blue Magpie, can frequently be seen on the foothills of the western Himalayas east to northern China, Indochina and south-east through to Thailand. The birds fly in small parties, following each other from one patch of woodland to another, with their long tails spread conspicuously behind them. They feed on a wide variety of animal and vegetable matter, and even take carrion. Gould quoted a report from India that the 'presence of a cheetah, or a bird of prey, is often discovered by the chattering of these beautiful creatures'.

YELLOW-BILLED OR GOLD-BILLED BLUE MAGPIE (WHITE-CAPPED BLUE PIE)

UROCISSA CUCULLATA

Urocissa flavirostris (Blyth)

PLATE 284

This magpie, now called the Yellow-billed or Gold-billed Blue Magpie, is similar to the Red-billed Blue Magpie, but lives at higher altitudes in the mountain forests of

284 *Yellow-billed or Gold-billed Blue Magpie* (HCR)

the western Himalayas from Pakistan to India, south-west China, Burma, north Vietnam and Nepal. Gould said that this species differed from other Himalayan blue magpies by its bright yellow bill, and 'the black cowl-like hood which occupies the crown of the head'.

Richter's illustration was drawn from some fine specimens presented to Gould by Captain Michael Tweedie of the Royal Artillery, who killed them at Kooloo, north of Simla. The plant, *Gardenia mangostana*, may have been copied from one of the fine botanical drawings in the Hon.

East India Company Library, a source which Gould acknowledged and used for *The Birds of Asia*.

Green Magpie (Hunting Cissa)
Cissa venatoria
Cissa chinensis (Boddaert)

PLATE 285

Now called the Green Magpie, this brilliantly coloured species is found in the mountainous country of India and south-

east Asia.

Gould described the colouring of its plumage as 'very evanescent'. The birds when newly moulted were a lovely emerald green, their wings bright sanguine red, and their bills and legs deep coral. Unfortunately, whether the birds were in the wild, in captivity, or mounted as specimens, their beautiful colours faded; the greens changed to a drab blue, and the reds to a dull brown.

These birds were easy to tame; in captivity they screeched or sang lustily with much gesticulation, and caused a great deal of amusement by their imitative sounds. Their habits were similar to jays or shrikes for they were highly carnivorous and would place pieces of food between the bars of their cages. A fine bird lived for some time at the Zoological Gardens, London, and Gould regretted that more examples were not sent to England, for they were very attractive and easily adaptable as aviary birds.

In the foreground of the illustration is a newly moulted male with bright colouring, and in the background is a duller bird showing faded plumage.

Gurney's Pitta
Pitta gurneyi
Pitta gurneyi Hume

PLATE 286

This pitta, an inhabitant of tropical forests in southern Burma and the Thailand peninsular was thought to be extinct in 1952, but was rediscovered in a bird market in 1986. There are believed to be as few as thirty pairs in the wild, but in Thailand pet-traders still claim they can procure them and sell them for about £100 each.

The pittas are secretive, shy birds, and forage for worms, snails and insects on the forest floor. Research in Borneo has shown that they are adversely affected by logging and deforestation but will return to breed in lightly disturbed or partially regenerated forest. Gurney's Pitta, however, has a limited distribution over about 310 miles (500 kilometres) in a zone between Thailand and Burma, and conservationists are very concerned about its future.

Gould, who was particularly interested in pittas, was most intrigued to hear of this 'new and magnificent' species, described in

285 Green Magpie (HCR)

286 *Gurney's Pitta* (HCR)

1877 by Allan Hume, editor of *Stray Feathers*, a magazine which contained many important articles on Indian birds. He was especially delighted when Hume presented him with an adult male and a female Gurney's Pitta, an addition to 'my already, I may say, unique collection of this beautiful family!'

The male Gurney's Pitta sports striking colours, with a black and yellow breast and a brilliant blue crest. The illustration depicts two colourful males and the duller female, which is barred with black and brown.

VOLUME VII

BULWER'S OR WATTLED PHEASANT

LOBIOPHASIS BULWERI

Lophura bulweri (Sharpe)

PLATE 287

In his biographical memoir of Gould, Sharpe related Gould's excitement when he was shown the British Museum's unique specimen from Borneo: 'It was always a real pleasure to see the delight which animated the old naturalist when, in his invalid days, I took some new form of bird such as Bulwer's Pheasant to be figured in *The Birds*

of Asia. On the latter occasion he exclaimed there was only one man in the world who could do justice to such a splendid creature and that was Mr. Wolf; who, at his request, at once designed a beautiful picture which appeared in *The Birds of Asia.*'

The pheasant has splendid colouring, its horns and wattles are ultramarine blue, its neck and body feathers are maroon or brown with metallic purple edges, it has a white tail and slender bright red legs.

During courtship display the blue wattles are dramatically engorged and enormously extended to form a vivid contrast with its bright red eyes and facial skin. The white tail of between thirty and thirty-two feathers, which is probably more feathers than the tail of any other bird, is flattened on the ground, then fanned to and fro, up and down, so that it looks like a flat white disc reaching above the back as far forward as the head.

Bulwer's Pheasants are now a threatened

LOBIOPHASIS BULWERI, *Sharpe*

287 *Bulwer's or Wattled Pheasant* (JW and WH)

EUPLOCOMUS VIEILLOTI, *G.R.Gray.*

288 *Vieillot's or Crested Fireback* (JW and HCR)

species in the wild, for their habitat occurs in the deep gullies of the forested interior of Borneo, where much damage has been caused by large contracts for logging. They have been bred in captivity, however, so there is hope that this species will survive. These birds were named after Sir Henry Earle Bulwer, Governor of Labuan, who presented the type specimen to the British Museum.

VIEILLOT'S OR CRESTED FIREBACK

EUPLOCOMUS VIEILLOTI

Lophuraignita (Shaw)

PLATE 288

Gould wrote that these pheasants lived for some time at the Earl of Derby's menagerie at Knowsley but that the flock had died out. Wolf's illustration was made from a single fine-plumaged male at the Zoological Gardens, London.

At the approach of the breeding season this male would become very restless and bear itself upright, and the fleshy parts round its eye would become very dilated. These swellings of cerulean blue would extend well above the crown of its head and below its neck to surround its contrasting eyes of bright scarlet.

Gould hoped that soon other pheasants would be added to the Zoological Society's aviaries for 'as fine or more ornamental bird could scarcely be found'.

The Fireback's name is a reference to its glowing or 'fiery' crimson back and rump. It was dedicated to Louis-Jean-Pierre Vieillot (1748–1831), a well-known French zoologist and author.

Today the Crested Fireback inhabits woods in Malaya, Borneo and Sumatra in the wild but its numbers have declined due to forest destruction.

SILVER (PENCILLED) PHEASANT

GENNAEUS NYCTHEMERUS

Lophura nycthemera (Linnaeus)

PLATE 289

This pheasant, now called the Silver Pheasant, is a well-known popular aviary bird, but its habits have been little studied in the wild. Its natural habitat is the mountainous areas of south China through eastern Burma and most of Indochina and north-east Vietnam.

Gould wrote that these pheasants had been successfully established for some time in European aviaries. He thought that it would be a mistake to allow them to become wild because male pheasants were often pugnacious, and fights between two species could end with the death of the weaker birds. They should best be kept as ornamental birds in aviaries or limited areas, 'for no good can result if they should

GENNÆUS NYCTHEMERUS.

J. Gould and H.C. Richter. del. et lith.

Hullmandel & Walton Imp.

hybridize with our Common Pheasant.'

The illustration was drawn from the finest male in the aviary of Edward Betts, of Preston Hall, near Maidstone.

GOLDEN PHEASANT

THAUMALEA PICTA

Chrysolophus pictus (Linnaeus)

PLATE 290

This male pheasant has a long, silky crest of amber or golden colour. The feathers at the back of its head and neck are of a rich orange-red, the ends edged with a narrow black line; during display these are raised and brought forward to form a gaudy ruff which nearly meets at the front and covers the beak.

The Golden Pheasant also has a magnificent tail; the upper tail coverts are rich crimson and the longer feathers are diagonally crossed with wavy bands of dark and buff brown. On its back are feathers of rich yellow and dark glossy green tipped with black; the plumage of its under-surface is intense scarlet.

In spite of their brilliant colouring these pheasants are secretive inhabitants of the forests of central China and little is known of their habits in the wild. They are popular and successful as aviary birds, and George Washington is said to have had some at Mount Vernon.

The illustration shows the great difference in colouring between the male and female. In the background two cocks are confronting each other; sometimes vicious fights occur, involving the use of the males' spurs.

LADY AMHERST'S PHEASANT

THAUMALEA AMHERSTIAE

Chrysolophus amherstiae (Leadbeater)

PLATE 291

This pheasant was named in honour of Lady Sarah Amherst (1762–1838), wife of Earl Amherst, a British diplomat in China in 1816 and Governor General of India from 1823 to 1828. Lady Amherst was an adventurous botanist and a keen ornithologist, and on her return to England in 1828 she brought a collection of Himalayan plants and two living male pheasants. The birds had originally come from Burma, and were given to her by Sir Archibald Campbell, who commanded the Burmese War. For two years they were kept in good health by Lady Amherst in India, but unfortunately, although they survived the journey, they died within a few weeks of their arrival in England.

The illustration shows a cock with its amazingly decorative plumage striding among trailing fernery towards a pool, and in the foreground is an exotic butterfly. Gould had not seen a female of the species, and hoped ardently that with new opportunities for exploration in remote areas of China, there would be more arrivals of these pheasants within his lifetime. He believed that this species could easily be adapted to life in aviaries in England.

Today Lady Amherst's Pheasant lives in the high mountains of south-east Tibet, south-west China and northern Burma. It successfully breeds in captivity.

THAUMALEA PICTA.

290 *Golden Pheasant* (HCR)

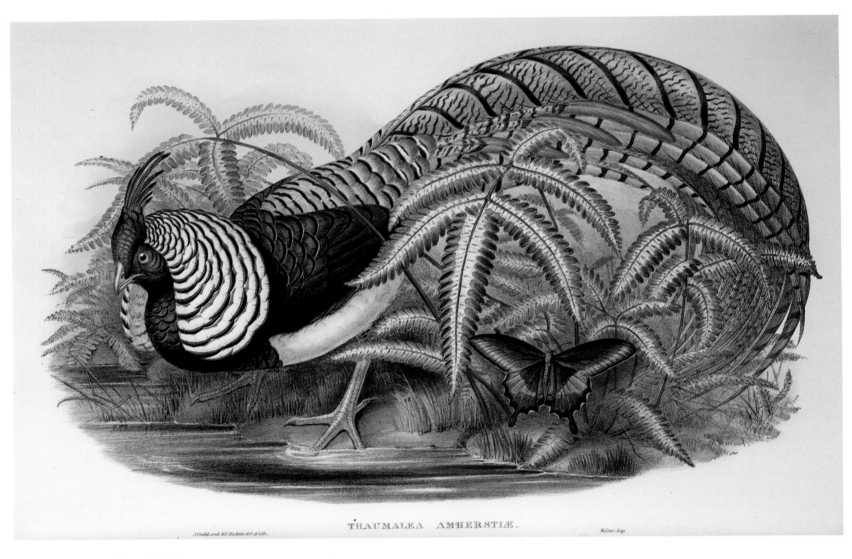

THAUMALEA AMHERSTIÆ.

291 Lady Amherst's Pheasant (HCR)

CASPIAN SNOWCOCK (CASPIAN SNOW PARTRIDGE)

TETRAOGALLUS CASPIUS

Tetraogallus caspius (Gmelin)

PLATE 292

These snowcocks live at high altitudes in the mountains of eastern Turkey, Armenia and northern Iran, and are similar to the snowcock of the Himalayas.

Wolf was able to study the birds 'in a fine state of plumage' at the Zoological Gardens, London, for during 1852 and 1853 two snowcocks from Persia (Iran) were living in the aviaries. In his picture, Wolf painted the snowcock in a wild mountainous background, for one of his favourite subjects was the depiction of birds in bleak conditions among the bare rocks and heathland. He enjoyed showing birds camouflaged in the snow as here, where the white blob of the back of a partridge is just visible in the distance as it scuttles away up the mountain.

Gould believed that these large snowcocks could be introduced into the Highlands of Scotland or hilly districts of Northumberland and the other northern English counties. He thought that if they were naturalized they could become of great economic importance as game birds and as a source of nutritious food.

REEVES'S PHEASANT

PHASIANUS REEVESII

Syrmaticus reevesii (Gray)

PLATE 293

This pheasant was named after John Reeves (1774–1856), a naturalist who lived in China and brought the first live male of this species to England in 1831. His son brought a female in 1838, and both pheasants lived at the Zoological Gardens, London. With the improvement of diplomatic relations with China many more

Reeves's Pheasants were imported to England, and in 1867 a male and two females presented to Queen Victoria lived in the Windsor Castle aviaries.

Gould believed that many years before the birds were seen in Europe their long central tail-feathers had been known and highly prized, for the Chinese presented them to foreigners as valuable gifts. He noted that the length of the male's tail varied from 4 or 5 feet (1.25–1.83 metres) to up to nearly 6 feet. Today, the record is 8 feet (2.4 metres), but the normal maximum for the male's tail is 5¼ feet (1.6 metres). The whole length of the male's tail could not be included in the illustration, so Richter drew some smaller birds in the distance to show their correct proportions. In the air the pheasants' flight is fast, but they can turn up their long tails as an effective brake or bend them to one side to make a sharp turning.

These birds are extensively hunted and trapped in northern and central China both for their flesh and for their showy feathers. They have been widely introduced as game and as ornamental birds into western countries. In some areas these pheasants have escaped from bird collections or have been released and have established small feral populations.

WESTERN TRAGOPAN
(HORNED PHEASANT)

CERIORNIS MELANOCEPHALA

Tragopan melanocephalus (Gray)

PLATE 294

Gould wrote that the only living example of the Western Tragopan that had reached England was a splendid male presented by Lord Hardinge to Queen Victoria on his return from India. Gould made a drawing of the live bird at Buckingham Palace gardens, and after its death he was allowed to examine it and make notes of its colours before they faded.

As the bird had survived for several years in the unlikely environment of a garden in the middle of a large city, Gould believed that if careful transport could be arranged from the Himalayas by way of the River Indus to Karachi, the species could be successfully introduced into English woods and aviaries.

The illustration shows the richly plumaged male, and two sombre-coloured females in the distance. During courtship display the male's horns become erect and brilliant azure-blue and the throat bib (or lappet) expands to show an incredible purplish-blue centre with pink margins and pale blue indentations; at other times they are a duller colour, hang loosely and appear shrivelled.

These pheasants live in the undergrowth of forests in the western Himalayas, Pakistan, India and south-west China. Their population and range has declined seriously in recent years, due to human persecution, the destruction of forests, and general disturbance by goats. The species is protected by law in Pakistan and India.

BLYTH'S TRAGOPAN
(HORNED PHEASANT)

CERIORNIS BLYTHI

Tragopan blythii (Jerdon)

PLATE 295

This illustration was drawn from a bird with fine plumage which lived for a short time at the Zoological Gardens, London. It had splendid golden colours on the naked parts of its face and around its throat.

The species had recently been discovered (1869) in the hills of Upper Assam and named after E. Blyth, a zoologist who was Curator of the Natural History Museum in Calcutta from 1842 to 1864. Some birds were obtained by Major Montagu of the Bengal Staffs Corps and transported with great care to London.

The male was described by Dr Sclater of the Zoological Society as being very courteous in his addresses to the female: 'When approaching her, he lowers all the feathers which are on the side nearest to her, almost hiding his legs, showing to great advantage all the beautiful markings of his plumage, and the admirable manner in which the colours blend into one another.'

TETRAOGALLUS CASPIUS.

PHASIANUS REEVESII, J.E. Gray.

Blyth's Tragopan is now rare in the forests of Assam and north-west Burma, where it has been hunted for food. Unlike many other of the ornamental pheasants, it is poorly represented in captivity.

GREAT ARGUS (PHEASANT)

ARGUSIANUS ARGUS

Argusianus argus (Linnaeus)

PLATE 296

The Great Argus has wings and tail-feathers patterned down the centre with a great chain of ocellated spots, and is named after the Greek god Argus who had one hundred eyes. The male of the closely related Crested Argus, *Argus rheinartia ocellata* has the longest central tail-feathers in

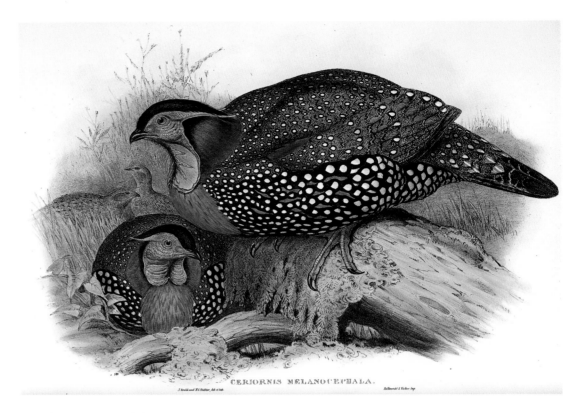

CERIORNIS MELANOCEPHALA.

J. Gould and H.C. Richter, del et lith.   Hullmandel & Walton Imp.

294   Western Tragopan (HCR)

CERIORNIS BLYTHI, *Jerd.*

J.Wolf & H.C. Richter, del et lith.   Walter, Imp.

295   Blyth's Tragopan (JW and HCR)

296 *Great Argus* (WH)

the world, regularly reaching 5¾ feet (173 centimetres), while their width of up to just over 5 inches (13 centimetres) makes them the largest feathers of any wild bird.

The male has a remarkable and rather complicated courtship display. Around dawn the male calls with loud, wailing sounds which serve to advertize his 'dancing-ground' or display site. If a female appears he performs a number of ritualised dances on his prepared ground cleared of leaves. The finale occurs when he faces the female spreading both wings vertically to form an oval, funnel-shaped fan with the two longest tail feathers visible between the wings. In this position the exquisite patterning and rows of 'eye-spots' on the feathers are fully displayed and appear to move as the whole tail is shivered. A successful courtship display will end in mating, after which the female departs to raise the brood on her own.

Unlike most other pheasants, the Argus Pheasant is not brilliantly coloured but instead is mainly brown and grey with exquisite black markings. It takes three years for the male to grow its full breeding plumage.

In the wild these pheasants live in Malaysia, Borneo and Sumatra but are becoming rare, as their forest habitat is destroyed through extensive tree-felling.

This illustration by Hart was published after Gould's death with notes by R.B. Sharpe.

HIMALAYAN OR IMPEYAN MONAL (MONAL)

LOPHOPHORUS IMPEYANUS

Lophophorus impejanus (Latham)

PLATE 298

The first attempt to introduce this pheasant to England was made at the end of the eighteenth century by Lady Impey, wife of Sir Elijah Impey, Chief Justice of Bengal from 1774 to 1789. This proved unsuccessful, but further attempts by Lord Hardinge, Governor General of India, brought many living birds of both sexes to England. By 1850 Prince Albert owned some Impeyan Pheasants; a pair were in the Zoological Gardens, London; and both Indian- and English-bred birds could be seen in the aviaries belonging to the Earl of Derby at Knowsley.

This illustration of the male in resplendent iridescent plumage and the female with dull brown markings was drawn and lithographed by Richter from 'a spirited sketch in oils, taken by Mr Wolf from the living birds in the Gardens of the Zoological Society'.

During display the cock fans and raises its rufous tail, droops its purple-blue wings to reveal its white back-patch, and fluffs out the magnificent iridescent red and golden neck feathers. In the Himalayas the birds are a remarkable sight when they fly over the forests, calling wildly and displaying their brilliant colours.

219

LOPHOPHORUS LHUYSI, *A. Geoff St. Hil.*

297 *Chinese Monal* (WH)

CHINESE (DE L'HUYS) MONAL

LOPHOPHORUS L'HUYSI

Lophophorus lhuysii Geoffroy Saint-Hilaire

PLATE 297

Gould wrote that recent exploration in China brought the prospect of many new species being found, but no one was prepared for the discovery of this beautiful Chinese Monal. 'It is to the distantly located French Consuls, and their still more enterprising missionaries that we are indebted for our first knowledge of the *Lophophorus l'huysi*.' It was previously thought by ornithologists that the Himalayan Monal, discovered in 1790, could not be excelled in the richness of its metallic colouring by any other species.

As no live examples had reached Europe, the illustration was drawn from skins brought from China by the missionary Père David (famous for the rare deer that bear his name), and lent to Gould by Dr D.G. Elliot, an American zoologist and publisher of some magnificent illustrated books on pheasants.

The Chinese Monal has a similar colouring to the Himalayan bird, but its crest is fuller and a rich purple to bronze colour, 'changing to a more brilliant or deeper shade as it is moved towards the light.'

The pheasant was named after E. Drouyn de L'Huys (1805–1881), a French zoologist. It is now rare in the wild, found only in the mountains of central China.

EGYPTIAN PLOVER OR CROCODILE-BIRD (ZIC-ZAC)

PLUVIANUS AEGYPTIUS

Pluvianus aegyptius (Linnaeus)

PLATE 299

Although these plovers are African, they were included among the birds of Asia because Gould thought some might inhabit the western Asian boundaries. He wished to use Wolf's illustration of the fable which originated from the Greek writer Herodotus. This related how the bird, known to the Egyptians as the zic-zac, was a friend of the crocodile and would fearlessly enter its open jaw to pick leeches and other parasites from its mouth.

Gould quoted one report that birds had never been seen perched in a crocodile's jaw, and that dissected crocodiles had teeth and mouths that were clean.

These plovers from north-east and central Africa are striking birds with blue-grey wings, pink-buff breasts, and bold black and white markings on their heads. They are extremely tame and frequent areas near rivers, lakes, and human habitation, feeding on insects and small creatures at the water's edge. An elaborate wing-raising display in which their white markings are shown to advantage is an essential part of their aggressive behaviour directed towards potential predators or food competitors.

298 *Himalayan or Impeyan Monal* (JW and HCR)

Wolf's original illustration depicted a life-size bird and smaller birds in the background 'around and in the mouth of the crocodile'. Gould did not know whether this 'oft-told tale' of the birds acting as tooth-cleaners was true or false. The story has still to be proved today. What is remarkable is the mutual tolerance shown by crocodile and what could be its prey, the Egyptian Plover.

PHEASANT-TAILED (CHINESE) JACANA

HYDROPHASIANUS SINENSIS

Hydophasianus chirurgus (Scopoli)

PLATE 300

This species of jacana or 'lily-trotter', now called the Pheasant-tailed Jacana, lives in marshy areas extending from Pakistan and India, south China and Taiwan south through south-east Asia to Sri Lanka, Java and the Philippines. During the breeding period the male has exceptionally long central tail-feathers which add 10 inches (25 centimetres) on to its normal 12 inch (30 centimetre) length.

Gould described this species of jacana as 'the most elegant yet discovered, and India may well be proud of so graceful an ornament to her marshes'. The lily-trotter was so light and had such large feet and toes that it could run across floating lily-leaves with the greatest facility.

Gould commented that the lily-trotters' wings seemed unsuitable for flying, but that when alarmed the birds dived and remained concealed with only their nostrils above water. Some species of jacana are known to run to safety holding their chicks tightly under their wing with only the spidery dangling legs of the chick being visible. This behaviour was first recorded in 1934 for the Australian Jacana and then in the 1960s for the African Jacana and has recently been dramatically filmed for the latter species.

The Pheasant-tailed Jacana has very unusual nesting habits, inverting the usual male and female roles of rearing a family. The females mate with several males, and do not take any part in incubating the eggs or looking after the chicks. As many as eight clutches of four eggs in a season are laid by the females, and the males rear about two broods annually. Two eggs are incubated under each of its wings and kept well away from the water.

MANDARIN DUCK

AIX GALERICULATA

Aix galericulata (Linnaeus)

PLATE 301

'The manners of this pretty species appear to be as gentle and loving as its dress is gay and beautiful, on which account . . . it is regarded by the Chinese as an emblem of conjugal fidelity.' Gould commented from his observations of the mandarin ducks mating habits that the tradition of their partnership for life appeared to be true, for even those kept in captivity seemed to be consistently moving about together in pairs.

Richter's print was made from 'a spirited and beautiful sketch by Mr. Wolf from the living birds in the Gardens of the Zoological Society'. During the summer months of 1851, Gould watched these birds swimming or perching on branches, and observed the drakes' colourful plumage change to drabness. But by the beginning of October the old drakes had regained their full colours and the young males of the two broods born that year were almost as splendid as the adults.

Gould hoped that these birds, would become fully naturalized in England, 'as an ornamental addition in our lakes and gardens'. This wish has been realized, for since 1971 the Mandarin Duck has been listed as a British bird, and settled populations have been established in several parts of the country.

TOP: *299 Egyptian Plover or Crocodile-bird* (JW and HCR)
MIDDLE: *300 Pheasant-tailed Jacana* (HCR)
BOTTOM: *301 Mandarin Duck* (JW and HCR)

PLUVIANUS ÆGYPTIUS.

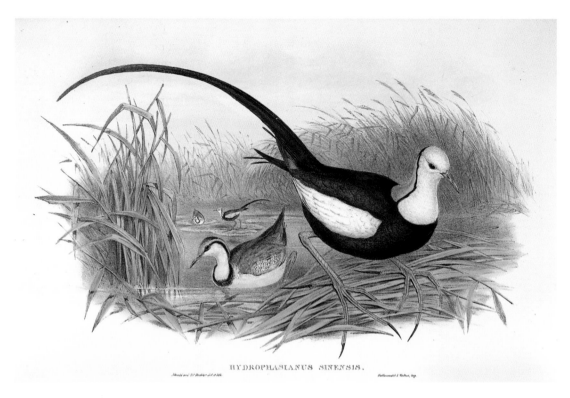

HYDROPHASIANUS SINENSIS.

THE BIRDS OF GREAT BRITAIN

Five volumes (1862–1873), 367 plates.

In late middle age, after the completion of many volumes of colourful tropical species, Gould turned his attention to the more sombre birds of his own country. Many British birds had already appeared some thirty years earlier in plates by Elizabeth Gould and Edward Lear in *The Birds of Europe*, but Gould had enlarged the scope of illustration by portraying a number of family groups including young birds, or chicks and nests, with the male and female.

Gould returned to the favourite haunts of his youth by the Thames between Maidenhead and Windsor to watch riverside birds, especially the nesting sand-martins, grebes, coots and moorhens. There, some twenty-five miles from his London office, he relaxed while fishing during the summers of the 1860s. His rough notes and sketches were compiled by his secretary Prince with other relevant material and are now in seven manuscript volumes at the Natural History Zoology Library, London, and the Academy of Natural Sciences, Philadelphia. Careful details about eggs and nests were recorded by Gould's son Franklin, who joined his father on expeditions to see

the Little Tern at Dungeness, and Dartford Warblers at Frensham Ponds, Surrey.

Fifty-seven illustrations of birds of prey, game and water birds were contributed by Joseph Wolf, an expert wildlife artist, whose powers of observation Gould greatly admired and respected. The hedgerow and garden species were illustrated by H.C. Richter, who enlivened the nondescript little brown birds by positioning them among sprays of exquisitely drawn wild flowers of the countryside. The last, elaborated plates, such as the congregation of Sand Martins, and the group of young Long-tailed Tits were by William Hart, whose detailed landscape backgrounds appeared in later series.

The Birds of Great Britain, the most popular of all Gould's works, with a list of 468 subscribers, was dedicated to Rowland, Viscount Hill of Hawkstone (kinsman of Sir Rowland Hill, originator of the 1840 penny postal system in England), a life-long friend and patron. It proved to be Gould's last fully completed work and perhaps his most satisfying and pleasurable achievement.

HALIAËTUS ALBICILLA.

J.Wolf and H.C.Richter, del. et lith.   Walter & Cohn, Imp.

302 *White-tailed Eagle* (JW and HCR)

VOLUME I

EGYPTIAN VULTURE
NEOPHRON PERCNOPTERUS
Neophron percnopterus (Linnaeus)

PLATE 303

Gould commented that the British Isles were not 'a favourite place of resort for any of the Vultures, their peculiar habits and mode of life being more especially adapted for the southern countries of Europe, Asia and Africa'. He included an illustration of the Egyptian Vulture among the British birds because it sometimes reached England and had been recorded in Somerset and Essex.

In October 1825, a young bird was discovered near Kilve, Somerset, 'feeding on the carcass of a dead sheep, and had so gorged itself with the carrion as to be unable or unwilling to fly to any great distance at a time, and was therefore approached and shot without any great difficulty'. A second young vulture, recorded in *The Zoologist*, 1868, was shot at Peldon, Essex, by a farm labourer who found a strange bird feeding on the blood of some geese he was killing. The latter

AQUILA CHRYSAËTOS, *Briss*

J.Wolf and H.C.Richter del et lith.   Walter & Cohn Imp.

304   *Golden Eagle* (JW and HCR)

303   *Egyptian Vulture* (JW and HCR)

vulture was sent to Gould for examination and Wolf depicted this immature bird in the illustration.

An unsigned crayon drawing of the adult bird's head and shoulders has survived among various sketches, cuttings and letters in a notebook for *The Birds of Great Britain*, which is now in the Natural History Museum Library, London.

The original plate showed an adult about two-thirds life-size and the darker young bird on a reduced scale. Today the Egyptian Vulture has a wide range including southern Europe, the Middle East, Africa, south-west and central Asia and India. It is a summer visitor in the north of its range,

and in winter it migrates south of the Sahara desert. Egyptian Vultures still occasionally fly to England, and one was recorded in June 1968.

GOLDEN EAGLE
AQUILA CHRYSAËTOS
Aquila chrysaetos (Linnaeus)

PLATE 304

'As civilization advances, this noble bird, the lord of our ancient forests, will either become extirpated or driven to seek an asylum in the parts of the country where nature still preserves a savage aspect. High cultivation and its presence are incompatible; the lamb and the Eagle can never dwell together in peace . . . The Highland shepherd and the keeper therefore do their utmost to destroy it, and the time is probably not far distant when it will no longer have a place in the avifauna of the British Islands.'

Gould, anxious about the future, pleaded that landowners should protect the remaining Golden and Sea Eagles in Scotland. He quoted figures revealing that 171 eagles were destroyed in the county of Sutherland between March 1831 and March 1834 in addition to fifty-three nestlings or eggs, and that a gamekeeper 'trapped fifteen Eagles in three months of 1847, and almost as many in the winter of 1850–51'. Gould thought that the Golden Eagle, if protected, could usefully preserve the balance of nature by preying on mountain hares which had become a pest.

Day by day, during the spring of 1862, Wolf watched and drew the Golden Eagle eyries at Black Mount, Glencoe, on the Estate of the Marquis of Breadalbane. Two

tiny downy eaglets in a large bulky nest perched on a crag can be seen in the background of the illustration. The foreground adult, three or four years old, was originally reproduced at about one-third life-size.

Today there are about 420 pairs left in Scotland, one of the largest populations in Europe, but they are threatened by egg collectors, deliberately contaminated carcasses and the destruction of their habitat. They are also found across Europe, north Africa, Asia, and North America, but they are nowhere very common.

WHITE-TAILED (SEA) EAGLE
HALIAËTUS ALBICILLA
Haliaetus albicilla (Linnaeus)

PLATE 302

The Sea Eagle, or White-tailed Eagle, was depicted by Lear in *The Birds of Europe* (see plate 14) some thirty years earlier than Wolf's illustration. Lear portayed two

eagles, an adult with its distinctive white wedge-shaped tail and a darker young bird. Wolf's two birds are both adults, and the white markings are most clearly seen on the outspread tail of the eagle flying into the distance.

Wolf's illustration was probaby based on a description sent to Gould by H. Osborne Jnr of Wick, Scotland, of an eagle soaring over a precipice and veering halfway between the tops of the cliff and the sea. 'Hardly had he made his appearance when a rush of birds seawards took place. Everything that could fly left the rocks; and the terror and confusion that ensued was remarkable. This continued during the whole course of his flight; and his appearance was the signal for a hurrying of the scared masses out of the reach of danger.' Wolf's Sea Eagle zooms towards a colony of Guillemots.

Gould wrote that the Sea Eagle was then more numerous in the British Isles than the Golden Eagle, and bred in north-west Scotland and Ireland. Since then it has declined in numbers throughout much of its range, but (as mentioned in the pre-

305 Osprey (JW and HCR)

306 *Common or Eurasian Buzzard* (JW and HCR)

307 *Northern Goshawk* (JW and HCR)

308 *Northern or Eurasian Sparrowhawk* (JW and HCR)

vious entry on the Sea Eagle) successful attempts have been made to re-establish it in west Scotland.

OSPREY

PANDION HALIAËTUS

Pandion haliaetus (Linnaeus)

PLATE 305

Gould regretted that the Osprey suffered from such unrelenting persecution by gamekeepers that it had almost become exterminated in Britain. He condemned such thoughtless killing, but hoped that the Osprey, then still found in Scotland, would always 'remain associated with the fine lochs and deserted castles of that country'.

The Osprey, or Fish Hawk, became extinct as a breeder in Britain in 1916, but in 1955 a pair returned to nest in tall pines at Loch Garten in the Scottish Highlands.

The site was declared a sanctuary, and later the Royal Society for the Protection of Birds made an observation hide for visitors to view further pairs nesting on specially prepared platforms. Since their return, forty pairs have been located in Scotland and nearly six hundred young have been raised.

The Osprey hunts over the water and dives with outstretched talons, rising with the fish firmly clutched in its grasp. In the illustration the bird's catch, a fine Scottish Trout, is portrayed by Wolf with the same care as its captor.

The Osprey migrates from Britain to West Africa. It is found breeding worldwide, in North and Central America, the Mediterranean, north and eastern Europe, Asia, Africa and the Australian coast; it winters southwards into Africa, India, south-east Asia, Australia and South Africa. The Osprey shares with the Peregrine Falcon the widest distribution of any bird of prey.

COMMON OR EURASIAN BUZZARD

BUTEO VULGARIS

Buteo buteo (Linnaeus)

PLATE 306

'Those who have travelled through Germany, France, and the central parts of Europe must have frequently seen a large, heavy bird perched on a dead stump, or on an exposed branch of a tree by the roadside or in a neighbouring field.' Gould believed that the Buzzard, a familiar sight in Continental Europe, had been so much persecuted in England that it was 'almost a bird of the past'. He believed that ignorant gamekeepers were the buzzard's greatest enemy, for they were unaware of the beauty of large birds of prey, and of their use in preserving the balance of nature. These men thought only of their employers' game interests: 'their greatest pride being a well-stored larder of Hawks, Jays and Pies, and a wood full of Pheasants'.

229

Gould described the Buzzard's plumage as very variable; some birds were nearly all purplish-black, some were 'narrowly rayed with brownish-white on their breast and thighs' and others had light breasts speckled and blotched with brown. Wolf illustrated a pair of light-coloured birds, the finest Gould had ever seen, owned by John Noble of Taplow, Buckinghamshire, which had lived for three or four years in a large cage. The other smaller bird in the background was drawn from a specimen with unusually dark colouring.

Gould remarked that the wild buzzard had few friends, for it preyed equally on leverets, rabbits, pheasants and other game birds, but he hoped that this 'troublesome fellow' would never be struck off the British bird list. Today it is the commonest large bird of prey in Britain and is seen in woodlands and open country in the west and north. Its breeding range extends through much of Europe and northern Asia to Japan.

NORTHERN GOSHAWK (GOSHAWK)

ASTUR PALUMBARIUS

Accipiter gentilis (Linnaeus)

PLATE 307

Gould described the Goshawk as a stealthy hunter; it did not hover like a Kestrel, or soar like the falcons, but sat motionless in a leafy tree scanning its surroundings, and at the sight of a hare, partridge, or any other small mammal or bird, sneaked 'upon its prey in a most artful manner'.

During a visit to an estate at Somerleyton, Suffolk, the keeper showed Gould a fine female Goshawk with beautiful 'lengthened lanceolate breast markings'. This bird had shown unusual temerity; it left the woods almost daily and flew 'skulkingly up the lanes to the farm steadings, just overtopping the buildings' to pounce 'upon a hen or poult as opportunity served – the great scurry, consternation and cackling of the mother hens bringing the housewife to the door just in time to see one of her feathered charges taken over the wall'. Once too often this foray was made, for the keeper was in waiting to shoot the culprit, and the Goshawk later became a carefully preserved exhibit.

The original illustration showed an adult

female, two-thirds life-size, and a young bird in the distance. The Northern Goshawk, possibly with nine subspecies, is found throughout the forests and open woodlands of the northern hemisphere, particularly in North America, Sweden, Finland and northern Asia. In Britain goshawks almost disappeared by the beginning of this century but have started to breed again in dense woods. They are threatened by human persecution, including egg collectors and robbers of young birds for falconry.

309 Gyrfalcon (Dark Race) (JW and HCR)

NORTHERN OR EURASIAN SPARROWHAWK (SPARROWHAWK)

ACCIPITER NISUS

Accipiter nisus (Linnaeus)

PLATE 308

The illustration shows an adult male in the foreground, and in the background a female seizes a Sparrow from the ivy-clad wall of a garden.

Gould contrasted the hunting and flight of the Sparrowhawks and Kestrels. The Kestrel hovered over wide spaces, fanning the air with its long wings, whereas 'the round-winged dashing Sparrow-hawk' was more reclusive. The Sparrowhawk sat in some leafy tree, watching a flight of

starlings or a flock of larks on which to prey, and winged its way over the fields, or surprised a finch 'by overtopping the hedge and securing the terror-stricken bird in the quickness of lightning', before it could shelter in the foliage.

Gould related that the Sparrowhawk showed remarkable spirit and daring when seeking its victims. 'I have heard of a Sparrow-hawk pursuing a Finch between the legs of a man, where it had flown for shelter; and in the course of my life I have known instances of its dashing through or killing itself against a pane of glass in pursuit of a bird, or when flying at a caged bird within.' He added that female Sparrowhawks were larger and more formidable than the male birds.

The Northern or Eurasian Sparrowhawk is widely distributed from north Africa through Europe to the Pacific coast of Asia, including Japan and the Himalayas. In Britain it is fairly widespread and one of the most common birds of prey.

GYRFALCON (GREENLAND FALCON)

FALCO CANDICANS

Falco rusticolus Linnaeus

PLATE 310

This illustration is one of Wolf's most majestic pictures; the white falcons perched on crags are magnificently silhouetted against the blues of the sky and sea in the background.

Gould described the plumage of the two foreground falcons. The middle falcon was 'an unusually light and beautiful young bird of the year, with teardrop-like markings on the whole of the upper surface'. The larger figure was an adult, with 'small, somewhat heart-shaped spots at the tip of each feather on the upper surface, faint specks of brownish-white on the under surface, and the tail creamy white'.

This light-coloured falcon with almost pure white plumage and black wing-tips is now described as a Gyrfalcon (White phase). Gyrfalcons are distributed through Greenland, Iceland, northern Scandinavia and Russia, also Alaska and northern Canada. They are rare visitors to England.

13.

FALCO CANDICANS, *J.F. Gmel.*

Greenland Falcon light race adult and young

J. Wolf & H.C. Richter, del et lith.

Walter Imp.

310 *Gyrfalcon (Light Race)* (JW and HCR)

311   Gyrfalcon (JW and HCR)

312   Peregrine Falcon (JW and HCR)

Gyrfalcon (Greenland Falcon)

Falco candicans

Falco rusticolus Linnaeus

PLATE 309

Gould was puzzled by the variations of light and dark colours and markings of the large northern falcons. Even dark race falcons were so inconsistent in their markings that he had never seen two specimens alike. However, he knew that these colour differences had no relation to age and that dark birds did not become white, because a falcon which had lived at the London Zoological Gardens for several years had not shown any sign of change in its plumage.

Gould greatly valued and admired Wolf's depictions of birds of prey. He first saw the artist's life-size illustrations in a magnificent book on the history of falconry

Traité de Fauconnerie (1844–1853) by Schlegel and Wulverhorst, drawn and lithographed by Wolf before he settled in England. Gould himself owned Wolf's superb watercolour study for this volume of a falconer's hooded Gyrfalcon perched on a gloved hand.

'I cannot conclude', Gould wrote, 'without calling attention to the admirable delineations of all these large northern Falcons, for which I am indebted to the pencil of Mr. Wolf, whose abilities as an artist are so justly celebrated, and who thoroughly understands the subject. I trust they will duly be appreciated by possessors of the present work.'

The Greenland Falcon is now described as a Gyrfalcon (dark phase). Though Gould entitled this illustration 'dark race' the birds depicted are intermediate in colour between the 'dark' and 'light' phases. For light phase see plate 310.

Gyrfalcon (or Norwegian Falcon)

Falco gyrfalcon

Falco rusticolus Linnaeus

PLATE 311

This is the last of Wolf's six illustrations of the northern falcons. Gould was greatly perplexed by the differences in their size and colouring and called them the Icelandic, Greenland and Norwegian Falcons. Today, all these falcons are accepted as different forms (or phases) of one species only: the Gyrfalcon *Falco rusticolus*.

Wolf depicted an adult and a crouching dark young bird with chest feathers of brown edged with white. As in several other Wolf illustrations, an isolated single feather is placed in front of the bird to show the colours in detail.

In July 1856, during a bird-watching trip in the mountains of Dovrefjeld, Norway,

Gould and Wolf were shown a large rock where the falcons nested. Unfortunately they did not see any of the falcons, but the setting of barren crags is reminiscent of the area in which they travelled.

Gould realized that Gyrfalcons, held in high esteem by falconers, were previously used in England to capture cranes, geese and bustards. However, as the sport of falconry had declined in Europe, and he had little knowledge of the subject, he referred readers to Schlegel and Wulverhorst's impressive *Traité de Fauconnerie*.

PEREGRINE FALCON

FALCO PEREGRINUS

Falco peregrinus Tunstall

PLATE 312

'The whole structure of the Peregrine', Gould wrote, 'is admirably adapted for aerial progression, its powerful pectoral muscles, unparalleled among birds of it size, together with its long and pointed wings, enabling it ordinarily to pass through the air with a rapidity estimated by some writers at the rate of 150 miles an hour; but this rate of progression is nothing compared to the impetuosity of its stoop when descending upon its quarry.'

The *Guinness Book of Records* states that the Peregrine is probably the world's fastest bird when stooping for prey, but accurate speed measurements are difficult to make, and the maximum is probably no more than 112 miles per hour (180 kilometres per hour). The male is the better flyer, and may make faster speeds in a display dive, but dives measured at 224 miles per hour (360 kilometres per hour) are debatable.

In the background of the picture Wolf illustrated a dramatic stoop which Gould had witnessed while shooting in the Scottish Highlands. A Mallard pursued with 'meteor-like quickness' by a male Peregrine was 'struck dead, its back being ripped open by a stroke of the Peregrine's hind claw'. Gould thought that this lightning strike in mid-air was the usual way the Peregrine attacked its victim.

Gould recorded that the female, shown about three-quarters life-size in the foreground of the original print was always larger than the male. Her average weight was 37½ ounces (1.06 kg) and length 19

inches (around 48 centimetres) compared to the male's average of 23 ounces (652 g) and length 16 inches (41 centimetres).

The *Peregrinne*, which has many subspecies, is found worldwide, In Britain the nominate race *F.p. peregrinus* is increasing again after a reduction in the use of pecticides commonly used in the 1960s, though it is still threatened by the theft of eggs and young for falconry.

NORTHERN OR EURASIAN HOBBY (HOBBY)

FALCO SUBBUTEO

Falco subbuteo Linnaeus

PLATE 313

'If an ornithologist were requested to name the most elegant species of Falcon inhabiting the British Islands, he would unquestionably reply, the Hobby; for the proportions of no other raptorial bird are more evenly balanced, or the colours more harmoniously distributed.'

Gould described the Hobby as very graceful; its long pointed wings enabled it to fly long journeys for it was a summer migrant to Britain. It preyed on small swift-flying birds and large insects. Wolf's picture shows a male Hobby with a dragonfly in its claws.

313 *Northern or Eurasian Hobby* (JW and HCR)

314 *Merlin* (JW and HCR)

The Northern Hobby winters in southern Africa, India and south-east Asia, and breeds in summer in much of Europe and Asia.

MERLIN

FALCO AESALON

Falco columbarius Linnaeus

PLATE 314

'Unlike the Hobby, whose habits lead it to frequent woodland districts, or the Peregrine which gives preference to rocks and trees in the neighbourhood of water, the Merlin affects the open moor and the fell: and the more wild and desolate the district, the greater is its charm for this bold little falcon.'

The illustration shows the Merlin's nest of a few crossed heather stalks laid on the bare ground on a bleak hillside. The male parent brings its prey of a small Serin Finch for the four white downy nestlings.

Gould believed that in Britain the Merlin was less persecuted by gamekeepers than other birds of prey because it lived in such remote areas, but today it is declining in numbers probably mainly through loss of habitat. The Merlin breeds throughout northern Europe and northern Asia, also in North America where it is known as the Pigeon Hawk. Most populations appear to migrate southwards in winter.

COMMON KESTREL (KESTREL)

TINNUNCULUS ALAUDARIUS

Falco tinnunculus Linnaeus

PLATE 315

Gould thought that few people could go for a country ramble without noticing 'a stationary object between them and the sky'. This was the Kestrel, or Windhover 'scanning the earth for a mouse, a lizard, or, if it be the season of summer, a young lark or other bird. For several seconds (sometimes for a minute or more) this speck in the sky appears motionless'.

The bird could become very tame and Gould quoted an account of some children

315 *Common Kestrel* (JW and HCR)

and a Kestrel which became devoted to them. In *The Zoologist* the Rev. H.H. Crewe of Derbyshire related that a young male which his children looked after was returned to the wild, but came back every day to the nursery window even three years later. The Kestrel entered, perched on the chairs or table, and sometimes on the heads of the little ones, who always had a piece of meat for him. When the family left home, and returned calling his name, he would come 'flying over the fields, squealing with joy to see them again'.

The male Kestrel, shown on a branch of a Scots pine, can be distinguished from the

female depicted in the background, by its grey head and the black bar across the end of its grey tail.

Today the Old World or Common Kestrel is the commonest and most widespread of the falcons both in Britain and throughout Europe, and is frequently seen hovering over motorway verges. It also ranges over Africa and parts of Asia, wintering southwards as far south as Africa, south-east Asia and the Philippines.

RED KITE (KITE)

MILVUS REGALIS

Milvus milvus (Linnaeus)

PLATE 316

Gould wrote that the 'soaring, buoyant and gracefully circling flights of the Kites' differed from the impetuous stoops of true falcons. The kites did not pursue their prey but circled high in the air scanning for carrion, dead fish, insects, small rodents and fledglings.

The Kite was once a common scavenger, and in Shakespeare's day was a familiar bird in London. In Britain its population gradually dwindled to a handful of breeding birds, but today some pairs of Red Kite are carefully protected in the hill country of central Wales where there are oak woods and open spaces. Their numbers are increasing in spite of theft by egg collectors and poison from baited carcasses. The Red Kite has a restricted range, and lives only in the western Palearctic region from Britain to western Ukraine and southwards to Spain, Italy, north-west Africa and Asia Minor.

Wolf's male bird, originally depicted two-thirds life-size, is rich red with a deeply forked tail. A nest in a tree fork, shown here in the background, was usually made of sticks lined with dry grass, wool and other soft materials. Gould quoted a description of a nest in Huntingdonshire, lined with 'small pieces of linen, part of a saddle-girth, a bit of a harvest glove, part of a straw bonnet, pieces of paper, and a worsted garter; and in the midst of this singular collection of materials were deposited two eggs'.

316 *Red Kite* (JW and HCR)

BLACK KITE

MILVUS MIGRANS

Milvus migrans (Boddaert)

PLATE 317

The Black Kite is a migratory bird and is widespread through most of Europe, Australia (where it is known as the Fork-tailed Kite), Africa (where two of the three races are known as Yellow-billed Kites) and Asia (Pariah Kite). Gould knew it had a large range, for in 1867 he received a specimen from Northumberland and shortly afterwards another from northern Australia. In Britain it has been recorded on only a few occasions, but it is conceivable that the fifteenth-century scavenging kites of London were a black, not red species.

In some areas the Black Kites are scavengers and found near village rubbish dumps feeding on mice, rats, lizards and grasshoppers. Gould quoted some comments by Henry Baker Tristram, who had watched them in the Holy Land: 'The Black Kite, never once seen in winter, returns in immense numbers from the south, and in the beginning of March scatters itself over the whole country, preferring especially the neighbourhood of villages, and certainly does not appear to attack the poultry, among which it may often be seen feeding on garbage. It is not strictly gregarious, though very sociable;

MILVUS MIGRANS, *Bodd.*

J.Wolf & W.Hart del et lith.

Walter Imp.

317   Black Kite (JW and HCR)

and the slaughter of a sheep near the tents will soon attract a large party of Kites, which swoop down regardless of man and guns, and enjoy a noisy scramble for the refuse, chasing each other in a laughable fashion, and sometimes enabling the wily Raven to steal off with the coveted morsel during their contention.'

country where it still lingers.'

Since Gould's day the Tawny Owl has adapted to living also in parks, cemeteries, and large wooded areas in city centres. They hunt after dark and prey mainly on small roosting birds. They are now one of the most common owls, with at least thirteen races described, and are found throughout Europe, north-west Africa into Asia and on to China, Korea and Taiwan.

The adult owls are depicted with three young in a tree hollow. Gould described the nestlings as 'clothed with a grey down upon which, as they progress in stature,

crescentic and circular markings of reddish brown gradually appear'.

Eagle Owl
Bubo maximus
Bubo bubo (Linnaeus)
PLATE 319

Gould commented that in the past the owl had been described as 'an emblem of all that is wise or learned' or as 'an omen of

318 *Tawny Owl* (JW and HCR)

Tawny (or Brown) Owl
Syrnium aluco
Strix aluco Linnaeus
PLATE 318

Gould was perturbed by the persecution of the Tawny Owls by gamekeepers because they preyed on young birds during the breeding season. He argued that this was a one-sided judgement because the owls also destroyed large numbers of mice, voles and rats. With the change in the countryside from woodland to arable land, and owls' habitat would be lost and it was better to protect than destroy them. 'Let us then cherish the Brown Owl as a bird designated for an especial purpose; let us still hear its hollow, rolling hoot in the twilight, or listen to the challenge note of the males — the only sound which breaks the stillness of midnight in those woodland parts of the

319 *Eagle Owl* (JW and HCR)

death and other evil forebodings', but he did not care to indulge in such fancies and preferred to consider the bird itself and its habits.

Gould probably had not seen the Eagle Owl in the wild, but there were many successfully kept in captivity including some at Arundel Castle and London Zoo. His friend Edward Fountaine of Norwich had reared thirty-five birds, and in May 1865 sent Gould a live young owl as a model for the illustration. The owl arrived safely and Fountaine suggested that Gould might like to keep it.

The three young birds with their fluffy white down and purplish blue bills have a prominent place in the picture. Wolf's family scene is very different from Lear's single bird illustrated about thirty years earlier in *The Birds of Europe* (see plate 18).

This large owl has a wide distribution from Europe, north Africa through Asia to eastern Siberia and China. At least twenty subspecies or races have been described, based on pronounced geographical variations in size and plumage, the colours correlating chiefly with climatic factors.

NYCTEA NIVEA.

LONG-EARED OWL

OTUS VULGARIS

Asio otus (Linnaeus)

PLATE 321

Gould maintained that pairs of Long-eared Owls should live in every large wood or fir plantation. Unfortunately their numbers were reduced in Britain by ruthless gamekeepers and sportsmen unappreciative of their beauty, and unconvinced of their use in catching mice and young weasels.

The Long-eared Owls have elongated tufts on their foreheads, which Gould pointed out were totally unconnected with their hearing. These 'ears' are now considered to be display tufts, which can be lowered or raised according to mood and may also be used to help the owls recognize each other.

Wolf illustrates two adult owls and a nest with four young that are about a fortnight old. These owls usually use old tree nests previously belonging to crows or other birds, but sometimes they nest on the ground in heathland. The young leave the nest when about four weeks old, and have a drawn-out mournful hunger cry 'peeee-e' which sounds like a squeaky gate with unoiled hinges.

Long-eared Owls are distributed in a belt across temperate Europe and central Asia as far as Japan and throughout North America.

SNOWY OWL

NYCTEA NIVEA

Nyctea scandiaca (Linnaeus)

PLATE 320

It is interesting to compare Lear's Snowy Owl for *The Birds of Europe* (see page 17) with Wolf's illustration of some thirty years later. Lear's soft downy birds were drawn from stuffed models, whereas Wolf had the opportunity to see the live birds in captivity. In *The Birds of Great Britain* Gould recorded: 'the Snowy Owl bears confinement remarkably well as evidenced by the state of contentment in which several examples lived in the Gardens of the Zoological Society for many years.'

Lear's owls are perched on sparse tree branches, but Wolf's are posed in front of a

OTUS VULGARIS.

321 Long-eared Owl (JW and HCR)

LITTLE OWL

ATHENE NOCTUA

Athene noctua (Scopoli)

PLATE 322

In Gould's day the Little Owl was known only as a captive bird and as an occasional visitor to Britain, although it was common in mainland Europe. Gould related that on the Continent the Little Owl was well known in towns and villages for it lived 'in old ruins, church steeples, and other lofty buildings'. It flew at dusk and its cry was so eerie that the superstitious regarded it as a bird of ill-omen. He himself disregarded such feelings and hoped the owl would be more frequently seen in England.

In the late nineteenth century the species was introduced to Britain: the first recorded breeding in Kent was in 1879, and the Little Owl spread so rapidly through England and Wales that widespread accusations were made of it killing many gamebird chicks. An investigation of its diet was carried out in great detail by the British Trust for Ornithology, and proved conclusively that these charges were unfounded. The owl's food consisted chiefly of insects (earwigs, beetles, craneflies), mammals up to the size of large rats and medium rabbits, but few birds were taken. Studies elsewhere show that the diet varies seasonally and with location, but in most, invertebrates were important throughout the year.

The original plate showed the adult bird, life-size. It holds a short-tailed field mouse for its young in a tree hole behind.

detailed arctic landscape. Wolf's background illustrates Gould's description of the polar regions where floating icebergs became detached from the ice-bound mainland. Gould narrated that in these solitary areas, the Snowy Owl 'in the company of Polar Bears . . . spends much of its time; and its whole structure, colouring and thick plumage are wonderfully adapted for such a mode of life'.

Gould added that in the breeding season the owls moved south to Norway, Finland and Russia, where their food of hares and lemmings was more abundant. He concluded by admitting: 'In the British Islands, therefore, my readers will be prepared to learn that it is only a chance visitor.'

The female is depicted in the foreground with the all-white adult male and what is probably a young male in the background.

322 Little Owl (JW and HCR)

VOLUME II

EURASIAN NIGHTJAR (NIGHTJAR)

CAPRIMULGUS EUROPAEUS

Caprimulgus europaeus Linnaeus

PLATE 324

The Nightjar was traditionally known as the goatsucker, due to an ancient belief that it sucked milk from goats' teats with its large mouth. Gould believed that this strange notion originated because nightjars frequented grazing land where their insect food was plentiful.

Like other nocturnal birds, nightjars were linked with superstition. Country folk said that those who harmed the Nightjar or its eggs could become 'puckeridge struck'; Gould interpreted this enigmatic phrase as a reference to the fact that horses when startled by nightjars had been known to throw their riders at night. He thought that only a few night travellers, about 'one in a thousand persons', ever saw the Nightjar, but its 'vibrating or chirring notes', which sounded like a spinning-wheel, could be heard at intervals from sundown to sunrise. During the day the bird rested quietly on the ground in barren

324 Eurasian Nightjar (HCR)

heaths, woods with open glades or copses near meadows.

The Nightjar was a summer visitor to Britain, arriving in May from Africa. It nested on the bare earth, and its two young, at first blind, were plentifully fed until they were able to move about and fend for themselves. Gradually they gained strength for their autumn journey south by hawking in the air on the abundant moths and other insects available in midsummer.

Nightjars are now becoming scarce in Europe; where their numbers are declining through habitat loss, disturbance and a decrease in insects due to pesticides. It is more accurately known as the Eurasian Nightjar for it breeds in much of Europe and through to central Asia and south to North Africa. Winter quarters are in Africa as far south as Cape Province.

BARN SWALLOW (SWALLOW)

HIRUNDO RUSTICA

Hirundo rustica Linnaeus

PLATE 323

The Swallow was indeed the 'true harbinger of spring', for in Britain it arrived in early or late April after wintering in Africa and often returned to the same nest site. Gould wrote: 'Like the prodigal child it has come again and we give it a true welcome.'

Swallows nested in 'the inner side of a smoking chimney, a shaft of a mine, the rafters beneath a bridge, barn or boat-house'. About mid-June the young left their cup-shaped mud nest, perched on neighbouring branches, took short flights and preened their feathers. Sometimes, as portrayed in the illustration, they were fed in mid-air by an adult. In the picture several other swallows are reflected in the stream as they fly over the surface of the water.

In the autumn the swallows collected in vast multitudes 'upon house-tops, church roofs, telegraphic wires, and trees beside rivers and ponds' in preparation for their long journey south to Africa. Some young birds from late broods were not strong enough to travel and their bodies were found in sheltered caves and crevices. Gould thought that these dead birds may have given rise to the widely held but absurd belief that swallows hid under the water, or hibernated in holes and caverns during the winter.

This species of Swallow seen in Britain, also known as Barn Swallow, has an extensive distribution from North America south to Mexico, throughout Continental Eurasia to Kamchatka and Japan, and south to north-west Africa and east to Iran, north-west India, China and Taiwan. Their wintering grounds are in South America, tropical and south Africa, Egypt, India and south-east Asia.

323 Barn Swallow (HCR)

SAND MARTIN

COTYLE RIPARIA

Riparia riparia (Linnaeus)

PLATE 325

The Sand Martin usually preceded the swallow and arrived in Britain at the end of March or beginning of April. Gould described the bird as the smallest of Britain's hirundines, yet despite its frail appearance it was 'a wondrous miner', and excavated numerous nesting holes of burrows in sandbanks or railway cuttings.

The illustration shows the martins as they gather together in thousands during the evenings for two or three weeks before their migration. Gould saw these larger twittering congregations by the Thames during August and September. 'Those who have not seen these vast assemblages can form but a faint conception of the sight . . . I have frequently observed masses of these birds collect high up in the air, and, having performed circular flights and other evolutions, descend, with a loud rushing sound, to the willow-beds like a shower of stones – the willows upon which they settle being completely covered and bowed down by the united weight of these little birds, which sit side by side for warmth and the occupation of the least possible space.' A young bird surveys the scene in the foreground.

In Britain the Sand Martin has recently declined in numbers and some long-established colonies are empty, perhaps due to prolonged periods of drought in the southern Sahara.

The species of Sand Martin seen in Britain is common in many parts of the northern hemisphere, breeding throughout Continental Eurasia to Kamchatka and Japan, south into northern Africa, northern India and south-east to China. The same species also breeds throughout North America; there is a southward movement to wintering areas in tropical Africa, India, south-east Asia and South America.

EURASIAN NUTHATCH (NUTHATCH)

SITTA CAESIA

Sitta europaea Linnaeus

PLATE 327

Gould described the Nuthatch as a very curious and amusing little woodland bird. It could be identified by its loud repetitious note and then spotted rushing 'round the boles and branches in a series of short jumps, or performing a dipping flight from tree to tree'. Unlike the Woodpecker or Treecreeper, the Nuthatch looked for insects by running obliquely over the main trunk and smaller branches, often with its head downwards and 'never making use of its tail as a support'. At other times it

325 *Sand Martin* (WH)

would search the ground for nuts and cherry-stones, wedge them in a chink, fork, or a slit in a railing, and peg away with its hatchet-like bill until the kernel was reached and eaten.

The illustration shows adult birds by a nest cavity. The Nuthatch nests in the hole of a tree, and like the Hornbill, often plasters up the opening with mud, leaving just enough room for the bird to enter.

In Britain the Nuthatch is found in woodlands throughout England and Wales but not in Scotland or Ireland.

The species, more accurately named the Eurasian Nuthatch, which has had many

326 Great Tit (HCR)

races described, breeds from southern Scandinavia east across Eurasia to Siberia, south into Morocco, Sicily through to Iran and in the Far East from Japan, China and Indochina to India.

GREAT TIT

PARUS MAJOR

Parus major Linnaeus

PLATE 326

Gould thought that the 'spirited, cheerful, sprightly' Great Tit, the largest British tit, was familiar to everyone living in the countryside. Its loud call was heard during spring in woods or hedgerows and described as like a saw sharpening, or the words 'sit-ye-down' or 'ox-eye'. These various descriptions caused Gould to comment that 'sounds uttered by birds strike the ear so differently that what would be music to one person is discordance to another'. Today the favoured onomatopoeic interpretation is 'tea-cher, tea-cher' or the sound of a bicycle pump!

The Great Tit was said to be no friend of the farmer, because it destroyed buds and picked holes in ripening fruit. Gould thought it untrue that tits harmed buds, because they attacked only those infected with insects and larvae, but he kept silent about its other activities as he wished to protect 'this very interesting species'.

The tits usually nested in a wall crevice or hole in a tree, but sometimes they chose very unusual places, and Gould had heard of them flying through a small hole to nest on cupboard shelves or in an inverted flower-pot. At Preston Hall, Kent, the keeper lifted the top off a box to show him a female nesting for the third year close to the piston rod of a pump that was constantly working.

This adult male and female are shown on a poplar branch gathered 'when it was loaded with catkins' in Ravensbury Park, Mitcham.

This variable and complex species, which may have as many as thirty-one subspecies, has a wide breeding range across the greater part of Eurasia from Britain to east Siberia, Japan and China, and southwards to north-west Africa, the Middle East, Iran, Iraq, and India through south-east Asia.

327 Eurasian Nuthatch (HCR)

328 Long-tailed Tit (WH)

Long-tailed Tit

Mecistura caudata

Aegithalos caudatus (Linnaeus)

PLATE 329

'Wonderful, indeed, is the architectural skill displayed by the Long-tailed Tit in the construction of its closely felted nest, so warmly lined with feathers, and externally bespangled with lichens. Who can behold it without feeling the highest admiration of the bird's skill and perseverance?'

The illustration shows an oval nest found on 2 May 1861 in the garden at Formosa, near Cliveden, by the Thames. Gould's son Franklin was set the task of counting the feathers in the lining, and found some two thousand belonging to the peacock, turkey, partridge, domestic hen, greenfinch, woodpigeon and other birds. The wall of the nest was made of moss and cow-hair, and the exterior composed of minute pieces of lichen fastened to the moss by spiders' silky cobwebs. It contained ten eggs and weighed 142 grains (¼ ounce or 6.5 grams).

As their nests had only a tiny side entrance, Gould could not imagine how twelve or thirteen newly hatched young could be fed at the bottom in utter darkness. Sometimes the adults roosted in the nest with their brood, and sat happily side by side with their tails uplifted. In the picture the young at the nest entrance wait with gaping mouths for caterpillars to be brought by their parents.

Long-tailed Tits breed fairly commonly in deciduous and mixed woodlands throughout Europe.

The species, which has had up to twenty subspecies described, has an extensive distribution across Eurasia from Britain, Scandinavia to Kamchatka, south to Sicily, southern Iran, northern Mongolia and in the Far East to the Yangtse in China, and Japan.

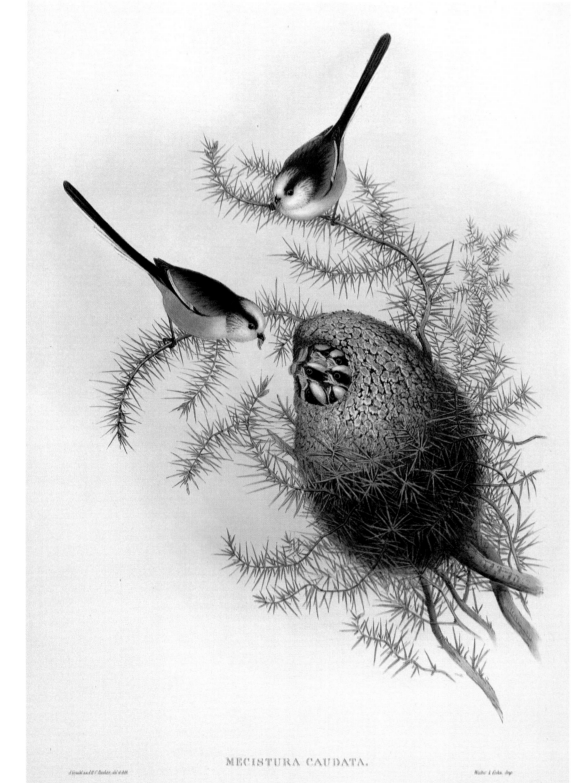

MECISTURA CAUDATA.

Long-tailed Tit

Mecistura caudata

Aegithalos caudatus (Linnaeus)

PLATE 328

The illustration shows a row of young Long-tailed or Bottle Tits which have just left their nest. Gould described how these young birds sat on the sunny side of a branch and were fed by their parents until they gathered enough strength to flit about and catch their own insects. At night they crowded together on a low branch 'in a huddled heap resembling a ball of feathers'. When the sun broke out in the early morning, the little tits could be seen sitting in a row facing the warmth, 'or perched alternatively head and tail so regularly as to astonish those who for the first time witness it'.

Hart's picture, added at the end of the series, illustrates Gould's field observations and is a charming divergence from Richter's frequently used formula of one or two birds and their young with their appropriate background.

329 *Long-tailed Tit* (HCR)

BEARDED REEDLING (TIT)

CALAMOPHILUS BIARMICUS

Panurus biarmicus (Linnaeus)

PLATE 330

Gould regretted that due to changes in farming and the draining of flat lands, particularly in Cambridgeshire, Huntingdonshire and Norfolk, the Bearded Tit had diminished in numbers. These elegant, delicately coloured little birds fed on insects in summer and reed seeds in winter

and depended on the fenlands for their habitat.

Today, the Bearded Tit, sometimes called the Bearded Reedling, is considered to be unrelated to the tit family and is akin to the Parrotbills of Asia. It lives among thick reed beds but suffers badly in severe winters. Recently numbers have been helped by the maintenance of reed beds in East Anglia and Kent bird reserves.

The illustration shows the adult male with its distinctive black drooping moustache, grey head and black under-tail

coverts. The female has buff under-tail coverts and a general fawn colour. In the distance are a number of young birds flitting past a nest set low among the reeds and bullrushes.

The species breeds locally from southeast England through Continental Europe across to southern Russia, Iran and Afghanistan to Siberia, Mongolia, northern China and south to Spain, Italy, the Balkan states, and Turkey. They winter within their breeding range and south to central China.

SONG THRUSH

TURDUS MUSICUS

Turdus philomelos Brehm

PLATE 331

Gould commented that few birds had inspired so much poetry as the Song Thrush. This was not surprising as it was one of the earliest spring birds to burst into powerful song in gardens, woods and hedgerows.

The blue speckled eggs were laid in a nest made of sticks, moss and leaves, and lined with pieces of rotten wood bound with mud and water. When the chicks hatched the thrushes ceased singing and attended to their young ones, which soon grew to the size of their parents. Thrushes often bred a second time and their distinctive song of repetitive phrases was again heard during summer and autumn. In the winter some birds migrated south to warmer districts.

Gould gave an account of the merciless shooting and trapping of migrant thrushes on the Continent for food. In some areas, particularly Belgium, it was a tradition for whole families to make snares, shoot and capture Song Thrushes. Even today the thrush can appear as an item on a Continental menu.

The illustration shows a male perched near the nest on a spray of dog rose, and above is a female singing. Song Thrushes live in woodlands, thickets, scrubland, parks and gardens. They breed from Britain, Scandinavia, and northern Spain across most of Europe through to western Siberia to Lake Baikal and extreme western China. They winter from west and southern Europe south to north Africa, Arabia and Iran.

330 Bearded Reedling (HCR)

331 Song Thrush (HCR)

BLACKBIRD

MERULA VULGARIS

Turdus merula Linnaeus

PLATE 332

Gould regarded the Blackbird as one of the most perfectly formed of birds: 'its bill is in just proportion to the size of its head; its wings, which are neither long or short, to that of its body; while its tail, legs, and feet are all in unison therewith.' With its balanced shape the Blackbird was equally at ease on the ground, in the air, or among the branches of the trees.

Gould described the Blackbird through the seasons. In winter its ebony blackness contrasted with the snow and its shivering

flight could be seen along the ditches and hedgerows. During spring it became spirited and bold, it ran and jumped over the lawn with its wings drooping and tail jerking. At midsummer every wood had a blackbird singing and answering, and by autumn it seldom rested without making a 'shrill, bickering, noisy chatter' in the evenings. The illustration shows the brown female sitting on her nest among the honeysuckle. The male is entirely black, except for the bill and the ring surrounding its eye, which are rich orange.

The species, which according to some authorities has up to sixteen subspecies, is found breeding from the Azores and Canary Islands, north-west Africa, throughout Europe eastward through Asia Minor to

Iran, Turkestan, northern Afghanistan, the Himalayas to Tibet and southern China. Some migrate south as far as Egypt, southern Iraq and south-east Asia.

WHITE-THROATED OR EURASIAN DIPPER (WATER OUZEL OR DIPPER)

CINCLUS AQUATICUS

Cinclus cinclus (Linnaeus)

PLATE 333

Gould described the Dipper as living in some of the most solitary, romantic and beautiful parts of the country, where the ornithologist could 'while away many hours in pleasureable delight' watching the bird by upland streams and lowland rivers.

Gould wrote: 'It is, indeed, very interesting to observe this pretty bird walk down a stone, quietly descend into the water, rise again perhaps at the distance of several yards down the stream, and wing its way back.' As its plumage seemed impervious to wet, the pearly drops which roll off into the stream' were the only evidence of its immersion.

Gould commented that the bird seemed to defy the laws of specific gravity by being able to stay and feed at the river bottom. Some naturalists thought that this was because it was able to cling to the pebbles with its sharp claws or make very rapid wing movements. However, modern studies have shown that when the bird walks upstream with its head down looking for food, the force of the current against its slanting back keeps it on the bottom.

The illustration shows a nest taken from a rock shelf on the River Usk, South Wales, and sent to Gould by Colonel Watkyns. It was domed and made of matted green moss lined with grasses and dead oak leaves, but had been trampled down and altered in shape by its tenants, the four vigorous youngsters.

The Dipper, more accurately and less parochially called the Eurasian or White-throated Dipper, is found in rapidly flowing rocky streams from Britain, Scandinavia, south to north-west Africa and the Mediterranean region, east to the Urals and south-west Asia to the Himalayas, central China and Mongolia.

332 Blackbird (HCR)

CINCLUS AQUATICUS.

333 White-throated or Eurasian Dipper (HCR)

NORTHERN WHEATEAR (WHEATEAR)

SAXICOLA OENANTHE

Oenanthe oenanthe (Linnaeus)

PLATE 334

Gould described the Wheatear's habitat as 'open downs, commons, heaths, and moorlands', and also solitary mountainous areas. 'If you ascend a glen in the Highlands from the sea-shore to its upper limits, the Wheatear is sure to be one of the few birds which greet you at every turn in the valley, and may be seen on every stony projection, livelily flirting its tail and showing the conspicuous patch of white on its rump, as it flits bobbingly from stone to stone or rock to rock.'

The Wheatears are migratory birds and make spectacular journeys. Gould related how they left tropical Africa in early spring and flew during summer to Britain, many parts of Europe, Iceland and even further north to the Arctic. They usually reached England in early March, when they could be seen on the downs around Brighton, Beachy Head and other parts of Sussex, before flying to Yorkshire and Derbyshire, where some bred while others continued northwards.

In the eighteenth century the Wheatear was considered a culinary delicacy, and Gould recounted how thousands had been trapped on the south coast during their migration. By the mid-nineteenth century numbers were already declining.

The illustration shows a male and female in the foreground with a Spider Orchid *Ophrys aranifera*.

The Wheatear, or more accurately the Northern Wheatear, has a wide distribution from northern North America, Greenland, Iceland, Spitsbergen through Europe to northern Asia and south to north-west Africa. It winters mainly in central Africa.

334 Northern Wheatear (HCR)

ERYTHACUS RUBECULA.

J.Gould & H.C.Richter, del. et lith.

Walter Imp.

335 European Robin (HCR)

EUROPEAN ROBIN (ROBIN)

ERYTHACUS RUBECULA

Erithacus rubecula (Linnaeus)

PLATE 335

'Of all the birds inhabiting our islands the Robin is the one most universally known, and the one which receives protection from every hand. The villager in his garden regards its presence with favour, and the lady in her greenhouse likes to see it hop before her from flower-stem to flower-stem. Its name is a hallowed one on our memories, from the pleasing associations imprinted thereon by the nursery rhymes and tales of our infancy. "Who Killed Cock Robin?" and the "Babes in the Wood" are never forgotten.'

The Robin was found in gardens, shrubberies, hedgerows, lanes, gullies and woods. Whether a garden pet or woodland bird it was fearless of intruders, and showed its curiosity by hopping from a twig for a crumb. It was usually alone, for it did not associate with other birds except the female during the breeding season.

'Every Robin has a limited area over which its reigns supreme, until a stronger one either kills or drives it away and takes it place.' The Robin was very pugnacious and a tyrant towards other birds. Gould thought its popularity perhaps stemmed from its sweet, intense song, which was heard thoughout the year, even in winter.

The illustration shows adult birds feeding their young in a nest among the common Ivy *Hedera helix.*

The Robin, more accurately known as the European Robin which distinguishes it from other robins, breeds from Britain and Scandinavia through Continental Europe into Russia and Asia Minor to western Siberia and northern Iran, and south to the eastern Atlantic islands, north-west Africa across to extreme south Russia.

RUTICILLA PHŒNICURA.

J. Gould and H.C.Richter del et lith.

Walter & Cohn, Imp.

COMMON REDSTART (REDSTART)

RUTICILLA PHOENICURA

Phoenicurus phoenicurus (Linnaeus)

PLATE 336

Gould described the Redstart as a migrant to Britain from Africa. It arrived in early spring when its fiery, red tail would be recognized in orchards, woods and gardens.

The Redstart nested in a variety of places and often returned to the same location. 'In the forest it is a small hole in the tree, in the village lane, a hollow space in pollard oak, in the garden, the cankered apple-branch, or between the upright boards of the tool-house.' Although a shy bird, it sometimes made its home near houses, and was even known to nest in the midst of a box of croquet balls in the orangery at Cliveden, near Taplow.

The illustration shows two males with their bright plumage, and the duller brown female in the nest cavity.

The Common Redstart breeds in the British Isles and northern Scandinavia through Europe to central Russia and Siberia to Lake Baikal, and south to north-west Africa, north Mediterranean region east to Iran and on into east Kazakhstan. It winters in southern Arabia and from Ethiopia, Kenya to west Africa.

336 *Common Redstart* (HCR)

DUNNOCK, HEDGE-SPARROW OR HEDGE-ACCENTOR

ACCENTOR MODULARIS

Prunella modularis (Linnaeus)

PLATE 337

The Hedge Sparrow was of very special importance for Gould as it brought back a happy childhood memory: 'How well do I remember the day when my father lifted me by the arms to look into the nest of a Hedgesparrow in a shrub in our garden! This first sight of its beautiful verditer-blue egg has never been forgotten; from that moment I became enamoured with nature and her charming attributes; it was then I

received an impulse which has not only never lost its influence, but has gone on acquiring a new force through a long life.'

Like the Robin, the Hedge Sparrow was a 'stay-at-home', living among the same surroundings summer and winter, and was so well known that it was 'part and parcel' of the countryside. It shuffled beneath the hedges, hopped over the lawn and gravel paths, 'never mounting to a conspicuous position, but creeping about more like a mouse than a bird'. As its food consisted chiefly of insects it was beneficial to gardens. The bird had a pleasing, simple song, though not 'so spirited and continuous as that of the Robin'.

Gould concluded by stating that the

common name 'sparrow' was incorrect for this species, for it was not related to true sparrows. Ornithologists today prefer the name Dunnock, a country word meaning 'dun-coloured bird', or Hedge Accentor, which was the alternative name Gould used in the title.

The Dunnock breeds from the British Isles through most of Continental Europe east to Asia Minor, the Caucasus and northern Iran. Partially migratory, northern populations winter south to the Mediterranean islands and north Africa.

WHITETHROAT OR GREATER WHITETHROAT

SYLVIA CINEREA

Sylvia communis Latham

PLATE 338

Gould described the Whitethroat as an interesting little bird found in bramble patches, blackthorn thickets and furze clumps. 'Its mirthful, hurried song', its 'scoldings and defiant actions' when its nest was disturbed, and the restless way in which it flew about and perched on the hedges 'with its erected crest and elevated tail' were familiar to all who strolled along a country lane or common.

The Whitethroats feed on aphids, flies and other insects, but also eat garden fruits and hedgerow berries. In September and October they fly to Africa, but droughts south of the Sahara have recently reduced their numbers.

The illustration shows adult birds with a bramble *Rubus caesius*. Richter was particularly adept at depicting little dull brown birds in an everyday patch of English hedgerow. The scene is enlivened by a bright Red Admiral butterfly.

The Whitethroat, sometimes called the Greater Whitethroat, breeds from the British Isles, and central Scandinavia and Iberia east to south-west Siberia, north Mongolia and extreme west China and south to north Africa, north Mediterranean region through Iran to north Pakistan and probably northern India. It winters in tropical and southern Africa.

337 Dunnock, Hedge-sparrow or Hedge-accentor (HCR)

338   *Whitethroat or Greater Whitethroat* (HCR)

339 *Wren or Winter Wren* (HCR)

Dartford Warbler

Melizophilus provincialis

Sylvia undata (Boddaert)

PLATE 340

Britain's first record of the Dartford Warbler was in 1773, on Bexley Heath, near Dartford in Kent. Gould related that it was so much sought after by bird and egg collectors that he feared it was becoming scarce in Wimbledon Common and Blackheath near London, although it was still abundant in many parts of Surrey and Hampshire.

Gould described the Dartford Warbler as 'shy, recluse and mouse-like'. It was also called the 'furze-wren' and lived among thick beds of furze or whin and in heathland. From a high spray, now and then, the male would pour forth a 'little warbling song', and could be seen 'bobbingly flying from place to place, each flight terminating in a dive down into the thickest part of the covert, through which it creeps and runs with the greatest facility'.

In May 1861, Gould and his son Franklin went to the heathlands at Frensham Ponds, near Farnham, Surrey, where the 'furze-wren' was known to be breeding. Near some hills called the Devil's Jumps they watched the warblers and found a nest with four eggs built in a bunch of thick heather.

The Dartford Warbler is now rare in England, and is resident only on commons and heaths in the southern counties. It is an entirely insectivorous bird and can be

340 *Dartford Warbler* (HCR)

badly hit by severe winters.

The Dartford Warbler is also found in thick scrub, dense thorn-scrub and shrubby salt-flats of south-west Europe and north-west Africa.

Wren or Winter Wren (Common Wren)

Troglodytes europaeus

Troglodytes troglodytes (Linnaeus)

PLATE 339

Gould thought that the name *Troglodytes* (one who creeps in a hole) was very appropriate for the Wren, for it liked to roost in holes, caverns and hollow stems of decayed trees.

The Wren was described as 'a cheery little bird', which could be both shy and familiar. Its shyness was shown by its habit of diving into a thicket and running mouse-like in and out of the plants, or of 'creeping through the interstices in a stone wall, and flying unseen to a distance'. It showed boldness, on the other hand, by announcing its presence with a 'sprightly warbling song' poured forth from a prominent position, or by looking for insects and spiders in flower-beds, greenhouses, barns and even pig-sties.

The Wren was often seen on the ground, where its brown colouring harmonized with 'the lower part of the heath, the ditch-bottom, and the decaying logs on which it dwells'. It nested in a bank of ivy, a crevice in a willow, or the thatch of a barn, and sometimes made additional domed roosting places or 'cock-nests', where the birds together gathered for warmth during the winter season.

The illustration shows adult birds feeding a young bird on the Common Hop *Humulus lupulus*.

The Wren or Winter Wren has an extraordinarily extensive range right through the Holaretic. Not surprisingly a species with such a wide distribution shows considerable clinal variation, and up to forty subspecies have been described. The validity of many is questionable.

Common or Eurasian Treecreeper (Tree-creeper)

Certhia familiaris

Certhia familiaris Linnaeus

PLATE 341

Gould described the Treecreeper as a little, creeping, mouse-like bird often seen 'traversing the boles and horizontal branches of the larger trees, the palings of an enclosure, or (among other places) the upright sides of an old wall', where it searched for spiders and other insects.

He also quoted a story which demonstrated the bird's mouse-like habits. Professor Richard Owen (later the first Superintendant of the Natural History Museum, London) related that while walking in his garden at Richmond Park, his son exclaimed 'Why! a mouse has just run between the bark and stem of that Acacia.' The Professor looked to see, and out popped a little treecreeper, which solved the mystery, and its nest was found 'snugly ensconced in the crevice'.

The illustration shows the male (below) and female feeding their young in the nest cavity of a tree covered with lichen.

The Common Treecreeper breeds through much of Eurasia from the British Isles and southern Scandinavia locally to southern Europe, east across to Sakhalm and south through to central and south-west China, north Pakistan, north India, south-east Tibet, north-east Burma and Japan.

CERTHIA FAMILIARIS, *Linn*.

J.Gould & H.C.Richter, del et lith.　　Walter. Imp.

341 Common or Eurasian Treecreeper (HCR)

253

VOLUME III

PIED WAGTAIL

MOTACILLA YARRELLI

Motacilla alba yarrellii Gould

PLATE 342

Gould thought that all those interested in birds must enjoy watching the Pied Wagtail as it tripped over the lawn, ran along by the riverside, performed 'its dipping flights from one place to another', or bobbed its tail up and down in constant motion. He believed that its delicately formed legs and feet, sharp eyes, and rounded short bill were ideally suited for catching small insects with quick-footed agility. By the water's edge it would rush about, apart from other birds, and sometimes run breast-high into the stream, leap on a floating leaf, stone, or a water-plant.

In 1837 Gould pointed out to other ornithologists that Pied Wagtails in Britain had slightly different markings from those in Europe. He marvelled that 'a mere strait of only some thirty miles should form a boundary' between a variation of colour.

The European race, the White Wagtail (*Motacilla alba alba*), differs from the Pied Wagtail by its pale grey rump and back. The White Wagtail is a common visitor to Britain on passage in the spring and autumn, and pairs sometimes stay to breed or individuals interbreed with the more residential Pied Wagtail. We now know the Pied Wagtail breeds throughout the British isles, and occasionally on adjacent Continental European coasts from northern France east to south Norway.

The illustration shows the male (right), young bird (centre) with yellow colouring on its face and throat, and female.

YELLOWHAMMER (OR YELLOW BUNTING)

EMBERIZA CITRINELLA

Emberiza citrinella Linnaeus

PLATE 343

Gould stated that 'Yellow Bunting' was the correct name for this species, but 'Yellow-Hammer' was the word generally known

342 *Pied Wagtail* (HCR)

343 *Yellowhammer* (HCR)

throughout Britain. The German for bunting was 'ammer' and the English name was derived from a corruption of this word.

The male Yellowhammer was described as a showy bird. In summer it looked very striking among the brambles in hedges of country lanes, where it often sang 'its singular ditty' (traditionally 'little-bit-of-bread-and-NO-cheese') from some prominent twig especially in the early mornings.

During autumn the Yellowhammers took to the open fields where they fed on grain and seeds, and in winter they mingled with other birds to join large flocks which were often seen in farmyards.

Gould remarked that the Yellowhammers varied very much in colouring. Some males had beautiful clear yellow heads,

some had 'a well-defined light chestnut moustache' on the lower part of the face, and others had 'the head and cheeks suffused with dark brown, without a trace of the moustache'.

The plate shows the female (below) with the male on a flowering branch of bramble. The flower on the ground is the Lesser Wintergreen *Pyrola minor* which was sent to Gould by Rev. H. Harpur-Crewe.

The Yellowhammer breeds in Europe and west Asia. The northern populations winter in the southern parts of their breeding range and beyond into north Africa and in south-west and central Asia.

SNOW BUNTING (OR SNOWFLAKE)

PLECTROPHANES NIVALIS

Plectrophenax nivalis (Linnaeus)

PLATE 344

Gould remarked that unlike the inhospitable Antarctic, the shores of the Arctic provided enough summer vegetation and insect life to nurture several small bird species. The most striking of these was the Snow Bunting, 'a species which, from its abundance and extreme tameness, must be to the Esquimaux what the Sparrow and Wagtail are to us.'

Gould described the severe winter conditions in the arctic from which perished his friends, the explorer Franklin and his crew, and nearly all other living creatures.

The Snow Buntings were more fortunate for they could fly to warmer areas. He related that during September and October Britain was visited by large numbers of these birds, particularly the eastern coast and 'the great promontory of Norfolk'. Gould quoted from Mr Saxby in the *Zoologist*: 'Seen against a dark hill-side or lowering sky, a flock of these birds presents an exceedingly beautiful appearance, and it may be then seen how appropriate the term 'Snowflake' is for this species.'

Gould found that the Snow Buntings had many different colourings according to age and season. The breeding plumage of the male was jet black and snow white. The female was browner, with dark streaks on the head and back and much less white on the shoulder, although the under surface was white like the male. In the illustration are four young birds, with olive-brown backs, tawny bellies and white shoulders. A small figure in the background shows the tawny colouring of the adult in autumn and winter.

Their breeding distribution is circumpolar in arctic and subarctic areas of the Eurasian and American continents and adjacent islands in the North Atlantic and Bering Sea, north to the summer limit of ice in Greenland, south to the continental

coasts of the Arctic Ocean, the Faeroes, Scotland and Scandinavia. They winter south to continental Europe, Asia and the U.S.A.

HOUSE SPARROW

PASSER DOMESTICUS

Passer domesticus (Linnaeus)

PLATE 345

'Would England be England without the presence of the saucy impudent Sparrow?' Gould asked. He described the sparrow as an 'institution' and so much part of everyday life that it was barely noticed. Nevertheless, the sparrow, like the dog, was man's constant companion and followed him in all his travels. The House Sparrow had left the clean air of the countryside to live in villages and thickly populated towns and cities.

Gould wrote that the sparrow had taken advantage of man's hospitality by becoming 'the most bold and impudent of our native birds'. It caused trouble through 'flooding our houses by stopping up our water-pipes with its huge nest', or 'disturbing our rest by its incessant bickerings

345 *House Sparrow* (HCR)

before our windows at the dawn of day'. At the very moment he was writing, on 15 August 1863, some young sparrows were noisily chirruping in a hole near his bedroom window in Charlotte Street, Bedford Square.

The sparrow was no mean-looking bird, but had many 'pleasing and harmonious colours' especially in summer. When the male displayed to the female, the silver-grey of its crown looked 'like a coronet', surrounded with streaks of chestnut and black. London birds were much duller due to their surroundings of 'smoke and other impurities'.

Gould described the nest as 'a very large, warm, and dome-shaped structure, composed of grasses wound round and round with the greatest ingenuity, and lined with feathers, bits of rags and other warm materials'. Nests in tree hollows or under the eaves of houses were not so large or elegant as those in tree branches. The garden nest in the illustration was such an amazing example of bird architecture that it was placed on exhibition in the British Museum.

This apparently ubiquitous species has been successfully introduced to many parts of the world though its original distribution was confined to Eurasia from the British Isles and Iberia east to north Manchuria, north to northern Russia and south to the Sahara, Sudan, Arabia and India.

344 *Snow Bunting* (HCR)

346 *Eurasian Goldfinch* (HCR)

EURASIAN GOLDFINCH (GOLDFINCH)

CARDUELIS ELEGANS

Carduelis carduelis (Linnaeus)

PLATE 346

In Victorian times the Goldfinch was a popular cage-bird, especially in the poorer areas of London. Gould described how vast numbers were captured by bird-catchers to be sold to bird-dealers for 'two shillings and sixpence or three shillings a dozen'. In the early morning the bird-catcher 'trudged by lamp-light through the streets of London, carrying his nets and cages on his back', to arrive in the country at day-break, when he set out his ground-nets or took young birds from their nests. Vivid details of the bird-catcher's life and conversation were recorded in Henry Mayhew's *London Labour and the London Poor*, 1851 – an epic work of social life referred to by Gould in his text. Gould found that sometimes these bird-catchers were 'excellent observers in their way' and could report on the arrival of unusual migrants from abroad.

The Goldfinches, which were present all year in Britain, moved to the open uplands and commons in small groups or 'charms' once the breeding season was over, and fed on their favourite plants, thistle, groundsel and plantain. The illustration shows the male (right) with the female on a wild Common Teasel *Dipsacus sylvestris*.

The Goldfinch, more strictly the Eurasian Goldfinch, breeds across Europe

347 *Western or European Greenfinch* (HCR)

through to Mongolia, Turkestan and the Himalayas north to western Siberia, east and south to the Atlantic islands, northwest Africa, the Near East, Iran, Afghanistan, north Pakistan, north India and west China. It is partially migratory with the northern populations wintering southwards.

WESTERN OR EUROPEAN GREENFINCH (GREENFINCH)

LIGURINUS CHLORIS

Carduelis chloris (Linnaeus)

PLATE 347

'The Greenfinch, as seen in our gardens during the month of April or at the time of pairing, is a very joyous and interesting bird. The male then displays itself to the greatest advantage, rising in the air with outspread wings and tail, frequently turning and pirouetting, as it were, and returning to the same tree or branch, uttering all the time its loud ringing whistle.' Gould remarked that in flight, the silvery under-

surface of the male's wing showed very clearly in contrast to the yellow and olive colours of its body.

'In winter', Gould continued, 'it frequents the fields, hedgerows and woods, and, if the weather becomes severe and the ground carpeted with snow, assembles in flocks round the farm-steadings and the immediate vicinity of houses.' Today, the Greenfinch is a frequent visitor to garden bird-tables and even drives away other birds!

The Greenfinch's nest, found in gardens and shrubberies, and even near the windows of houses, was usually made of roughly interlaced roots and moss, and lined with wool or hair. In the illustration the male and female birds are shown with their nest and young birds on a branch of the pink-flowering May.

More correctly termed the Western or European Greenfinch, this species breeds throughout Europe to the Urals and through Asia Minor, northern Iran and southern Transcaspia to Turkestan south into northern Africa. Though generally resident some move south in winter into north Africa, Iraq and southern Iran.

EURASIAN OR NORTHERN BULLFINCH (BULLFINCH)

PYRRHULA VULGARIS

Pyrrhula pyrrhula (Linnaeus)

PLATE 348

Gould wrote that the Bullfinch lived in woodlands, especially among larch trees, but also liked hedgerows and plantations both in lowland and hilly districts. In spring it often caused damage to fruit trees in gardens by eating the flower buds. Gould remarked: 'This trait in its character has very justly obtained it many enemies.'

The Bullfinch's nest was usually placed in a shrub or low tree. The beautifully constructed nest in the illustration was found in April 1859, on a branch of a box-tree in the woods of Taplow Court near the Thames. The platform for the nest was made of the dead stalks of Traveller's Joy *Clematis vitalba*, arranged with the heads outwards. The nest itself was composed of fine roots, tendrils and hair.

Many years later, in 1872, John Ruskin visited the elderly naturalist, and was shown this nest as a superb example of architecture. Ruskin waxed lyrical at the complexity of the withered wild clematis twigs, which he typically described as like 'an intricate Gothic boss of extreme grace and quaintness, apparently arranged both with triumphant pleasure in the art of basket-making, and with definite purpose of obtaining ornamental form'!

Gould thought that this pair of Bullfinches had indeed an innate taste for ornamentation, for after this nest was taken they immediately began to construct another. The second nest had a platform of old flower-heads of alder equally regularly arranged in a beautiful circle.

The Eurasian or Northern Bullfinch breeds throughout much of Eurasia east to Kamchatka, north to the Arctic Circle, south to Italy, the Balkans, Caucasia, northern Iran, southern Siberia and Japan. Largely resident, some do move just south of the breeding range in winter however to Korea and China.

COMMON STARLING (STARLING)

STURNUS VULGARIS

Sturnus vulgaris Linnaeus

PLATE 349

Gould described the Starling as 'quick and nimble in all its actions, pert and inquisitive'. On the ground, while searching for food it pried into every tuft of grass and every hole or crevice. Flocks moved quickly from one part of a field to another, 'those foremost in the van finding abundance of food, and leaving little behind them, the hinder birds are constantly rising, and

pitching in front, until the whole field has been examined'. Gould believed that Starlings were of immense value to farmers by consuming wire-worms, grasshoppers, flies and other insects.

In the spring the Starling was equally at home building its untidy nest in the turret of a royal castle as on the roof of a humble cottage. Other favoured nest sites were church eaves, house rain-pipes, decayed trees, or the deserted holes of woodpeckers.

On summer mornings these birds were often perched, sentinel-like, on the crown of a weather-cock, or the letters of the compass-points. Later in the day they took to the fields, and were often seen standing on the backs of sheep in the pasture.

On winter evenings they formed flocks so vast it was impossible to estimate their numbers. In the air they performed 'many graceful evolutions, sweeping, dipping, and turning with rapidity and ease . . . the dark cloud of birds instantly changing their position by a concerted plan only known to themselves'.

Starlings went through many plumage changes from youth to maturity. The illustration shows the yellow-billed, brilliantly speckled, adult birds in spring with their young brood.

The Common Starling has been introduced into many parts of the world and so successfully that this originally Palaearctic species is in some countries considered to be a serious agricultural pest and a threatening competitor to native birds.

350   *Common or Black-billed Magpie* (HCR)

COMMON OR BLACK-BILLED MAGPIE (MAGPIE)

PICA CAUDATA

Pica pica (Linnaeus)

PLATE 350

Gould greatly admired the Magpie although he knew it was unpopular among gamekeepers and landowners. He pointed out that it was a very attractive bird, and its colours were 'a striking contrast to the greens of the countryside. It was not merely black and white but a variety of beautiful colours. The illustration attempted to portray the purple, blue and green of its tail, and the blue and bronzy-green sheens of its wings, as well as the pure white and intense black of the rest of its plumage.

The Magpie's nest shown in the background was an elaborate construction. The foundation of crossed sticks was topped with shreds of bark, clay and moss, and lined with fine roots and tendrils. Above this a thick dome was linked to the rim of the nest to form a spherical mass with one or two entrances. Gould thought that such skilled basket-work, made mostly of thick hedge cuttings, was worthy of exhibition in a museum.

Gould described the Magpie as prying, inquisitive, pert and cunning. Its flight although graceful, was short and laboured, but it could leap from branch to branch with the utmost agility when chased into a wood by a hawk or falcon. In spring it was garrulous, and when excited uttered 'a peculiar chattering noise'. The Magpie's main food was worms, grubs and insects, although it would readily take carrion, and also the eggs and young of birds, or pilfer fruits and berries in gardens.

The Magpie or, to distinguish it from other magpies, the Common or Black-billed Magpie, has a wide distribution with up to thirteen races or subspecies. The species is found in much of Europe and Asia, north-west Africa, western Arabia and western North America.

COMMON OR EURASIAN CUCKOO (CUCKOO)

CUCULUS CANORUS

Cuculus canorus Linnaeus

PLATE 351

The Cuckoo traditionally heralded the coming of summer, and its familiar notes were welcomed from Land's End to the Hebrides in Britain, and from Killarney to the Giant's Causeway in Ireland.

Gould commented that although it was well known that the cuckoo was a parasite, and placed its eggs to be hatched in smaller birds' nests, 'the why and wherefore of its habits' were still a great mystery.

Gould made his own observations in a garden at 'Formosa', near Maidenhead on the Thames, in 1860. At the beginning of June some wagtails built a nest among the espalier apple-trees, and five eggs were found, four belonging to the wagtail and one similar egg to a cuckoo which had been noticed nearby. On 18 June, all the eggs were hatched simultaneously; but after three days, in the early morning, the four wagtail nestlings were found dead on the ground. The parasite then had the nest all to itself, and by 6 July was able to hop out and even fly a short distance.

Gould marvelled at how the baby Cuckoo could have the strength to push out the other nestlings. 'As to how they are ejected there is much diversity of opinion; the general belief is that they are shouldered out by the parasite; but from this I entirely dissent, for the simple reason that, judging from my own observation, I do not believe that at the end of the third day the parasite has the physical power requisite to eject the rightful possessors from a deep cup-shaped or a domed nest.' Gould believed that the foster-parent, over-anxious to care for her parasite fledgling, inadvertently caused the death of her own young by clearing out of the nest all debris and extraneous matter.

The illustration shows the male in the foreground, and a young Cuckoo in the distance being fed by a wagtail.

The Common or Eurasian Cuckoo, with its eight subspecies, breeds throughout Eurasia and north-west Africa, from Scandinavia, the British Isles, Iberia and Morocco eastwards to north-east Siberia, Japan, Burma and south China. All winter in east and south Africa except the eastern Asiatic populations which winter in south-east Asia south to the Philippines.

COMMON OR EURASIAN CUCKOO (CUCKOO)

CUCULUS CANORUS

Cuculus canorus Linnaeus

PLATE 352

This illustration was added at the end of the series to show a Meadow Pipit and her nest, with the parasite baby Cuckoo expelling the pipit fledglings.

After Gould had published his text on the Cuckoo, he was forwarded an eye-witness account and a tracing of a sketch by Mrs Hugh Blackburn, of a young cuckoo actually seen in the act of throwing out some Meadow Pipit fledglings. In his introduction Gould admitted that his previous theories were erroneous, and inserted Hart's lithograph based on Mrs Blackburn's sketch into the third volume. The extra picture showed the grisly sight of the Hercules-like baby Cuckoo standing up and, with embryonic arm-like wings, heaving the other less developed fledglings overboard.

Mrs Hugh Blackburn (Jemina Wedder-

351 *Common or Eurasian Cuckoo* (HCR)

PICUS MAJOR, *Linn.*

352   Common or Eurasian Cuckoo (WH)

353   Great Spotted Woodpecker (HCR)

burn) (1823–1909), the wife of Hugh Blackburn, Professor of Mathematics at Glasgow University was a watercolourist who had a keen sense of observation of natural history and social life in nineteenth-century Scotland. Her account and picture of the Cuckoo incident, which took place on a hillside above Roshven, on the west coast of Scotland, was published in *Birds from Moidart and elsewhere*, but not until 1895, six years after Gould's death.

However, in the sixth edition of *The Origin of Species* (1872) Darwin referred, in his chapter on instinct, to Gould's change of mind which presumably was based on her account of the young Cuckoo's ability to eject its foster siblings. Since then studies have shown that the host's eggs or young can be ejected from the nest of the newly hatched cuckoo when it is only between eight and ten hours old.

GREAT SPOTTED WOODPECKER
PICUS MAJOR

Dendrocopos (Picoides) major (Linnaeus)

PLATE 353

'In its habits there are few birds more shy and reclusive; unlike the Green Woodpecker, it seldom approaches the dwelling of man, but keeps to the topmost branches of large trees; occasionally, however, it deviates from this kind of life and descends to the pollard oak, the willow, or the fence-tail, and in autumn resorts to gardens, for the sake of the wall fruit.' Gould related that the woodpecker hopped and rambled over the surface of trees, carefully scrutinizing every crevice for spiders and insects, clutching the bark with its strong claws, and supported against the trunk by its stiff tail-feathers. Gould regretted that

their hammering noise, produced by a rapid succession of strokes of its bill on dead branches, were not heard in every wood, but 'the collector, the keeper, and the sportsman' were unable to refrain 'from levelling their guns' at this attractive woodpecker. He thought that the dense woods of Norway were its only safe refuge.

Woodpeckers do not make a nest but lay eggs in bored holes of decayed trees. The illustration shows the adult male with bright red on the back of its head (right) and the female (centre) with a young male with red crown (left).

The Great Spotted Woodpecker, which may have up to fourteen subspecies, breeds in Eurasia and north-west Africa from the Atlantic to the Pacific north to the tree line in Europe and Siberia and south to the Canaries, across to China, Burma, Vietnam and Japan.

VOLUME IV

BLACK GROUSE (BLACKCOCK)

TETRAO TETRIX

Tetrao tetrix Linnaeus

PLATE 354

Gould associated the Blackcock, now known as the Black Grouse, particularly with the highlands of Scotland, where it could be found among the heather and sedge on hillsides and in valleys. The Blackcocks perched on trees, bushes or stone walls, and their food consisted of buds, shoots, seeds and berries. The male's lyre-shaped tail was a traditional Scottish emblem and worn in highlanders' bonnets.

Wolf's illustration shows males gathered together before the females at a communal display ground or 'lek'. They challenge each other by fluffing up their white under-tail coverts, raising their lyre-shaped tails and puffing out their necks, while the hens watch from a distance. Sometimes the males use their bills and claws, making feathers fly in all directions. After mating the polygamous males take no part in nesting duties.

On the right is a black male with a

354 *Black grouse* (JW and HCR)

scarlet comb and lyre-shaped tail. The brown female on the left has a smaller, slightly forked tail.

The range of the Black Grouse extends through Eurasia from Britain and Scandinavia east to the Kolymar and Lena rivers and Ussuriland, south to the Kirghiz Steppes and Turkestan, north Mongolia, northeast China and north Korea.

ROCK PTARMIGAN (PTARMIGAN)

LAGOPUS MUTUS

Lagopus mutus (Montin)

PLATE 356

Gould described the Ptarmigan as the pride of the Scottish highlands. It no longer lived in England and its southern limit was the Grampian mountains. He recommended a few hours' train journey from London as an 'easy, pleasant and exhilarating' trip to these hills, especially when the heather was 'radiant with blossoms' in summer and the Ptarmigan could be seen in its finest plumage.

Wolf illustrated the Ptarmigan in the different seasonal dress it wore for summer, autumn and winter. He took 'the utmost pains' to depict these changes of plumage in relation to the appropriate scenery. One of his favourite subjects was avian camouflage, and he found a real delight in painting the subtle white shades of a Ptarmigan crouched in the snow, hidden from the eyes of a Golden Eagle. He also explored the theme of the struggle for survival, and nature's protection of smaller species from larger predators in the harsh conditions of the high mountains.

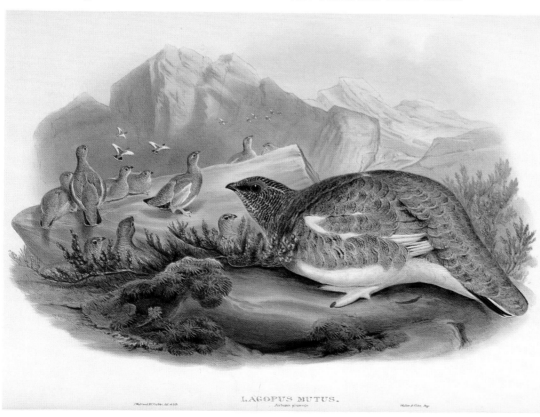

355 *Rock Ptarmigan* (JW and HCR)

356 *Rock Ptarmigan* (JW and HCR)

ROCK PTARMIGAN (PTARMIGAN)

LAGOPUS MUTUS

Lagopus mutus (Montin)

PLATE 355

The Ptarmigan needed to be particularly wary in autumn, Gould wrote, when sportsmen climbed the rugged hills and would not be content to leave without 'making a bag'.

Wolf illustrated the Ptarmigan's camouflage in this season, when both adults and young had mottled grey bodies, and their colours harmonized with the grey-browns of mountain rocks and boulders. This was a transitional stage between the female's tawny brown and the male's blackish-brown in summer, and their white plumage in winter. Wolf studied the grey-plumaged Ptarmigan in the Scottish highlands near Loch Stack, in the west of Sutherland.

The Ptarmigan or Rock Ptarmigan has a distribution which is circumpolar through northern Eurasia, and northern North America, Greenland and Iceland.

GREAT BUSTARD

OTIS TARDA

Otis tarda Linnaeus

PLATE 358

Gould related that the Great Bustard was once seen on the open plains and heaths of East Anglia and Wiltshire, the downs of Berkshire, Hampshire and Sussex, and the Yorkshire wolds. During the mid-nineteenth century its numbers gradually decreased, for it was an easy target for shooting by landowners, farmers and poachers. Bustards were omnivorous, feeding on grasses and crops, worms, insects, mice and small reptiles.

In the background of the illustration Wolf depicts the males in a 'state of excitement' during the breeding season, when their necks were enormously inflated, and their white under-tail coverts were spread out like a fan. The female nested in open country in a depression of the ground, and she is shown here with two young in the foreground.

A programme of captive-breeding leading to re-introduction has in recent years been initiated by the Great Bustard Trust; as yet no successful breeding with the captive birds has occurred but the prognosis is optimistic.

The Great Bustard does still breed across Eurasia, with broken and relief distribution in parts; migratory in east of its range, it is dispersive or resident elsewhere.

EURASIAN OR GREAT BITTERN (BITTERN)

BOTAURUS STELLARIS

Botaurus stellaris (Linnaeus)

PLATE 357

'The clearing of forests, the draining of marshes, and the damming back of encroaching seas have a tendency to alter the condition of every country where such operations are carried on . . . the result being a great disturbance to our natural productions both animal and vegetable . . . Before these changes took place, the greater part of the country was in a state of nature, and the Bittern was common; and no bird was more secure from molestation; for it dwelt in fastnesses where few enemies could approach, situated as they were in the midst of many square miles of waving reeds or forests of tangled herbage.'

Gould pleaded for the protection of the Bittern in the reed beds of Norfolk and Lincolnshire. 'Pray, then, let us still see this weird bird in some part of England; let there still be a marsh where the *will-o'-the-wisp* may exercise its delusive powers, and the boom of the Bittern be heard; for both fever and ague would the ornithologist risk to see the bird in a state of nature.'*

Today there are very few breeding Bitterns left in Britain, and these are mainly in East Anglia. Their numbers may be increased by winter visitors from Europe, when they are forced out by freezing conditions. There appears to have been a general decline in numbers at least in the western part of their extensive breeding range across Eurasia. A subspecies, *Botaurus stellaris capensis*, which is in appearance only slightly different from the nominate *B. s. stellaris*, is found in southeast Africa.

*A characteristic of the male Bittern is its territorial 'booming' call, a hollow noise which sounds like a foghorn.

357   Eurasian or Great Bittern (HCR)

NORTHERN LAPWING (LAPWING OR PEEWIT)

VANELLUS CRISTATUS

Vanellus vanellus (Linnaeus)

PLATE 359

The Lapwing's habitat, Gould related, was 'the upland moorland, the wet grassy mead, the marsh . . . over which it trips and enlivens the solitude with its plaintive cry of *pee-wit*'. He described how during summer the Lapwing's eggs, which were esteemed a great delicacy for a 'wedding breakfast, and the festive supper', were sought after by collectors who came in great numbers to the nesting sites. The bird, naturally distrustful and protective of its eggs, 'employed many artifices to draw the intruder away . . . in the course of which it performs many singular and interesting evolutions, tumbling, dipping, and turning with great rapidity'.

In autumn and winter great masses of Lapwings were seen in the air, 'passing from one feeding ground to the other'. Their broad rounded wings and flapping movements made them conspicuously different from any other birds.

The plate shows a female and her four nestlings, which have distinctive white collars.

The Lapwing, or more accurately the Northern Lapwing, breeds throughout most of Europe east across Asia to the Pacific Ocean. Most populations are migratory wintering from Europe, south Asia and Japan to north Africa, India, Burma and south China.

OTIS TARDA, *Linn.*

358   Great Bustard (JW and HCR)

359   *Northern Lapwing* (HCR)

360   *Common or Eurasian Oystercatcher* (HCR)

361 *Pied Avocet* (HCR)

COMMON OR EURASIAN OYSTERCATCHER (OYSTERCATCHER)

HAEMATOPUS OSTRALEGUS

Haematopus ostralegus Linnaeus

PLATE 360

Gould described the Oystercatcher as a 'strikingly showy bird, whether seen on the low rocky promontories of the coast or the shingly beach'. In summer the adults had jet-black throats and heads, but in winter they had white collars. Throughout the year they had orange bills, red eyes and pinky flesh-coloured legs, and their plumage was at its brightest prior to the beginning of the breeding season.

Gould questioned why they were called Oystercatchers for they ate a wide variety of other food, including worms, cockles and mussels. They were particularly fond of limpets left by the receding tide, which they dexterously prised from rocks with their long bills.

The illustration shows the adult in summer plumage in the foreground and in winter plumage behind.

Oystercatchers, similar to the Common or Eurasian Oystercatchers, occur in most parts of the world, though some forms are entirely black. They are all grouped in one genus *Haematopus*, with up to eleven species currently recognized, though some

authors consider there to be as few as three or four species.

The subspecies shown in Gould's illustration breeds in Europe east to Pechora in northern Russia.

PIED AVOCET (AVOCET)

RECURVIROSTRA AVOCETTA

Recurvirostra avosetta Linnaeus

PLATE 361

'How much it is to be regretted that a bird so attractive in its general appearance, and so singular in its form as the Avocet, should be nearly extirpated from our island! Yet such is unhappily the case; for, although it was formerly abundant, it is now very rarely to be met with.' Gould wrote that formerly the Avocets bred in small communities on the marshes and sandy dunes of the east coast; but they had been the victims of wanton shooting because their feathers were thought suitable for artificial flies and their flesh considered worth eating. He wrote that up to 1854 a few pairs continued to visit East Anglia, but within the last ten years even these few had departed.

Today, through protection and habitat management the Avocet has successfully

regained a foothold in Britain. In 1947 two groups totalling twenty-eight pairs were discovered breeding in East Anglia after many years of absence. Arrangements were made to improve their nesting and feeding conditions, and now reserves at Minsmere and Havergate Island, Suffolk, have over a hundred breeding pairs. The Avocets have spread to other areas, particularly in north Norfolk.

Gould described the Avocet's upcurved bill as only suitable for probing in 'oozy, muddy flats of estuaries, bays and similar situations, where it can patter about with its wide-webbed feet, and gather small crustaceans and sea-worms'. As it moved about it constantly swept its bill from side to side through the water.

The illustration shows an adult and young birds about three weeks old, which have already developed characteristically long legs and toes.

The Avocet, or Pied Avocet, is a Palearctic and Afro-tropical species breeding on the coasts of the North Sea and the Baltic, around the Mediterranean and from the Caspian Sea eastwards to north China as far south as Iraq and Baluchistan. There are also local populations in Africa from Ethiopia through to southern Africa. They are migratory in the northern parts of their breeding range, more dispersive in the south.

362 *Dunlin* (HCR)

DUNLIN

PELIDNA CINCLUS

Caladris alpina (Linnaeus)

PLATE 362

'During the months of autumn and winter the sea-shores of most parts of our island are constantly enlivened by flocks of Dunlin, which at one moment are winging their way out to sea, and at the next sweeping round towards the beach, showing their grey-brown backs as they go away, and their silvery-white breasts as they approach; at another time the oozy mudflats are covered by these little birds of elegant form, sprightly actions, and a disposition at once tame and unsuspecting.'

The Dunlin was illustrated by two plates, in summer when its rich browns harmonized with the colours of heathland, and in winter when its duller plumage blended with the starker landscape.

The adult birds in winter are depicted with their four fledglings, 'which can run

about nimbly the day they are excluded from the shell, and are surprisingly pretty'. The flowering plant is the Common Butterwort *Pinguicula vulgaris*.

The breeding distribution of this species is circumpolar, mainly on arctic tundras, though with a southerly extension of range into the Baltic coastal regions, Denmark and the British Isles. They winter from Europe, south Asia and Japan south to east Africa, India and Taiwan, the Hawaiian Islands, and along both coasts of North America south to north Mexico and the West Indies.

BLACK COOT (COOT)

FULICA ATRA

Fulica atra Linnaeus

PLATE 363

Gould watched a pair of Black Coots by the Thames near Taplow, and described the progress of their young from birth to maturity. The Coots built their high, flat

nest with a mass of herbage among the reeds and the female laid up to eight eggs in the following few days. While she sat, the male swam 'noiselessly but constantly before her, keeping off all intruding Coots, and protecting her to his utmost from every danger'. In about a fortnight, the young birds hatched, and Gould was delighted with their beautiful colouring and interesting markings. He drew attention to the illustration as the most faithful portrait of nestlings three or four days old 'as the pencils of Mr. Wolf or Mr. Richter could render them'. Later the red, blue and flesh tints of the head gave way to other markings, and the red wispy hairs and down were replaced by feathers.

These common birds of large still waters and slow rivers are found through the greater part of Europe, Asia and Australasia. Four subspecies are recognized with slight geographical variations in colour and size. The subspecies of Britain, *Fulica atra atra*, is found throughout Eurasia and North Africa, west to the Azores, east to Japan and south to Sri Lanka.

MOORHEN

GALLINULA CHLOROPUS

Gallinula chloropus (Linnaeus)

PLATE 364

Gould wrote that the Moorhen was found by 'the sedgy banks of lakes and rivers, reedy ponds, moats, beds of osiers, wet ditches etc.'. It was naturally shy and reclusive, and often hid from observation by retreating into a thick reed covert.

'On the water the Moorhen is as buoyant as a cork, and its powers of swimming are as perfect as those of most water-birds'. Gould commented that it was also quite graceful on land, and sometimes left the waterside to walk over the grass and garden lawns 'with all the ease of a land-bird, flirting its tail from side to side, and conspicuously displaying the white under-coverts, especially during the season of courtship'. The Moorhen was a neat, trim little bird, and its 'richly coloured bill, and red-gartered green legs' contrasted with its sombre plumage.

The illustration shows the adult birds with their brood of about four or five days old. Gould related: 'Immediately on emerging from the shell, these infant birds take to the water, and follow their parents

FULICA ATRA.

363   *Black Coot* (JW and HCR)

through labyrinths of thick and tangled herbage, at one part of the day sunning themselves on prostrate rushes, at another threading the floating leaves of the water-lilies . . . as night approaches, their sensitiveness to cold prompts them to seek shelter under the wings of a careful mother.'

The Moorhen has an almost worldwide distribution, apart from Australasia, and is found in Eurasia, Africa, south Asia and the Malayan Archipelago and the Americas from Ontario to Argentina. There are, considerable geographical variations over such a large area and twelve subspecies or races are currently recognized.

364   *Moorhen* (JW and HCR)

VOLUME V

MUTE SWAN

CYGNUS OLOR

Cygnus olor (Gmelin)

PLATE 365

For Gould the Mute Swan was not only the 'most majestic, stately and graceful' member of the genus, but a fine example of aquatic design: 'its body, and indeed its whole structure, is so admirably adapted that the hand of man has never been able to improve upon such a model of buoyancy.' The text mentions 'the most noble swannery' of Abbotsbury in Dorset, which still remains today Britain's large colony of breeding Mute Swans.

Wolf's illustration shows a breeding pair with two of their brood on the mother's back. Gould explains: 'If they become fatigued they scramble on the back of the mother and nestle among the secondary feathers by which means they obtain both warmth and shelter — a practice which is continued for two or three weeks.' The devoted parents work as a team, the female incubating the eggs while 'the male is in constant attendance . . . occasionally taking her place upon the eggs, or guarding her with jealous care, giving chase and battle if necessary to every intruder.'

365 *Mute Swan* (JW and HCR)

Gould was keen to defend the reputation of the Mute Swan against accusations of being a pest. 'Much has been written respecting the harm done by Swans in the destruction of fish in our rivers; but I firmly believe that this occurs to only a limited extent . . . and that on the contrary they effect much good by clearing thick beds of weeds.' Today the situation is reversed and the effects on swans of lead poisoning caused by lost fishing weights has recast some anglers as a danger to swans. In Britain the Mute Swan population has declined in recent years and some of the Thames herds have almost disappeared.

The Mute Swan is found breeding discontinuously across Europe east to central Asia. Partially migratory, wintering within the breeding range and beyond, it has been introduced to eastern America, Australia, South Africa, and elsewhere.

COMMON SHELDUCK (SHELDRAKE)

TADORNA VULPANSER

Tadorna tadorna (Linnaeus)

PLATE 366

'It must, I think, be admitted that the Sheldrake is one of the most attractive and ornamental of the *Anatidae* indigenous to the British Islands – the breadth of its markings, the purity of the white portions of its plumage, the rich red of its bill and legs, all combining to render it a creature of great beauty.' Gould commented that whether the Sheldrake walked over the grass, swam buoyantly in the water or rose in the air, its bright colours were displayed to the greatest advantage.

Gould described the Shelduck's natural habitat as the arid seacoasts and sand-dunes, but domesticated or pinioned birds bred readily on lakes and ponds. This species was particularly attractive to the owners of ornamental waters because, unlike many other ducks, both sexes had the same bright plumage and retained their fine colours throughout the year.

Shelducks nest in burrows, haystacks

TADORNA VULPANSER.

366 *Common Shelduck* (HCR)

367 *Mallard* (JW and HCR)

and holes or under the shelter of boulders or bushes, always near salt or brackish water either on shallow coasts and estuaries or inland seas and lakes. The ducklings led by their mother sometimes join other broods to form a crêche, which can be up to a hundred strong.

The Common Shelduck breeds from the British Isles and western Europe across, though discontinuously, to Asia. Some populations are sedentary, others are migratory, wintering south to north Africa, northern India and Burma.

MALLARD (OR WILD DUCK)

ANAS BOSCHAS

Anas platyrhynchos Linnaeus

PLATE 367

Gould stated that the Mallard had a very extensive distribution and had an important relationship with man, for in many

countries where it was not indigenous it had become 'thoroughly domesticated'. The European settler had introduced it to foreign lands where it formed 'part and parcel of his surroundings, contributing to his enjoyment and constituting no considerable portion of his subsistence'.

In Gould's day the Mallard was important for its culinary use, and bred throughout Britain. He related that 'vast numbes, both of the old and young birds (or "flappers" as they are termed) are annually sent to our markets, through the agency of the gunner and the decoy man.'

Wolf's illustration shows the strikingly different markings of the drab female and the colourful male. In summer, after the drake has bred, 'his finery is exchanged for a sombre dress of various shades of brown, and his appearance so resembles that of the female that they are scarcely distinguishable one from the other.'

The Mallard or Wild Duck's, opportunistic adaptability allows it to exist in a wide range of habitats throughout the northern hemisphere.

COMMON or GREEN-WINGED TEAL (TEAL)

QUERQUEDULA CRECCA

Anas crecca Linnaeus

PLATE 368

Gould gave a description of the daily routine during autumn of the Common or Green-winged Teal, Britain's smallest resident duck. At daytime it rested, remaining 'on the surface of the water, rising and falling with every ripple', or sat quietly on the river bank. As evening approached the teals became more animated, their whistling 'crick' call was heard, and at night they simultaneously rose, 'and quit the waters for the morass, the ploughed field, the oozy mud-bank, or wherever they may obtain a supply of food'. At daylight they returned 'to their usual sanctuary, where they preen their feathers, and the males swim around each other in circles before settling to rest for the day'.

In spring the teal nested among tufts of heather or tussocks of grass, sometimes at some distance from the water. Soon after hatching the young brood were conducted to a small pool, a 'wet and sloppy morass' or 'little rill of water', where they were guarded by their parents from the attacks of harriers and any other animals by which their lives may be endangered'.

The illustration shows the male Common Teal in the foreground with young, and the duller female in the background.

This species breeds throughout the Holarctic; the suspecies *Anas crecca crecca* in Europe and north Asia and the subspecies *A.c. carolinensis* in North America. The latter, the American Green-winged Teal is distinguished from the Eurasian Green-winged Teal by the vertical white stripe at the side of the breast and the absence of a horizontal white stripe on the scapulars.

368   *Common or Green-winged Teal* (HCR)

COMMON EIDER (EIDER DUCK)

SOMATERIA MOLISSIMA

Somateria mollissima (Linnaeus)

PLATE 369

'The Eider Duck has special claims to our notice, first, because it is a really fine bird, and, secondly, on account of the important part it plays in commerce.' Gould described the Eider as an oceanic bird, which ranged round the northern coasts of Europe, Asia and America, 'its principal places of resort being a few degrees within and without the arctic circle'.

During the breeding season the female plucks down from her breast to form a warm covering for her eggs and to protect them from the cold. In Iceland the Icelanders made special islands for nesting eiders by constructing promontories and isthmuses away from the mainland and the intrusion of dogs, foxes and predators. The female eiders had become so tame that they allowed their down to be gathered, first soon after incubation, and again after the eggs had hatched and the ducklings had departed with their mother.

Gould was full of praise for the qualities of the eider's feathers, which were made into bed coverings. 'Few of those who feel the comfortable warmth of an Eider-down coverlet ever give thought to the matter of where it is composed — a material so wonderfully elastic that the entire contents of the quilt may be compressed into the closed hand.'

COMMON GOLDENEYE (GOLDEN-EYE)

GLANGULA GLAUCION

Bucephala clangula (Linnaeus)

PLATE 370

The plate shows the male and female in the foreground, and two males in courtship display in the background. Gould attempted to depict accurately the males in one of their '*outré* positions . . . then the head is thrown back on the lower part of the back, with the bill at a right-angle to the body, an attitude which is repeatedly assumed as the males approach each other, or slowly pirouette, as it were in circles round the female'.

Gould enjoyed watching 'the statelyswimming old Drakes, with their large green heads and full golden-coloured eye through an opera glass'. Prism binoculars were patterned in 1859, but this is the first reference to Gould using them. Gradually they replaced the gun as essential equipment for the ornithologist.

The Common Goldeneye breeds throughout the Holarctic region, and though two subspecies have been described, one in Europe and north Asia, and the other in North America, the differences are slight.

369   *Common Eider* (HCR)

SMEW (OR NUN)

MERGUS UMBELLUS

Mergus albellus Linnaeus

PLATE 371

'I think it was a happy simile when this bird was compared to a nun; for where can we find one more chaste in its colouring, more graceful in its form? . . . Romance apart, this is really one of the prettiest, if not the most beautiful of water-birds; to see it, however, with its plumage pure and unsullied it must be seen in a state of nature. How different is the bird when seen in our Museums!' Gould wrote that unfortunately the Smew was not commonly seen in Britain, for it did not breed there but only arrived in winter, particularly during severe weather.

The plate shows the striking males in the foreground and the duller female in the background. The male has white plumage with black markings in winter, but in summer after breeding it loses these fine colours and becomes grey and brown like the female. Gould commented that the tranquil winter scene illustrated in the picture completely changed during spring, when the males exhibited 'the greatest animation, stretching forth their necks, erecting their crests, and swimming and circling in the water as if their bodies turned on a pivot'.

The Smew breeds in the extreme north of Fenno-Scandia and across parts of Russia

370   Common Golden-eye (HCR)

and Siberia to Anadyrland and Kamchatka; they winter south of their breeding range.

GREAT CRESTED GREBE

PODICEPS CRISTATUS

Podiceps cristatus (Linnaeus)

PLATE 374

Gould expressed great anxiety for the future of the Great Crested Grebe. In mid-Victorian times the grebe was trapped and killed, since its ear-tufts and head-feathers were in great demand as decoration in hats and jewellery, and its silky white skins were cut up into narrow strips as trimmings for muffs and pelisses. 'How much this is to be regretted!' Gould protested. 'Wholesale destruction like this almost amounts to extermination: such wicked acts are most reprehensible; for, besides its cruelty, it is killing the goose that lays the golden egg.'

Fortunately, Gould's fears were not realized, although the British population was reduced to just forty pairs by 1860. Shortly afterwards a Bird Protection Act was passed, fashion changed, and today the grebes have increased enormously in number and are plentiful on rivers, inland lakes, reservoirs and flooded gravel pits.

Gould related that the grebe's nest was a large heaped-up mass of weeds which floated on water. The nestlings had extraordinary striped markings and when only a day old could swim and dive with astonishing agility. When they wanted to rest, they would scramble on the back of their mother, and sail about in the sunshine, or, if in danger, dive with her beneath the surface of the water.

The Great Crested Grebe has a rather odd distribution, throughout Eurasia and north Africa, and discontinuously into the Afro-tropical and Australasian regions.

371   Smew (HCR)

372 *Great Northern Diver or Common Loon* (HCR)

URIA TROILE.

373 *Common Guillemot or Common Murre* (HCR)

GREAT NORTHERN DIVER OR COMMON LOON

COLYMBUS GLACIALIS

Gavia immer (Brünnich)

PLATE 372

'In the seas surrounding the British Islands, and especially in the firths and salt-water lochs of the eastern and western parts of Scotland, they may be seen, courageously breasting the waves, or making lengthened dives in search of the fish, crustaceans, and molluscs on which they principally live.'

Gould described the Great Northern Diver as a voracious feeder, for it lived on herrings, sprats and other fish, as well as shrimps, crabs, and molluscs. When it visited fresh water it was very unpopular with fishermen and landowners. Its diving powers were exceptional and it would often avoid being hunted by diving under the boat containing its pursuers, and reappearing where least expected.

The adult diver is illustrated in summer with its dark head and fine spotted plumage. In winter it has a grey head and white under-parts.

The Great Northern Diver or Common Loon, as it is called in America, is a breeding bird of the Nearctic region into Greenland and Iceland, wintering south of its breeding range to the Atlantic and Pacific coasts of Canada and the USA, with regular occurrences off the coasts of northern Europe.

COMMON GUILLEMOT OR COMMON MURRE

URIA TROILE

Uria aalge (Pontoppidan)

PLATE 373

'It will be observed that my figures represent the two birds known by the names of the Common and the Bridled or Ringed

Guillemot', Gould commented. The illustration shows one of the guillemots with a white line of feathers outlining its eye and stretching back on its head like spectacles. The 'Bridled' Guillemot is not a separate species but a plumage form of the Common Guillemot, and the precise factors governing the ratio of the two types are not well understood.

The guillemots are depicted in their breeding plumage, when their dark upper-parts have short, smooth, velvety-brown feathers, a contrast to their white shaggy necks and throats of winter. In the background of the picture guillemots crowd on the rocky precipices where they incubate their large pear-shaped eggs.

Gould quoted from Robert Gray's description of Ailsa Craig, a Scottish island where thousands of sea birds congregated. 'The Guillemot and Razorbill breed on narrow ledges of rock occupying the entire face of the highest precipices of Ailsa Craig, and presenting, when viewed from the sea, a very remarkable and orderly appearance. They make no nest, but lay their single egg upon the bare ledge, which is seldom more than six inches [15 centimetres] in breadth, so that each bird is compelled to sit erect when incubating.' The guillemot's eggs were described as 'very variable in colour, and of all shades from pure white to dark green, many being spotted with fantastic characters and intricate lines, which baffle description or portraiture'.

The Common Guillemot (Common Murre in North America) breeds on the coasts and islands of the North Atlantic, west Arctic and North Pacific Oceans, locally south to Portugal, Hokkaido, California and Newfoundland. They winter at sea mainly within the southern limits of their breeding range.

374 *Great Crested Grebe* (HCR)

SULA BASSANA, *Linn.*

J.Wolf & H.C.Richter, del et lith.

Walter, Imp.

376 *Black-headed Gull* (JW and HCR)

NORTHERN (SOLAN) GANNET

SULA BASSANA

Morus (Sula) bassanus (Linnaeus)

PLATE 375

Edward Lear illustrated the adult white gannet and dark younger bird in *The Birds of Europe* (see no. 000). The large birds are outlined against a distant setting of rocky cliffs which is only faintly indicated. In contrast, Wolf's picture shows a background of a noisy colony in some detail, with the dark young birds mingling among the lighter adults.

Gould related that in spring the gannets were found in vast numbers on the rocks off the coasts of Scotland and on the Bass Rock and islands of St Kilda and Ailsa Craig, where they lay a single dull-white egg in a shallow nest composed of grass and seaweed. He quoted a passage by Robert Gray that described the numbers of gannets on the Bass Rock as estimated between ten and twenty thousand, with at least as many on Ailsa Craig. The gannets gathered in early spring: 'Early in February many thousands have been observed in one flock off the village of Ballintrae, assembling over a shoal of fishes and precipitating themselves from a great height into the sea

in search of their prey.' After a few minutes' submersion they reappeared, throwing back their heads and gobbling their prey with incredible rapacity.

The Northern Gannet breeds on the rocky coasts and marine islands on both sides on the North Atlantic; at other times they are found in open seas.

BLACK-HEADED GULL

CHROICOCEPHALUS RIDIBUNDUS

Larus ridibundus Linnaeus

PLATE 376

The Black-headed Gull was so widespread over the shores of Britain that Gould thought it pointless to name any particular localities. During autumn and winter it frequented the bays and mouths of large rivers, where it paddled about over the oozy mud in search of marine worms, crustaceans and small fishes, all of which it devoured with avidity. It was also seen in fields looking for worms and insects, where like the rook it followed the ploughman, and 'not unfrequently both the sable and silvery-bodied birds' were seen on the same furrow.

Gould quoted a passage by William Yarrell about a breeding area at Scoulton Mere, Norfolk, which was probably the setting for Wolf's illustration. In the middle of this mere, on a boggy island of some seventy acres covered with reeds, birch and willow trees, were 'favourite breeding places of the Brown-headed Gull'. These gulls arrived about mid-February and searched for food over several miles in the surrounding countryside. About the middle of May their eggs were found in great abundance, and a man and three boys found constant employment in collecting them, 'sometimes upward of a thousand a day', for sale as delicacies. Large numbers of young birds hatched and immediately took to water, and by July they flew off with the adults to the sea coast.

The gull's head plumage changes through the seasons. In winter it is white, but in the spring and summer the white is gradually replaced by a chocolate-brown hood. Yarrell's name, 'Brown-headed Gull, is probably a better description than the modern 'Black-headed Gull'.

There has been a marked increase in numbers, especially in northern Europe, since the early nineteenth century and the Black-headed Gull now breeds in Greenland (recently), Iceland across Europe and northern Asia. It winters as far south as the Canaries, Gambia, Nigeria and the Nile valley, India and Malaysia, and is regularly seen on coasts of eastern North America.

ROSEATE TERN

STERNA PARADISEA

Sterna dougallii Montagu

PLATE 337

Gould thought that this tern was appropriately called *paradisea* because of its elegant form and beautiful colouring. It was named 'roseate' because of the pink flush on its breast but this was only seen during the breeding season.

Gould knew that the Roseate Tern, although nowhere very numerous, had a wide range extending over the seashores of northern Europe, north America, Africa and India, but he believed it was becoming scarce in Britian. 'Formerly there was scarcely a large sand-spit or rock promontory in the British Islands . . . that had not

its little colony of Roseate Terns . . . Now it is to be feared that they have either been killed off from many of these favourite localities, or they have deserted them.'

Today the Roseate Tern is very rare and the causes of its continued decline are not fully understood. Some are killed in winter in West Africa, especially in Ghana by small boys with snares and baited hooks on fishing lines. In Britain they are killed by predators and disturbed by human activity, and have to compete for breeding sites with the expanding gull populations, but some colonies have been deserted for no apparent reason.

LITTLE TERN

STERNULA MINUTA

Sterna albifrons Pallas

PLATE 378

'How joyous are the emotions of the sailor when, towards the end of a long voyage, he sees the Little Tern flapping its long wings over the surface, or descending headlong

into the ocean. Light-hearted is he now; for he knows that this aerial sprite is a never failing indication that the shore is near at hand, and that in a few hours he may get a short relief from his monotonous sea-life.' Gould went with his son Franklin in June 1864 to visit a breeding colony on the shingle beds at Dungeness, Kent, where they saw many Little Terns incubating close to each other. Their two eggs were placed in the midst of the shingle, 'being deposited in a little depression, without a nest other than a few bits of shells arranged neatly around'. The buffy stone-coloured eggs looked so similar to the sand and the shingle that it was very difficult to detect them. Dotted over the shore were many more terns, and others were crying and wailing overhead.

The illustration shows the adult feeding the downy marbled brown chicks on the shingle. In the distant background is Dungeness lighthouse.

The Little Tern has a wide distribution and is virtually cosmopolitan, with the northern populations having extensive winter migrations to warmer waters.

377 Roseate Tern (HCR)

378 Little Tern (HCR)

THE BIRDS OF NEW GUINEA

Five volumes (1875–1888), 320 plates.

PAROTIA LAWESI, *Ramsay.*

The Birds of New Guinea and the Adjacent Papuan Islands, Gould's last great work, was completed after his death. Richard Bowdler Sharpe, Gould's protégé and devoted friend, then in charge of the bird collection at the British Museum, assumed the authorship halfway through the series in 1881, after the twelfth part had been issued. Sharpe was more than forty years junior to Gould, whom he had met when he was only fifteen, and they both shared a passionate interest in ornithology. In his last years, although an invalid and often in pain, Gould was always pleased when Sharpe visited him to look at his collection of skins and discuss the latest bird discoveries.

'The halo of romance which for nearly a century has centred round New Guinea and its animals does not get dimmed as time speeds on, indeed it shines more brightly than ever', wrote Sharpe in his introduction. The most remarkable species were the birds of paradise which had first become known to Europe in the sixteenth century when the Spanish ship *Vittoria* brought a gift of skins (minus their legs) to the king of Spain from a sultan of the Moluccas. Their feathers and plumes were so beautiful that the Spaniards said they must have come from paradise. The first description by a European naturalist of a bird of paradise's display was by Alfred Russel Wallace, whose exploration of the Malay Archipelago (1854–1862) included stops in the western Papuan region. His discoveries and the rivalry between the Dutch, German and British colonial powers encour-

aged professional explorers and naturalists to penetrate the rainforests and mountains of the interior. New species of birds of paradise, cassowary, bowerbirds, pygmy parrots and paradise kingfishers were discovered.

In the 1850s Wallace observed the New Guinea natives hunting birds of paradise for their beautiful plumes, which were prized as decorative headdresses. At the end of the nineteenth century trading in plumes reached enormous proportions when an increasing demand by European collectors and fashionable milliners meant that between 25,000 and 30,000 birds were exported annually. Fortunately, even though native hunting still continues, the bird of paradise population does not seem to have decreased, but today there is a greater danger to their numbers from deforestation and the destruction of habitat.

Gould's and Sharpe's descriptions of the New Guinea birds were those of 'closet' naturalists, working from specimens and knowing little of their habits and lifestyle in the wild. The text is often dull compared to the panache of earlier writings. Gould must have missed the assistance of his invaluable secretary Prince, who had helped to prepare and edit his previous work but who had died in 1874. The paucity of the narrative is fortunately redeemed by the richness of Hart's pictures. Gould delighted in brightly coloured birds and these final highly decorative illustrations provided a triumphant flourish at the end of a long publishing career.

ERYTHROTRIORCHIS DORIÆ

W. Hart del. et lith.

Mintern Bros. imp.

379 *Doria's Goshawk* (WH)

VOLUME I

(MARQUIS) DORIA'S GOSHAWK
ERYTHROTRIORCHIS DORIAE

Accipiter doriae (Salvadori and D'Albertis)

PLATE 379

This illustration published after Gould's death depicts an immature and an adult male. The immature bird in the foreground was drawn from the type specimen lent by the Marquis of Doria, Director of the Museo Civico, Genoa, which had been discovered in south-east New Guinea by the Italian traveller Luigi D'Albertis (1841–1901). Some authorities now regard Doria's Goshawk as being generically distinct from other *Accipiter* and keep it in a separate genus *Megatriroratis*.

The adult bird in the background with darker brown chocolate streaks was drawn from a specimen in the British Museum which was brought by Andrew Goldie from the Astrolabe Mountains.

The hawk, measuring 20–27 inches (51–69 centimetres) is of average size but has a very long tail with ten to twelve black bars.

(NEW GUINEA) HARPY EAGLE
HARPYOPSIS NOVAE GUINEA

Harpyopsis novaeguinea Salvadori

PLATE 380

Hart's illustration of this very large bird of prey, measuring 30–35 inches (76–89 centimetres) was originally two-thirds natural size. The most powerful of all eagles, it lives in undisturbed forest areas flying at or below canopy level. It has broad wings and huge talons, which are probably the strongest of any raptor. The name Harpy is of Greek derivation, meaning the 'Snatchers', and in mythology the harpies were interpreted as hideous winged monsters. These eagles are adept at snatching their prey from branches or cavities in trees and can carry off mammals such as ground wallabies and even piglets.

Sharpe wrote the text after Gould's death and marvelled at how this bird had such a close similarity to the Harpy Eagle of South America, yet they lived so far apart and in different environments. It presented for him 'a problem of geographical distribution which our present knowledge has no means of explaining'.

380 *Harpy Eagle* (WH)

BLACK SICKLEBILL × ARFAK ASTRAPIA BIRD OF PARADISE (ELLIOT'S PROMEROPS)
EPIMACHUS ELLIOTI

Epimachus fastuosus × *Astrapia nigra*

PLATE 381

During the late nineteenth century thousands of skins were shipped to Europe; some birds thought to be rare or undiscovered species were found actually to be hybrids. These hybrids occurred because most male birds of paradise are polygamous and during their courtship dance they verge on a state of trance, mating with any hens available which are sometimes of other species. The bird in the illustration was drawn from a skin which Gould believed to be a unique type specimen, although he knew little of its habitat or origin. In fact, this bird is now thought to be a cross between the Black Sicklebill and the Arfak Astrapia Birds of Paradise.

Many hybrid birds are themselves sterile and are of no value to species survival. One explanation for the bright colours and long plumes of the birds of paradise is that their obvious differences help females to recognize the males of their own species. If the females select suitable mates hybridization is avoided, and the fertility of their offspring is ensured. After mating the females lay their eggs and feed the chicks unaided, while the males, who take no part in rearing, continue with their display and the courtship of other birds.

BLACK SICKLEBILL (GREAT PROMEROPS)
EPIMACHUS SPECIOSUS

Epimachus fastuosus (Hermann)

PLATE 384

In the foreground is depicted a splendid male with a very long tail. It is almost entirely glossy black and has iridescent patches of blue and green. During courtship the male erects the fans of feathers and epaulettes glossed with green and violet at each side of its breast, and these form a huge screen round its head. Another male and female are shown on a smaller scale in the background.

Gould wrote that due to the meagre knowledge of the bird in the wild, and the imperfect skins that had reached Europe for many years, the flamboyant males and dull

381 *Black Sicklebill X Arfak Astrapia Bird of Paradise* (WH)

females had often been identified as separate species. He added that 'we have had to wait until quite recently for the gladdening of our eyes by the receipt of the perfect bird.' This species is now called the Black Sickle-billed Bird of Paradise which marks its long curved beak.

Magnificent (New Guinea) Riflebird

Craspedophora Magnifica

Ptiloris magnificus (Vieillot)

PLATE 382

Riflebirds derive their name from their high-pitched call which resembles the whine or whistle of a rifle bullet.

This species generally known as the Magnificent Riflebird is found throughout the lowlands of New Guinea and also in the rainforests of north-east Queensland, Australia. The cock has an erectile fan-like shield on its throat and an upperbreast of iridescent blue-green, separated from its purplish belly by two bands of bronze-green and deep-red. In the background the cock shown on a high branch is performing its courtship dance by posturing with its wings spread wide and its head thrown back to catch the rays of sunlight on its throat. It also shakes its plumage to make a sound like heavy rustling silk. The female has brownish colours and looks very dull compared to the showy male.

Twelve-wired Bird of Paradise

Seleucides Nigricans

Seleucides melanoleuca (Daudin)

PLATE 383

The illustration shows two flamboyant males which have six ornamental bright yellow plumes from each flank, each with six projecting thin black wire-like shafts. During display the shafts bend sharply forward and the breast-plate of iridescent black and green throat feathers is expanded.

The traveller D'Alberti found many of these birds by the Fly River in southern New Guinea, where they perched on the dead branches and their calls resounded in the forests shortly after dawn. They were also seen by Alfred Russel Wallace in north-west New Guinea among the flowering trees and sago palms of swampy lowland areas feeding on nectar, fruit and insects.

GRASPEDOPHORA MAGNIFICA.

SELEUCIDES NIGRICANS.

382 *Magnificient Riflebird* (WH)

383 *Twelve-wired Bird of Paradise* (WH)

EPIMACHUS SPECIOSUS.

J. Gould & W. Hart, del. et lith.

Walter Imp.

ARFAK ASTRAPIA BIRD OF PARADISE (GORGET PARADISE BIRD)

ASTRAPIA NIGRA

Astrapia nigra (Gmelin)

PLATE 385

This little recorded bird lives in the high forests of the Arfak Mountains in north-west New Guinea at altitudes above 5,000 feet. The male shown in the foreground has erectable neck feathers, which during display expand into a magnificent collar.

In the distance are shown another male and the dull blackish-brown female.

385   Arfak Astrapia Bird of Paradise (WH)

SUPERB BIRD OF PARADISE

LOPHORHINA SUPERBA

Lophorina superba (Pennant)

PLATE 386

Gould was continually amazed by the extraordinary diversity of ornamentation among the birds of paradise. This bird stood apart from all others with its velvety black cape which it could elevate behind its head like a large ruff, and its remarkable iridescent triangular blue-green breast-shield.

This species is widespread in forest areas throughout New Guinea, and the male calls frequently from canopy perches

386   Superb Bird of Paradise (WH)

throughout the day.

The male in the foreground is shown 'in a state of excitement', and in the background another male and the dull female are depicted on a smaller scale.

KING BIRD OF PARADISE

CICINNURUS REGIUS

Cicinnurus regius (Linnaeus)

PLATE 387

'Although one of the smallest of the Paradise Birds, the present species yields to none in the beauty of its plumage or elegance of its form; while its wire-like caudal plumes are just as remarkable in structure as any of the fantastic decorations which adorn the larger kinds.' The brilliantly coloured scarlet male appears almost tail-less, but has two long tail wires which are each tipped with a curly green feathered disc. These tail wires are almost as long as its body, and during display when the tail is shaken, the wires and green discs tremble and trace a wide arc high above the bird's head.

Gould quoted from Alfred Russel Wallace's *Malay Archipelago* in which the explorer relates his delight at finding the live bird so different from Linnaeus's description which had been based on a mutilated skin prepared by natives. Alfred Russel

Wallace observed that the King Bird frequented the lower trees of the less dense forests, and was very active, 'flying strongly with a whirring sound'. When it fluttered its wings it often erected the beautiful fans on either side of its breast. 'These two ornaments, the breast fans and the spiral-tipped tail wires, are altogether unique, not occurring on any other of . . . the eight thousand species of birds . . .' Wallace's enthusiasm much amused his hosts of the Aru Islands who saw nothing unusual in the King Bird of Paradise or 'Goby-Goby', for to them it seemed as ordinary as the Common Robin or the Goldfinch was in England.

387   King Bird of Paradise (WH)

LAWES PAROTIA OR LAWES SIX-WIRED BIRD OF PARADISE

PAROTIA LAWESI

Parotia lawesii Ramsay

PLATE 388

This Lawes Six-wired Bird of Paradise also called Lawes Parotia has three wire-like plumes growing out of each side of its head, each tipped with a black racket. During courtship the males puff out their back and breast feathers to make a shape like an umbrella or a crinoline so that they look like black cones. They display in a cleared arena or dance area while the females look down from a perch. The males dance in a set pattern with short hops to the left and right, then bob up and down on the spot, and sway their heads rapidly from side to side. They repeatedly flick their long head wires making them vibrate and the rackets at the ends bob about crazily until they are lost in a blur.

This illustration was made after Gould's death and has Hart's signature on the lower right-hand side. The text which was prepared by R.B. Sharpe relates that the birds were drawn from male and female specimens in the British Museum collected by Carl Hunstein in the Astrolabe Mountains of south-east New Guinea.

This species was named after Rev. William George Lawes, a British missionary in New Guinea from 1874 to 1906.

GOLDIE'S (GREY CHESTED) BIRD OF PARADISE

PARADISEA DECORA

Paradisea decora Salvin and Godman

PLATE 389

R.B. Sharpe wrote the text after Gould's death: 'The discovery of a new Bird of Paradise must always be a matter of interest to naturalists, and especially when the species proves to be so fine a character as the present bird.'

This species is now called Goldie's Bird

PARADISEA DECORA, *Salv. et Godm.*

389   *Goldie's Bird of Paradise* (WH)

388   *Lawes Parotia or Lawes Six-wired Bird of Paradise* (WH)

of Paradise after its discoverer, Andrew Goldie, who was a botanical and zoological collector in New Guinea from 1876 and became a storekeeper at Port Moresby in 1882. He found the birds in the mountains of the isolated Fergusson Island, one of the D'Entrecasteaux Archipelago. Today, in the wild, this species is still found only on two islands (Fergusson and Normanby) off the east coast of New Guinea.

LESSER (PAPUAN) BIRD OF PARADISE

PARADISEA PAPUANA

Paradisaea minor Shaw

PLATE 391

This species, known as the Lesser Bird of Paradise, is widespread in New Guinea, and skins have been known in Europe since the sixteenth century. The French naturalist, René Lesson, was the first European to describe seeing the birds in the wild when he spent two weeks ashore in Western New Guinea while voyaging through the Pacific with the *Coquille*, 1822–15.

Alfred Russel Wallace, the British zoologist and explorer who, with Darwin, put forward the theory of evolution by natural selection, brought the first live birds to England in 1862. Gould quoted from Wallace's fascinating description of his journey with the two adult birds which he had bought for £100 in Singapore. The birds were fed with rice, bananas, and cockroaches. Bananas were bought in

Bombay during a break in the journey, but cockroaches were difficult to find on the Peninsular and Oriental steamers. Wallace set traps in the storerooms, and hunted at night in the forecastle but found scarcely enough for a single meal. Eventually, during a stop in Malta Wallace managed to procure several full biscuit-tins of cockroaches from a bakehouse; the birds survived the unsettled weather and the ship's poor accommodation to live for several years at London Zoo. There they became quite tame, their plumage grew and they often displayed their fine feathers to the delight of visitors.

GREATER BIRD OF PARADISE

PARADISEA APODA

Paradisaea apoda Linnaeus

PLATE 390

Skins of this species were some of the first birds of paradise to reach Europe. As the natives packed and preserved the skins with no legs or wings the birds were thought to be footless and wingless. The legend arose that they glided through the air on the wind with their long plumes, and floated towards the sun never coming down to rest or land. They fed on air and dew and one writer said that the eggs were laid and hatched by the female in a hollow of the male's back while they flew. Linnaeus named them the footless (*apoda*) Paradise Birds for in 1758 no perfect specimens had ever been seen in Europe.

Alfred Russel Wallace was probably the first European naturalist to observe the display of the male Greater Bird of Paradise in the wild when he watched a communal courtship or lek on the Aru Islands. On his return his descriptions and his fine specimens, exhibited at the British Museum, aroused great interest. It became clear that many birds of paradise mounted in Europe had erroneously been given other birds' feet, and Gould was relieved to write that at last 'complete skins are the rule and badly prepared ones the exception.'

RAGGIANA OR COUNT (MARQUIS DE) RAGGI'S BIRD OF PARADISE

PARADISEA RAGGIANA

Paradisea raggiana Sclater

PLATE 392

Gould considered this species to be one of the grandest of the paradise birds. 'That so large and splendid a species should have remained unknown up to the period of Signor d'Alberti's visit to the southern parts of New Guinea (1876–1877) serves to show the probability that other treasures remain for future explorers in this great unknown land.'

The males display communally in canopy trees of the lower forests. Up to twenty males may be watched by several females, and as many as a dozen males gather in a single tree, shrieking and post-

PARADISEA APODA, *Linn*

390 *Greater Bird of Paradise* (WH)

PARADISEA PAPUANA.

J. Gould & W. Hart del et lith.

Walter, Imp.

391   *Lesser Bird of Paradise* (WH)

PARADISEA RAGGIANA, *Sclater.*

J.Gould & W.Hart del. et lith.

Walter imp.

392 *Raggiana or Count Raggi's Bird of Paradise* (WH)

uring competitively. The trembling red feathers are raised above their heads and their wings are clapped together.

Today the Raggiana's ornamental red plumes are still much sought after by hunters and traders for warriors' head-dresses worn at ceremonial gatherings and dances. Fortunately, although large numbers of males with their full plumage are killed, the young male birds are jealously guarded, and their overall numbers do not seem to have substantially diminished.

TRUMPETBIRD (PURPLE AND VIOLET MANUCODE)

PHONYGAMA PURPUREOVIOLACEA

Phonygammus (manucodia) keraudrenii
(Lesson and Garnot)

PLATE 393

The Purple and Violet Manucode appears to be a violet-blue colour but it also has green and purple glossy shades. The male has red eyes and a shaggy mane of loose neck feathers. These manucodes live in the lowland forests of New Guinea and northeast Australia where they eat fruit and berries, particularly figs, seeds and insects. During courtship display the male raises and spreads its wings, erects its body-feathers and calls loudly. Unlike most birds of paradise which are polygamous, the

394 *Vogelkop Gardener Bowerbird* (WH)

manucodes are monogamous.

This species is now called the Trumpetbird or Trumpetbird Manucode because of the male's loud resonant trumpeting squawk. 'Manucode' is derived from a Malay name meaning 'a bird of the gods'.

The illustration of an adult male in two positions was made by Hart after Gould's death from a specimen in the British Museum and is probably the subspecies *Phonygammus keraudrenii purpeoviolaceus* from the mountains of south-eastern Papua New Guinea.

VOGELKOP GARDENER (GARDENER) BOWERBIRD

AMBLYORNIS INORNATA

Amblyornis inornatus (Schlegel)

PLATE 394

The Gardener Bowerbird is so-called because of the elaborate floral and fruit decorations it places on a front 'lawn' specially made of plucked green moss at the entrance to its bower.

These birds, also known as Vogelkop Gardener Bowerbirds, build the most ingenious of all bowers, a conical hut resembling a small wigwam about 3 feet (1 metre)

high and 5 feet (1.6 metres) in diameter with a wide front entrance. The trunk of a sapling is used as a central pillar to support the roof made of twigs laid methodically in a radiating pattern, and orchid stems are draped over the outside. The hut floor is kept meticulously clear of all debris. The carefully arranged bright flowers, fruit, and

393 *Trumpetbird* (WH)

395 *Striped Bowerbird* (WH)

fungi at the entrance and on the lawn are frequently tidied and replaced when faded.

Observations on the courtship display of these dull brown birds are very limited but they are known to be clever mimics, reproducing calls of many other birds. They live in a restricted area of the Vogelkop and Wandammen mountains.

Gould's description and illustration were adapted from an article by Dr Beccari in the *Gardener's Chronicle*, 16 March 1878.

STRIPED (ORANGE-CRESTED) BOWERBIRD

AMBLYORNIS SUBALARIS

Amblyornis subalaris Sharpe

PLATE 395

R.B. Sharpe wrote about this species after Gould's death, and described how Andrew Goldie had discovered a female in the Astrolabe mountains but it was many years

before a pair was found and identified. The male has a splendid orange crest which is erected during display.

The Orange-crested Bowerbird, now called the Striped Bowerbird, now lives in a limited mountainous area of south-east New Guinea. The male builds a rough hut-like bower of sticks and a mat of stems which is placed at the entrance and decorated with flowers and fruit.

396 *Flamed or Golden Bowerbird* (WH)

FLAMED OR GOLDEN BOWERBIRD (GOLDEN BIRD OF PARADISE)

XANTHOMELUS AUREUS

Sericulus aureus (Linnaeus)

PLATE 396

Gould wrote that the Golden Bird of Paradise had been known for many years from dried skins which gave little idea of its beauty. He was grateful to Count Salvadori of Turin who visited London in 1877 and brought him the fine specimens which were used in the illustration. These birds are now called the Flamed or Golden Bower Bird, and are uncommon forest birds about which little is known. The male is spectacularly orange and gold whereas the female has drabber colours. A small bower built by the male is of an 'avenue' type made with walls of sticks; he decorates the entrance with coloured objects.

NEW IRELAND OR RIBBON-TAILED DRONGO

DICRANOSTREPTUS MEGARHYNCHUS

Dicrurus megarhynchus (Quoy and Gaimard)

PLATE 397

Gould wrote that this large species of drongo was first described in 1830 by Quoy and Gaimard in their account of the voyage of the *Astrolabe*. It is resident in New Ireland, an island of the Bismarck Archipelago, lying to the north-east of New Guinea.

The drongos are usually black with bright metallic sheens of green to purple. They have long forked tails, and strong beaks with bristles. Their diet consists mainly of insects, but they will take frogs, and lizards which they hold with one foot and tear to pieces with their beak before swallowing.

VOLUME III

(MYSORE ISLAND) BLACK SUNBIRD

CINNYRIS MYSORENSIS

Nectarinia aspasia (Lesson and Garnot)

PLATE 398

This illustration was drawn from specimens which came from Biak Island, one of the Geelvink Islands in north-west New Guinea. They were collected for Leiden Museum by Baron von Rosenberg's expedition and are the subspecies *Nectarinia sericea mysorensis*.

The two male sunbirds have showy colours of glossy black, emerald green and purple whereas the females are dull brown and grey. They are hummingbird size, about 4½ inches (11 centimetres). Their habitat is in lowland forest areas, gardens and mangrove swamps where they search for nectar and arthropods.

397 New Ireland or Ribbon-tailed Drongo (WH)

398 Black Sunbird (WH)

SCLATER'S OR SCARLET-THROATED MYZOMELA (SCLATER'S HONEYEATER)

MYZOMELA SCLATERI

Myzomela sclateri Forbes

PLATE 399

These small honeyeaters live among flowering trees in lowland forests on Karkar Island off the north coast of New Guinea and other islands to the north of New Britain. They are only 4½ inches (11 centimetres) long and resemble tiny sunbirds in their activities of searching for nectar, insects and spiders.

Hart's illustration was published in the year of Gould's death; it was based on a surviving lively pencil sketch made by Gould in old age for he never lost enthusiasm for classifying and illustrating newly discovered species. This bird was named after Dr P.L. Sclater, Secretary of the Zoological Society, London.

399 *Sclater's or Scarlet-throated Myzomela* (WH)

VOLUME IV

GREAT OR IVORY-BREASTED PITTA

PITTA MAXIMA

Pitta maxima Müller and Schlegel

PLATE 400

One of Gould's last projects was the un-completed *Monograph of the Pittidae* (1880–1881). Only one volume was published with ten illustrations of pittas from various countries reprinted from plates in other series.

The pittas had stocky bodies, long legs, stumpy tails and brilliant colours. This species was found by Alfred Russel Wallace in the Moluccan Island of Gilolo (Halmaheras), and described in the *Malay Archipelago* in 1869, as one of the most beautiful birds of the east. Although they

PITTA MAXIMA, *Mull. and Schleg.*

400 *Great or Ivory-breasted Pitta* (HCR)

had vivid colours of black, white, azure blue and crimson they were difficult to capture as they moved quickly through the tangled undergrowth of the dense forest.

Blue-breasted or Red Bellied (Blue-backed) Pitta

Pitta cyanonota

Pitta erythrogaster cyanonota G.R. Gray

PLATE 402

This species came from Ternate, a small island of the Moluccas and specimens were procured by Alfred Russel Wallace and other explorers. Gould noted that these pittas had distinctive white patches on their shoulders which could be seen when the wings were stretched. The species has a wide distribution in the Malaysian archipelago, New Guinea and north-east Australia and a number of subspecies have been described. The pittas forage in the undergrowth of lowland forests for worms or insects, and break snails' shells open by banging them against a rock.

The illustration demonstrated that Hart was particularly adept at showing birds in vivid imaginary landscape settings although he himself had never visited New Guinea or the Moluccan Islands.

402 *Blue-breasted or Red-bellied Pitta* (WH)

401 *Common Paradise Kingfisher* (WH)

Common Paradise (Port Moresby Racket-tailed) Kingfisher

Transiptera microryncha

Tanysiptera galatea Gray

PLATE 401

The Racket-tailed Kingfishers, now called the Paradise Kingfishers, are characterized by their bright blue plumage and central tail streamers. This species also has spatulate tips at the ends of its very long streamers.

Gould's specimen was an adult bird from south-east New Guinea. It is depicted on an exposed perch ready to swoop down on its quarry.

Rufous-bellied (Gaudichaud's) Kingfisher

Sauromarptis gaudichaudi

Dacelo gaudichaud Quoy and Gaimard

PLATE 403

Gaudichaud's Kingfisher is a noisy bird and is sometimes named Gaudichaud's Kooka-burra. They inhabit the swampy jungle where their loud call can be mistaken for a dog's bark when heard in the distance. They perch on branches in the lower forest canopy and feed on crabs, lizards and insects. This large kingfisher was disco-vered by Quoy and Gaimard in the Astro-labe 1832–1835.

403 *Rufous-bellied Kingfisher* (WH)

404 *Shovel-billed Kingfisher* (WH)

SHOVEL-BILLED (SPOON-BILLED) KINGFISHER

CLYTOCEYX REX

Clytoceyx rex (Sharpe)

PLATE 404

Gould thought that the description given by a previous ornithologist of 'spoon-bill' was inappropriate, as this kingfisher's bowl-like beak was very different from the flattened spatulated bill of the familiar species of spoonbill. Today this bird is known by the more suitable name of Shovel-billed Kingfisher.

These birds dig with their massive stubby bills for crabs, reptiles, worms and grubs especially in muddy river banks. Gould commented that the beaks of his specimens were usually still covered with dried earth.

The male has a bluish tail whereas the female's is rufous. Gould also remarked that the male and female Australian Laughing Kookaburra could be identified by these different tail colours in the same way.

405 *Yellow-capped Pygmy Parrot* (WH)

VOLUME V

YELLOW-CAPPED PYGMY PARROT (PYGMY PARROT)

NASITERNA PYGMAEA

Micropsitta keiensis (Salvadori)

PLATE 405

Gould remarks that the pygmy parrots have many unusual characteristics. They are very small, only 3½ inches (9 centimetres) long, and have disproportionally large bills compared to the size of their bodies. Their feet have long outer hind toes and the central four to six feathers of their tails have spiny ends.

The Yellow-capped Pygmy parrot now lives in the lowland forests. They creep up trees like woodpeckers, and roost in holes and hollow tree trunks.

ECLECTUS RIEDELI, *Meyer.*

W. Hart del. et lith.

Walter Imp.

407 *Red-breasted Pygmy Parrot* (WH)

Red-breasted (Bruijn's) Pygmy Parrot

Nasiterna Bruijnii

Micropsitta bruijnii (Salvadori)

PLATE 407

This species was considered by Gould to be the most beautiful of the pygmy parrots. It was named after Dr J. Bruijn (1811–1895) a Dutch zoologist and collector.

Gould recalled having seen many thousands of similar pairs of small parrots in Australia, 'breeding in the spouts of the decayed branches of the gum-tree'. However, there are no Pygmy Parrots in Australia, and Gould was probably remembering seeing fig-parrots or lorikeets.

Eclectus (Riedel's) Parrot

Eclectus Riedeli

Eclectus riedeli Gray

PLATE 406

This species of large parrot is unusual because while the female's plumage is mainly red, the male's is mainly green. The female has a black beak and the male an orange one. First knowledge of the species was from a red and blue hen sent by Mr Riedel to Dr Meyer at Dresden. The green male was discovered later and the illustration was made from a pair of specimens brought back from Timor Laut by Mr H.O. Forbes, and are probably the subspecies *Ecleldus roratus riedeli*.

408 *Vulturine or Pesquet's Parrot* (WH)

Vulturine or Pesquet's Parrot

Dasyptilus Pesqueti

Psittrichus fulgidus (Lesson)

PLATE 408

This black and red parrot, now also called the Vulturine Parrot, has a vulture-like profile with a large body, long neck and small head, with a large curved bill and unfeathered skin on its face. Its loud harsh cry is audible from a long distance in scattered mountain forests throughout New Guinea. The bird's tail and wing quills are in great demand for traditional head-dresses and also sell for high prices to traders. Even today hunting pressure is considerable and it is one of the New Guinea's threatened species.

Collectors in the late nineteenth century found great difficulty in obtaining examples. One parrot which lived for a short time in the London Zoo was carefully mounted and placed on exhibition at the British Museum.

CACATUA TRITON, *Temm*.

W. Hart. del. et lith.

Mintern. Bros. imp.

409   Triton Cockatoo (WH)

CARPOPHAGA RUBRICERA, *Gray.*

W. Hart del et lith.

Mintern Bros. imp.

Triton Cockatoo

Cacatua triton

Cacatua galerita triton Temminck

PLATE 409

This magnificent cockatoo, illustrated by Hart from life, was brought from New Guinea by C.T. Kettlewell in his yacht *Marquesa* and presented to the London Zoo in 1884.

The first description of the Triton Cockatoo was made by Temminck in 1849, who named it after a Dutch ship which surveyed the coast of New Guinea. Sharpe (who wrote the text after Gould's death) considered it to be different from the Australian Sulphur-crested Cockatoo because of the naked blue skin surrounding the eye, its slightly smaller size and stronger bill. In most other respects the two are similar, and the Triton Cockatoo is now considered to be merely a subspecies of the Sulphur-crested Cockatoo.

Red-knobbed Imperial (New Ireland Fruit) Pigeon

Carpophaga rubricera

Ducula rubricera (Bonaparte)

PLATE 410

This pigeon is one of a group of large imperial pigeons which mainly inhabit woodlands and the subcanopy of the forests. They feed entirely on large fleshy

411 Pied Imperial, Nutmeg, or Torres Strait Pigeon (WH)

fruits digesting the soft parts and passing the seed. Hart's illustration was drawn from a specimen in the British Museum which came from New Ireland in the Bismarck Archipelago.

Pied Imperial, Nutmeg, or Torres Strait (Yellow-tinted White Fruit) Pigeon

Carpophaga subflavescens

Ducula spilorrhoa G.R. Gray

PLATE 411

Now called the Pied Imperial Pigeon, Nutmeg Pigeon, or Torres Strait Pigeon this species is distinctive for its white plumage, black flight feathers and black tail-band. This species can be seen in north and north-eastern Australia and in the mangroves and coastal lowland forests of New Guinea and the satellite islands.

In late winter and early spring large numbers fly south across the Torres Straits and other waters to nest on offshore islands of northern Australia. During the breeding season the pigeons provide an exciting spectacle when they fly in flocks from their island colonies to mainland feeding areas.

Southern or Double-wattled (Two-wattled Pygmy) Cassowary

Casuarius bicarunculatus

Casuarius casuarius (Linnaeus)

PLATE 412

This cassowary differs from other species by having two wattles on its neck. Hart's illustration was based on drawings made by Gould of live cassowaries at the London Zoo. The picture shows their heads and necks on a large scale to indicate their distinctive wattles, casques or bony crests and bright neck colouring. Gould was particularly interested in the family of the *Casuariidae* and made plans for a separate monograph which was never completed.

Dwarf or Bennett's (Painted-throated) Cassowary

Casuarius picticollis

Casuarius bennetti Gould

PLATE 413

The bird portrayed in this illustration lived in the London Zoo from May 1874 to October 1876. The colours on the neck of the cassowary vary according to age and species, and as these could only be studied from living birds or heads preserved in spirits, Gould was anxious to have a permanent record of this rare species.

412 Southern or Double-wattled Cassowary

413 Dwarf or Bennett's Cassowary

A lithograph of John Gould by T.H. Maguire, aged 45.

FURTHER READING

BLUNT, Wilfrid *The Ark in the Park. The Zoo in the Nineteenth Century*. Hamish Hamilton, London, 1976. A lively history of the London Zoo.

CHISHOLM, Alec H. *The Story of Elizabeth Gould*. The Hawthorne Press, Melbourne 1944. Includes 12 letters from Elizabeth Gould to England from Australia which describe conditions in the early colony and reflect her homesickness.

CHISHOLM, Alec H. *Strange New World. The Adventures of John Gilbert and Ludwig Leichhardt*. Angus & Robertson, Sydney, 1944. A moving account of Gould's explorer's last expedition.

DANCE, S. Peter *The Art of Natural History: Animal Illustrators and their Work*. Country Life Books, London, 1978. A comprehensively illustrated natural history art book.

DANCE, S. Peter *Classic Natural History Prints, Birds*. Studio Editions Ltd., London, 1990.

DANCE, S. Peter *Classic Natural History Prints, Wolf's Birds of Prey*. Studio Editions Ltd., London, 1991. A selection of Wolf's finest birds.

GOTCH, A.F. *Birds – Their Latin Names Explained*. Blandford Press, Poole, Dorset, 1981. A fascinating list of Latin names, with their origins and brief biographies of the people after whom the birds are named.

HINDWOOD, K.A. *Emu: Gould Commemorative Issue*. Articles: John Gould in Australia, Mrs. John Gould, The letters of Edwin Prince to John Gould, Some Gouldian Letters, and Gouldiana.

HYMAN, Susan *Edward Lear's Birds*. Weidenfeld and Nicolson, London, 1980. An attractively illustrated book with a text somewhat biased in Lear's favour against Gould.

JACKSON, Christine Elisabeth *Bird Illustrators: Some Artists in Early Lithography*. W.F. & G. Witherby, London, 1975. An account of Gould and his books, and many other personalities in bird lithography during the nineteenth century.

JACKSON, Christine Elisabeth *Bird Etchings: The Illustrators and their Books. 1655–1855*. Cornell University Press, New York and London, 1985 and 1989. An insight into the life and work of many of Gould's contemporaries.

EBES, Hank *The John Gould Collection from his personal Library*. Ebes Douwma Antique Prints & Maps and Sotheby's Australia, Melbourne, 1987. A sale catalogue with illustrations of all Gould's Australian and New Guinea prints of birds and mammals.

LAMBOURNE, Maureen *John Gould – Bird Man*. Osberton Productions, Milton Keynes, 1987. Issued in connection with an exhibition at the Natural History Museum, London, and includes illustrations of preliminary sketches and watercolours.

LYSAGHT, Averil Margaret *The Book of Birds: Five Centuries of Bird Illustration*. Phaidon, London, 1975. An enjoyable history with well chosen pictures.

McEVEY, Allan 'John Gould's Contribution to British Art. A note on its authenticity'. *Art Monograph 2. Australian Academy of the Humanities 1973*. Sydney University Press, 1973.

NOAKES, Vivien *Edward Lear, the Life of a Wanderer*. Collins, London, 1968. Revised editions Fontana 1979 and BBC Publications 1985. An account of Lear's adventurous life and strange personality.

NOAKES, Vivien *Edward Lear 1812–1888, Royal Academy of Arts, Exhibition*. Weidenfeld and Nicholson, London, 1985. Includes a biliography with a list of Lear's contributions to natural history books.

NOAKES, Vivien *Edward Lear. Selected letters*. Clarendon Press, Oxford, 1988. Included are some of Lear's witty letters to Gould from Rome.

PALMER, A.H. *The Life of Joseph Wolf, Animal Painter*. Longmans Green & Co, London, 1895. A vivid description of the wildlife painter.

SAUER, Gordon C. *John Gould: The Bird Man. A Chronology and Bibliography*. Henry Sotheran, London and Landsdowne Editions, Melbourne, 1982. A wonderful compendium of information about Gould and his publications.

SHARPE, R. Bowdler *An Analytical Index to the Works of the late John Gould. F.R.S.* Henry Sotheran, London, 1893. Sharpe also includes a short biography based on his friendship with Gould in old age.

SCHERREN, Henry *The Zoological Society of London. A sketch of its Foundation and Development, and the story of its Farm, Museum, Gardens, Menagerie and Library*. Cassell, London, 1905.

SITWELL, Sacheverell, BUCHANAN, Handasyde and FISHER, James *Fine Bird Books, 1700–1900*. Collins, London, 1953.

SKIPWITH, Peyton *The Great Bird Illustrators and Their Art, 1730–1930*. Hamlyn, London, 1979. A wide selection of bird illustrators with their biographies.

TATE, Peter *A Century of Bird Books*. Witherby, London, 1979.

TATE, Peter *Birds: Men and Books. A Literary History of Ornithology*. Henry Sotheran, London, 1986.

TWYMAN, Michael *Lithography 1800–1850*. Oxford University Press, Oxford, 1970.

TWYMAN, Michael *Charles Joseph Hullmandel: lithographic printer extraordinary*. Lasting Impressions, ed. P. Gilmour, London, 1988. A biography and description of Hullmandel's establishment where Gould's early works were printed.

INDEX

Page numbers in *italic* refer to the illustrations

ACKNOWLEDGEMENTS

I would like to thank Christine Jackson, James Helyar, Allan McEvey, and Gordon Sauer for sharing their friendship, erudition and enthusiasm over many years. I am very grateful to Ann Datta, Zoology Library, National History Museum, London, her staff, Carol Gokce, Paul Cooper, Janet Lloyd-Davies, Coral Black, Nick Stead, and Effie Warr at the Zoology Library, Tring, for showing me Gould's monumental volumes, also Miss Sylvia FitzGerald and Cheryl Piggott for their help at the Library and Archives, Royal Botanic Gardens, Kew. Peter Olney has been of invaluable assistance in providing updated information on the species and the scientific names.

The publishers would like to thank the following for their kind permission to reproduce the original prints in their possession: The Spencer Library, University of Kansas for the sketches and print of the Elegant Pitta in the introduction; The Marquess of Bath, Longleat House, Warminster, Wiltshire for plates 1–4, 6–10, 12–17, 19–73, 104–7, 110, 112–116, 118–29, 131, 133–35, 138–66, 168–98, 200–4, 206–7, 209, 211–18, 220–26, 229–38, 240–50, 253–55, 258, 312–13, 318–19, 322–24, 336–43, 345–74 and 376–78. The Mitchell Library, Glasgow for plates 5, 11, 86–103, 108–9, 111, 117, 130, 132, 136–37, 167, 263, 265–66, 269–301, 344 and 379–413; Maureen Lambourne for the photograph on page 298 and plates 74–85; The Natural History Museum London for the portrait on page 5 and plates 18, 199, 205, 208, 210, 219, 227–28, 239, 251–52, 256-57, 259–62, 310, 320, 335 and 375; Henry Sotheran Limited, London for plates 264, 267–68, 302–9, 311, 314–17 and 321; The National Portrait Gallery, London, for the portrait on page 7.